VISUAL IMPAIRMENTS:
DETERMINING ELIGIBILITY FOR SOCIAL SECURITY BENEFITS

Committee on Disability Determination for Individuals with Visual Impairments

Peter Lennie and Susan B. Van Hemel, Editors

Board on Behavioral, Cognitive, and Sensory Sciences
Division of Behavioral and Social Sciences and Education
National Research Council

NATIONAL ACADEMY PRESS
Washington, D.C.

NATIONAL ACADEMY PRESS 2101 Constitution Avenue, N.W. Washington, D.C. 20418

NOTICE: The project that is the subject of this report was approved by the Governing Board of the National Research Council, whose members are drawn from the councils of the National Academy of Sciences, the National Academy of Engineering, and the Institute of Medicine. The members of the committee responsible for the report were chosen for their special competences and with regard for appropriate balance.

The study was supported by Contract No. 0600-99-38810 between the National Academy of Sciences and the U.S. Social Security Administration. Any opinions, findings, conclusions, or recommendations expressed in this publication are those of the author(s) and do not necessarily reflect the view of the organizations or agencies that provided support for this project.

Library of Congress Cataloging-in-Publication Data

Visual impairments : determining eligibility for social security benefits / Peter Lennie and Susan B. Van Hemel, editors ; Committee on Disability Determination for Individuals with Visual Impairments, Board on Behavioral, Cognitive, and Sensory Sciences, Division of Behavioral and Social Sciences and Education, National Research Council.
p. ; cm.
Includes bibliographical references and index.
ISBN 0-309-08348-6 (pbk.)
1. Vision disorders—Diagnosis. 2. People with visual disabilities—Evaluation. 3. Disability evaluation—United States. 4. Social security—United States.
[DNLM: 1. Vision Disorders—diagnosis—United States. 2. Disability Evaluation—United States. 3. Eligibility Determination—United States. 4. Social Security—United States. 5. Vision Tests—United States. WW 140 V8345 2002] I. Lennie, Peter. II. Van Hemel, Susan B. III. National Research Council (U.S.). Committee on Disability Determination for Individuals with Visual Impairments.
RE91 .V525 2002
617.7'15—dc21

2002005466

Additional copies of this report are available from National Academy Press, 2101 Constitution Avenue, N.W., Washington, D.C. 20418

Call (800) 624-6242 or (202) 334-3313 (in the Washington metropolitan area)

This report is also available online at **http://www.nap.edu**

Printed in the United States of America

Suggested citation: National Research Council (2002) *Visual Impairments: Determining Eligibility for Social Security Benefits*. Committee on Disability Determination for Individuals with Visual Impairments. Peter Lennie and Susan B. Van Hemel, editors. Division of Behavioral and Social Sciences and Education. Washington, DC: National Academy Press.

THE NATIONAL ACADEMIES

National Academy of Sciences
National Academy of Engineering
Institute of Medicine
National Research Council

The **National Academy of Sciences** is a private, nonprofit, self-perpetuating society of distinguished scholars engaged in scientific and engineering research, dedicated to the furtherance of science and technology and to their use for the general welfare. Upon the authority of the charter granted to it by the Congress in 1863, the Academy has a mandate that requires it to advise the federal government on scientific and technical matters. Dr. Bruce M. Alberts is president of the National Academy of Sciences.

The **National Academy of Engineering** was established in 1964, under the charter of the National Academy of Sciences, as a parallel organization of outstanding engineers. It is autonomous in its administration and in the selection of its members, sharing with the National Academy of Sciences the responsibility for advising the federal government. The National Academy of Engineering also sponsors engineering programs aimed at meeting national needs, encourages education and research, and recognizes the superior achievements of engineers. Dr. Wm. A. Wulf is president of the National Academy of Engineering.

The **Institute of Medicine** was established in 1970 by the National Academy of Sciences to secure the services of eminent members of appropriate professions in the examination of policy matters pertaining to the health of the public. The Institute acts under the responsibility given to the National Academy of Sciences by its congressional charter to be an adviser to the federal government and, upon its own initiative, to identify issues of medical care, research, and education. Dr. Kenneth I. Shine is president of the Institute of Medicine.

The **National Research Council** was organized by the National Academy of Sciences in 1916 to associate the broad community of science and technology with the Academy's purposes of furthering knowledge and advising the federal government. Functioning in accordance with general policies determined by the Academy, the Council has become the principal operating agency of both the National Academy of Sciences and the National Academy of Engineering in providing services to the government, the public, and the scientific and engineering communities. The Council is administered jointly by both Academies and the Institute of Medicine. Dr. Bruce M. Alberts and Dr. Wm. A. Wulf are chairman and vice chairman, respectively, of the National Research Council.

COMMITTEE ON DISABILITY DETERMINATION FOR INDIVIDUALS WITH VISUAL IMPAIRMENTS

PETER LENNIE (*Chair*), Center for Neural Science, New York University
IAN L. BAILEY, School of Optometry, University of California, Berkeley
JOHN A. BRABYN, The Smith-Kettlewell Eye Research Institute, San Francisco
RICHARD V. BURKHAUSER, College of Human Ecology, Cornell University
VELMA DOBSON, Department of Ophthalmology, University of Arizona
RICHARD D. GONZALEZ, Department of Psychology, University of Michigan
KAREN JACOBS, Sargent College of Health and Rehabilitation Sciences, Boston University
CHRIS A. JOHNSON, Devers Eye Institute, Portland, Oregon
FRANK J. LANDY, SHL/Landy Jacobs, Inc., Boulder, Colorado
PAUL P. LEE, Duke University Eye Center
GORDON E. LEGGE, Department of Psychology, University of Minnesota
DENNIS M. LEVI, School of Optometry, University of California, Berkeley
CYNTHIA OWSLEY, Department of Ophthalmology, University of Alabama, Birmingham
SHEILA K. WEST, Wilmer Eye Institute, Johns Hopkins University
M. ROY WILSON, School of Medicine, Creighton University

SUSAN B. VAN HEMEL, *Study Director*
WENDY E. KEENAN, *Senior Project Assistant*

CONTENTS

PREFACE

This report is the product of over two years' work by a committee of 15 diverse experts in vision and other subjects, convened by the National Research Council in response to a request from the Social Security Administration. The committee was tasked to review the tests and criteria used to determine visual disability for purposes of eligibility for Social Security benefits. The committee evaluated the tests currently used to determine disability for people with visual impairments and examined other possible ways to assess such disability, including new tests of visual functions and the direct measurement of vision-dependent task performance. Special attention was given to finding ways to improve the reliability and validity of tests of visual function and to reviewing evidence bearing on the ability of such tests to predict job performance capabilities.

The committee would like to acknowledge the contributions of a number of people who helped us to complete the work reported here. First, we are grateful to the consultants who provided information and guidance on issues under study, several of whom prepared commissioned or pro bono reviews and analyses for the committee: Andrew Houtenville of Cornell University; Denis Pelli and Marisa Carrasco of New York University; Barbara Altman and Beth Rasch of the Centers for Disease Control and Prevention; August Colenbrander of the Smith-Kettlewell Eye Research Institute; Richard Jeanneret and Kevin Rook of Jeanneret & Associates; and Carol Mangione and Peter Gutierrez of the University of California, Los Angeles.

We also wish to thank the staff of the Social Security Administration (SSA) Office of Disability: Sandra Salan, project sponsor, and her associates, Michelle Hungerman and Cara Fireison. They provided much useful information on how SSA programs really work and also improved our description of SSA disability programs and procedures. Also at SSA, Terry Dodson, Carole Jones, and Susan David prepared data analyses from SSA statistical files in response to our queries, and Leo Hollenbeck of the SSA library helped us uncover historical information on SSA programs.

In the service and advocacy community, we are grateful to all of the organizations that nominated speakers and otherwise supported the public forum the committee held on November 15, 2000, and to the individuals at those organizations who provided valuable information to help us in planning the forum. We are especially grateful to the forum participants, listed in Appendix B, who gave thoughtful and expert responses to the difficult questions we posed, providing the committee with valuable insights into the issues that are most important to people with visual impairments.

We also would like to acknowledge the officials and others associated with disability benefit programs in other countries who responded to our questions about their programs: Mansel Aylward, Chief Medical Advisor, Department of Social Security, United Kingdom; Örjan Bäckman, KnowledgeCentre, Uppsala, Sweden; Barbro Lutteman and Kristina Tornquist, Örebro University, Sweden; Doug Taylor, Director, Income Security Programs, Disability Benefits Division, Human Resources Development Canada.

At the National Research Council, Susan B. Van Hemel was the study director for this project. Special thanks are due to Gooloo Wunderlich, of the Institute of Medicine, for sharing her knowledge of SSA disability programs and policies, to Christine Hartel, director of the

Board on Behavioral, Cognitive, and Sensory Sciences, for her guidance and support, to Christine McShane, for editing our manuscript with great skill and insight, and to Wendy Keenan, our skilled and professional project assistant, whose contributions to this study were invaluable. I would also like to recognize the committee members, who provided an exemplar of how an interdisciplinary process should work: they debated ideas on their merits, shared insights from different viewpoints, and were consistently respectful of each other's expertise.

This report has been reviewed in draft form by individuals chosen for their diverse perspectives and technical expertise, in accordance with procedures approved by the Report Review Committee of the National Research Council (NRC). The purpose of this independent review is to provide candid and critical comments that will assist the institution in making the published report as sound as possible and to ensure that the report meets institutional standards for objectivity, evidence, and responsiveness to the study charge. The review comments and draft manuscript remain confidential to protect the integrity of the deliberative process.

We thank the following individuals for their participation in the review of this report: Aries Arditi, Thomas J. Watson Research Center, IBM Corporation, Yorktown Heights, NY; Monroe Berkowitz, Rutgers University; Karen J. Cruickshanks, Department of Ophthalmology and Visual Sciences and Department of Population Health Sciences, University of Wisconsin; Eleanor E. Faye, Lighthouse International, New York, NY; Gregory Goodrich, Veterans Administration Palo Alto Health Care System, Palo Alto, CA; Marilyn Mets, Department of Ophthalmology, Northwestern University Medical School; Gary S. Rubin, Institute of Ophthalmology, London, England; Frank Thorn, New England College of Optometry, Boston, MA.

Although these reviewers listed above have provided many constructive comments and suggestions, they were not asked to endorse the conclusions or recommendations nor did they see the final draft of the report before its release. The review of this report was overseen by Robert Sekuler of Brandeis University. Appointed by the National Research Council, he was responsible for making sure that an independent examination of this report was carried out in accordance with institutional procedures and that all reviewers' comments were considered carefully. Responsibility for the final content of this report, however, rests entirely with the authoring committee and the institution.

Peter Lennie, Chair

Committee on Disability Determination for Individuals with Visual Impairments

VISUAL IMPAIRMENTS

EXECUTIVE SUMMARY

Disability insurance has been a part of the Social Security insurance system in the United States since 1956. The Social Security Administration (SSA) has an obligation to establish criteria for eligibility that will ensure that people who are truly disabled are provided benefits. SSA recently initiated several studies of the processes and criteria that are used to determine disability benefit eligibility. The SSA asked the National Research Council to study its methods of determining disability for people with visual impairments, to recommend changes that could be made now to improve the process and outcomes, and to identify research needed to develop improved visual disability determination methods over the long term.

Two major concerns motivated this study. SSA's first concern is about the *reliability* of the tests as they are now used—the tests used for many years to determine visual disability, as now performed in optometrists' and ophthalmologists' offices, may not be as reliable as they could be. The second concern is about the predictive *validity* of current tests—at present, SSA measures the impairment of visual functions, but the relationships between such impairments and disability in the performance of real-world visual tasks in the workplace have not been clearly established. Deficiencies in these vital areas would diminish the fairness and credibility of the disability determination process.

TESTS OF VISUAL FUNCTIONS

Measurements of visual acuity and visual fields are fundamental and should continue to be the primary tests for disability determination. The reliability and value of both tests would be greatly improved by the adoption of standardized testing procedures using modern instruments.

The measurement of contrast sensitivity can detect aspects of visual impairment that are not expressed in measurements of acuity or visual fields. In certain circumstances, this measure adds important information to the assessment of claimants who do not show severe impairments of visual acuity or visual fields.

Impairments of other aspects of visual function—disorders of binocularity, glare sensitivity or recovery, color vision, visual search—are on their own not generally disabling, the literature provides little evidence that they are major contributors to disability, and these functions do not warrant primary assessment. However, impairments in these aspects of vision can contribute to disability under some circumstances.

The current procedure for computing "visual efficiency" does not permit adequate characterization of the visual performance of persons with severe low vision. The current procedure also makes distinctions, no longer necessary, between the performance of aphakic (lacking natural lenses) and phakic eyes.

The relationships between visual functions and real-world functional capacity do not suggest a natural cutoff point for disability. There are no sharp inflections in performance scores or self-reports of performance abilities corresponding to specific acuity, field, or contrast sensitivity scores. The setting of criterion scores for disability is a policy decision to be made by SSA.

VISUAL TASK PERFORMANCE

The committee examined whether disability due to visual impairments could be measured directly, rather than by estimating it from tests of visual function. The committee explored tasks in four domains: reading, mobility, social participation, and tool use, having concluded that these adequately capture important visual requirements of everyday life and jobs. Acceptable tests of performance are not yet available in most of the domains examined. Tests of reading are the closest to being ready for use.

- Reading tests are available that would be usable for disability determination after modest additional research and development (mainly standardization and norming). Tests of reading ability could provide important information for the assessment of functional capacity in the "vocational factors" steps of the disability determination process.
- For safe and efficient orientation and mobility, the most important aspects of visual function are contrast sensitivity, visual fields, and acuity. Our recommended tests of visual function assess these.
- For driving, at present there are no standard tests of driving ability available for determining driving fitness in those who are visually impaired.
- For tool use and manipulation, the data are insufficient for us to recommend any battery of performance-based tests that would determine visual disability in this domain.
- Social participation should not be a high priority for testing at this time, but it may be worthy of reconsideration in the future, as candidate tests emerge.

OTHER MEANS OF ASSESSING DISABILITY

The committee evaluated the usefulness of two other means of assessing disability: job analysis databases, which include information on the importance of vision to job tasks or skills, and measures of health-related quality of life, which take a person-centered approach to assessing visual functioning.

- Data from the Position Analysis Questionnaire were helpful in determining the importance of some visual functions in the workplace, but the proprietary nature of the dataset permitted only limited inferences about today's employed population.

- Health-related quality of life instruments could be useful in efforts to identify important everyday and work tasks affected by visual impairment and possibly to quantify relationships between visual functions and task performance. However, such tests would not be useful in the disability determination process for individual claimants.

High-quality data on visual function and employment for a random sample of the working-age population could help efforts to identify the relationship between visual function and employment outcomes. Because serious vision limitations are relatively rare in the working-age population, no current nationally representative datasets contain adequate samples of people with significant vision limitations. Without information on a random sample of working-age people with serious visual limitations that includes information on the social environment in which they work, it is not possible to establish the relationship between visual function and employment.

TESTING OF INFANTS AND CHILDREN

Most school-age children (i.e., at least 6 years of age), can be tested with standard adult tests of visual acuity and contrast sensitivity, as well as with short versions of adult procedures for testing visual fields. Although vision improves slightly between the early school years and adulthood, adult standards for disability determination are appropriate to apply to children whose visual acuity, visual fields, and contrast sensitivity can be tested with adult methods. A child whose vision subsequently improves beyond the level of disability status will be identified in the review that is required by law to be conducted by SSA at least every three years for beneficiaries under age 18 years.

Methods for assessing visual acuity in infants and children who cannot be assessed with adult tests have been developed, validated, and normed. These methods can be used for disability determination. There are no standardized, widely available methods for assessment of visual fields in children who cannot perform adult perimetry procedures. For these children, disability determination must, of necessity, be based on the clinician's judgment about the child's peripheral vision based on clinical tools. The use of contrast sensitivity information in determining disability in children who cannot be assessed with adult techniques is not appropriate, due to the absence of standardized, normed tests for young children and to the absence of data indicating the effects of poor contrast sensitivity on activities of everyday life in this population.

Sound statistical principles have been used in establishing SSA's recently published guidelines for disability determination in children, which set criteria of two standard deviations below the same-age norm performance for "marked" impairment and three standard deviations below it for "severe" impairment of function.

RECOMMENDATIONS

Tests of Visual Functions

For testing **visual acuity,** our recommendations are similar to those of the Committee on Vision in its 1980 and 1994 reports (National Research Council, 1980; 1994). We recommend that visual acuity charts should contain the same number of optotypes in each row; the space between optotypes in a row should be at least as wide as the optotypes in that row; and the size of the optotypes should decrease in 0.1 log unit steps from row to row. Chart luminance should be at least 80 cd/m^2, with 160 cd/m^2 optimal, free from glare, with a level of contrast between optotypes and background that is above 80 percent. The person being tested should be encouraged to read as many optotypes on the chart as possible and to guess at an optotype if he or she is unsure. Acuity results should be scored on an optotype-by-optotype basis, since this scoring procedure produces lower test-retest variability than does row-by-row scoring.

For disability determination, visual acuity should be tested under binocular conditions, since this provides the most representative measure of an individual's everyday vision. However, if acuity must be tested monocularly rather than binocularly, the acuity of the better eye should be used for disability determination.

Given the history and legislation behind the current SSA standard of "20/200 or worse distance acuity" as the principal criterion for visual disability, the committee recommends continuation of the 20/200 cutoff criterion. Since we recommend a visual acuity chart design that would include optotypes at the 20/160 level, applying the "20/200 or worse" criterion literally to scores obtained with such a chart would set the effective criterion to "worse than 20/160 distance acuity." The scoring of the charts currently used in disability determination sets the effective criterion at "worse than 20/100." The recommended charts have a 20/100 line that would allow SSA to maintain the effective criterion at its current position, but SSA must make the decision on whether this should be done.

For testing **visual fields,** the committee recommends that the current SSA standard should be revised so that disability determinations are based on the results of automated static projection perimetry rather than Goldmann (kinetic, nonautomated) visual fields.

We propose the following criteria for any perimeter to be used by SSA for disability determination:

- The automated static perimeter should be capable of performing threshold testing using a white size III Goldmann target and a 31.5 apostilb (10 cd/m^2) white background.
- The perimeter should be capable of measuring sensitivity for the central 30° radius of the visual field with equal numbers of target locations in each quadrant of the field, and target locations no more than 6° apart.

- The perimeter should be a projection perimeter or should produce measures that are equal to those obtained on a projection perimeter.
- The perimeter should have an internal normative database for automatically comparing an individual's performance with that of the general population.
- The perimeter should have a statistical analysis package that is able to calculate visual field indices, particularly mean deviation or mean defect (MD), which is the average deviation of visual field sensitivity in comparison to normal values for the central 30° radius of the visual field.
- The perimeter should demonstrate high sensitivity (ability to correctly detect visual field loss) and specificity (ability to correctly identify normal visual fields).
- The perimeter should demonstrate good test-retest reliability.
- The perimeter should have undergone clinical validation studies by three or more independent laboratories with results published in peer-reviewed ophthalmic journals.

We recommend that SSA use the MD (mean deviation or mean defect) score to characterize impairment.

The committee recommends that **contrast sensitivity** be assessed as a supplementary basis for disability determination for claimants with visual acuity between 20/50 and 20/200 and other evidence or self-report of visual impairment greater than would be expected from the acuity score. The following criteria should be met:

The test used should

- be simple to administer;
- require no sophisticated equipment;
- be well-standardized, reliable, valid, and sensitive to visual loss;

- be relatively insensitive to changes in focus, viewing distance, and illumination;
- provide a single score that can be compared with normative data.

Currently, one available test—the Pelli-Robson Contrast Sensitivity Test—is known to meet these criteria.

SSA should use log contrast sensitivity score in determining disability.

Severe impairments in **other visual functions**—disorders of binocularity, glare sensitivity or recovery, color vision, visual search—could be taken into account as "adjustments" in the disability determination process.

In the matter of combining scores on multiple visual impairments to arrive at an aggregate impairment score and setting cutoff scores for disability determination, the committee recommends that:

- SSA no longer calculate central visual efficiency and visual field efficiency. Because the recommended indices of visual acuity, visual fields, and contrast sensitivity use logarithmic scales, appropriately weighted addition of scores will provide a simple, direct aggregate measure of impairment.
- Research be undertaken to examine directly how different kinds of impairments interact in determining overall visual performance. In the absence of such research, SSA should continue to treat impairments of different aspects of visual function as though they operate independently in determining overall visual performance.
- SSA support research to inform policy decisions about the levels of impairment of visual functions that should qualify as disability.

The committee also makes the following recommendations for all testing of visual functions.

- All tests should be administered under standardized conditions using modern instruments and with the claimant wearing the best tolerable correction.

- Tests such as acuity should be administered and scored binocularly unless circumstances dictate that this is not appropriate (e.g., in diplopia, in which binocular performance would be worse than that of the better eye). If binocular scores are not obtainable, the better eye score should be used in disability determination.

- To improve the reliability and accuracy of testing, SSA should develop and promote, through both regulations and its professional relations function, clear guidelines or criteria for visual function test materials and procedures (charts, perimetry equipment, test protocols, etc.). SSA should consider establishing a test quality assurance advisory panel with both scientific and clinical expertise in vision testing to evaluate new tests and approve those that meet SSA's needs.

- SSA should consider developing standards for test administration, in consultation with the ophthalmological and optometric communities, and explore ways to ensure that such standards are met by the professionals who test SSA claimants. This could greatly improve the reliability of testing. Possibilities range from initiating an accreditation or certification system for providers and their test facilities to establishing dedicated test centers that would operate under SSA supervision.

The committee recommends the following additional research efforts related to visual function testing:

- SSA should support research relating the outcome of visual assessment with such tools as visual acuity charts to an individual's ability to function in the workplace and in society. This will allow future evaluation of the adequacy of the present cutoff criterion of 20/200.

- SSA should support research on the visual functions for which testing is not now recommended, to explore how they contribute to disability and how they can best be measured. This would provide scientific support for any future decision to include such measures in determination of visual disability.

Visual Task Performance

The committee strongly recommends that SSA invest in the development of tests of visual task performance for future use in disability determination.

- Appropriate tests exist to measure reading disability. Reading speed, reading acuity, and critical print size all are potentially relevant to the evaluation of disability. SSA should support research to develop a normative database for promising reading tests.
- As soon as tests are available that meet SSA needs, a test of reading vision should be included as a component in the assessment of individuals with vision impairment who receive vocational assessment when they fail to meet the medical listings.
- There is a need for tests of driving ability to determine fitness in those who are visually impaired. SSA should support research and development of driving tests for use in vocational assessment.
- Standard, performance-based tests of tool use developed for use in personnel selection and placement should be studied for possible utility in helping to determine disability due to vision.

Testing of Infants and Children

- Use same-age norms, not age equivalents, in evaluating visual acuity performance in children too young to be assessed with adult visual acuity tests.
- Until standardized tests are available for younger children, do not test fields by perimetry until children are old enough to be assessed with static perimetry—between 6 and 8 years of age.
- Until standardized tests are available for younger children, do not test contrast sensitivity until children are old enough to be assessed with adult tests of contrast sensitivity—between 6 and 8 years of age.

1

INTRODUCTION

The problem of visual loss is recognized as a significant issue by the American public. The federal government recognized the potential disability associated with visual loss when it incorporated Aid to the Blind into the Social Security Act of 1935 (Koestler, 1976, p.45). Thus, the issue of the appropriate determination of disability for individuals with visual impairment is an important one for the Social Security Administration (SSA).

This report assesses the existing disability determination process used by SSA to identify individuals with visual impairments in the context of current scientific knowledge and clinical practice. The charge of the Committee on Disability Determination for Individuals with Visual Impairments was to:

- Evaluate current scientific understanding of the visual demands of everyday tasks, including information that can be obtained from quality-of-life measures.

- Examine the adequacy of the current tests of central visual acuity and visual field as measures of the capacity to work.

- Explore other existing tests of visual function as means of simply and reliably estimating visual capacity, alone or in combination with other tests.
- Examine the potential value of new measures and procedures for estimating visual disability.
- Identify where more work might be required to better characterize visual impairments, to better estimate functional capacity, and to better characterize the visual requirements of work and everyday tasks.

This report is the committee's response to these challenges.

ISSUES THAT PROMPTED THE STUDY

SSA administers benefits programs for people with long-lasting disabilities that severely affect their ability to work or, for children, to perform everyday activities like their peers. Under Title II of the Social Security Act, workers covered by Social Security may qualify for benefits called Social Security Disability Insurance (SSDI, often referred to as DI). Under Title XVI, adults and children who are not eligible for DI may qualify for Supplemental Security Income (SSI) benefits, which are means-tested disability benefits. For each person who comes to SSA to request disability benefits (formally referred to as a "claimant"), SSA must determine whether he or she is eligible under the program regulations that implement the laws Congress has enacted for Social Security disability benefits.

SSA was concerned that, while its criteria are intended to identify claimants whose visual impairment severely reduces their ability to work, the agency has little information about the relationship between performance on medical tests of vision and performance of vision-dependent tasks on the job. The SSA Office of Disability is also aware that the criteria it uses are based on old medical practices and that new and refined methods of testing visual function are being used in the medical and rehabilitation communities.

Predicting Performance in the Workplace

The overall goal of disability assessment is to establish functional capacity (fitness for work). The committee examined how best to do that, whether through the use of simple tests of visual function, such as acuity and visual fields, or through testing more complex, visually dependent skills, such as reading and driving, or even through the direct measurement of visual performance in the workplace.

A good deal is now known about the visual requirements of work-related tasks like reading and mobility, as well as about the visual capabilities most missed by people with impaired vision. Much work has also been done to assess the impact of different degrees of visual impairment on a person's quality of life, by using questionnaires and by observation of behavior in different everyday contexts. Although the measurement of overall performance has been a major focus of research on people with low vision and has become central to the assessment of disability in children (discussed below), it has not been systematically examined as a means of assessing visual disability in adults.

Adequacy of Current Tests

The SSA disability determination process uses basic tests of *visual acuity* and *visual fields* that were standardized in the 1950s. The SSA regulations specify quite precisely some conditions under which tests should be administered but provide little guidance on others, particularly those for the measurement of acuity. Understanding of what the tests measure has advanced greatly since the SSA regulations were formulated, and the instruments used for measurement have been much improved, offering the prospect of more refined and reliable assessment.

Recognizing this, in 1994 SSA sought advice from the National Research Council's Committee on Vision on the testing and scoring procedures that should be used to obtain reliable measures of central visual acuity and visual fields. The resulting report (National Research Council,

1994) noted that the current standards have important weaknesses, in addition to making recommendations about how tests should be administered in ways that conform to the standards. That report served as a point of departure for the current study, and its findings informed our investigation of visual disability determination methods.

Limited Range of Visual Functions Tested

The tests of central visual acuity and visual fields described in SSA's medical listings assess key aspects of visual performance, but they do not touch on other dimensions of vision that may be relevant to overall functioning in everyday life and the workplace. In its 1994 report, the Committee on Vision commented on some of these, which we mention here.

An important element of normal vision is the capacity to distinguish small differences in the brightness of adjacent regions in a scene. The better one's *spatial contrast sensitivity*, the better one can distinguish an object from similar surroundings, and the better one can distinguish fine detail. Contrast sensitivity has been studied systematically since the 1960s, and its potential importance in clinical assessment has only recently been recognized. Impaired contrast sensitivity can result in poor vision that is not readily detected by such measures as visual acuity.

Other visual capabilities that are potentially important include binocular vision, which is the use of two eyes to provide normal vision. Disruptions of binocular vision can lead to double vision and impaired capacity to distinguish small differences in depth. The SSA criteria take no account of impairments of binocular vision other than those that might arise through paralysis of the eye muscles.

Impairments of color vision, both congenital and acquired, are not uncommon, especially among males. These generally result in one's being unable to distinguish colors that are readily distinguished by people with normal color vision. The SSA criteria take no account of the weaknesses of color vision, either as isolated impairments or in conjunction with others.

There are at least two issues related to the brightness or darkness of the environment in which a person is trying to see: adaptation and glare. The normal visual system is able to adjust its sensitivity rapidly (adapt), so that one can see well over the very wide range of light intensities encountered in normal life. Impairments of adaptation can leave one unable to see well at low or high light levels. The SSA criteria do not touch on impairments of light or dark adaptation.

Light from a bright source in the field of view can be scattered within the eye. This scattering, known as *glare,* reduces the contrast in the retinal image. Some people are very susceptible to glare and their vision can be much impaired by it. The SSA criteria do not provide for the measurement of susceptibility to glare.

Visual search is another aspect of visual function that may be important in everyday life and work. It allows one to locate and select objects of importance in the environment, in order to respond appropriately to them. This function is not now part of the testing for disability determination.

PREVALENCE AND SIGNIFICANCE OF VISUAL IMPAIRMENTS

Estimates of Visual Loss

There are many different estimates of the number or prevalence rates of people in the United States with visual impairments, all supporting the assertion that this population is significant, is likely to be greater in underserved populations, and increases markedly with age. The variation among estimates is in part due to differences among the surveys in the assessment of vision (self-report of vision loss versus loss based on standard visual testing), differences in definitions of blindness and visual impairment, and differences in the age, socioeconomic status, and racial/ethnic mix of the populations studied.

The committee reviewed several population-based studies that included detailed examination of visual status, not all of them based on U.S. populations. They include the Baltimore Eye Survey (Rahmani et al., 1996; Tielsch et al., 1990), the Beaver Dam Eye Study (Klein et al., 1991), the Rotterdam Study (Klaver et al., 1998), the Blue Mountains Eye Study (Attebo et al., 1996), the SKI study (Brabyn et al., 2000), Proyecto VER, a study of Hispanic populations in Arizona (Munoz et al., 2002; Rodriguez et al., 2002) and the Salisbury Eye Evaluation Study (Rubin et al., 1997). Because visual loss is strongly dependent on age, most of these studies are based on older population samples, ranging from age 40 and older in the Baltimore study to age 65 and older in the Salisbury study. Each of these studies except one examined sample sizes of 2,500 or more subjects, with four each having over 4,000 subjects. Table 1-1 shows their reported rates for blindness and measured visual impairment, according to the study definitions. Rates cannot be directly compared, however, because the actual age structure may differ among study populations.

The rates of blindness and visual impairment as reported in the age-specific analyses in these studies suggest that blacks and Hispanics have more vision loss than whites. The data are difficult to summarize for several reasons: the studies used different definitions of visual loss, the age distributions are different (e.g., the Hispanic population age 40 and older is much younger than other populations age 40 and older), some studies are decades older than others and are affected by the rise in the rate of cataract surgeries, and the age ranges vary from 40 and older to 65 and older. Overall, the prevalence of blindness varied from 0.3 percent in a population age 40 and older to greater than 1.7 percent in a black population age 65 and older. Blindness rates in the populations less than age 65 are unstable because vision loss is rare; most studies report rates of less than 0.3 percent.

The studies in which detailed ophthalmological examinations have been carried out to determine causes of visual loss were most informative as to major causes of vision impairment in adults. These causes will change with age, as cataract, glaucoma, and age-related macular degeneration (AMD) assume more prominence in the older age groups. There are also shifting trends over time related to changes in medical practice, as cataract surgery has become more frequent in the past 15 years, leading to less cataract blindness and visual loss over time.

The ranking of causes is quite different in the 40 to 65 age group than in the older group, with AMD and cataract, disorders commonly related to age, accounting for much less of the total impairment in the younger age group. Diabetic retinopathy and other causes of visual loss were much more important at younger ages. AMD was the leading cause of blindness among whites, and cataract, glaucoma, and diabetic retinopathy the leading causes among blacks. For Hispanics, the leading cause of blindness was glaucoma; the leading cause of visual loss was cataract, followed by diabetic retinopathy and AMD.

The committee recognizes that many people with visual impairments have other impairments as well. We considered this in our evaluation of tests, noting when particular tests require capabilities in addition to vision, such as motor skills or literacy. We have given the most attention to this issue in the discussion of tests for infants and children, for whom multiple impairments are especially important (Chapter 4). We have not, however, considered how the results of tests for visual impairments might be combined with those for other impairments to produce composite disability scores. This issue is beyond the scope of work the committee was asked to perform.

Self-Reported Visual Problems

In addition to actual ophthalmological determination of visual loss are people's perceptions of visual problems and the self-reported impact on function that such problems may cause. Various health surveys have used different phrases, such as "cannot see at all," when asking respondents whether they are blind. One estimate of the numbers of persons with disability due to self-reported visual impairments[1] is based on the 1992 National Health Interview Survey

---

[1]The committee prefers to use the term "impairment" only to refer to measured loss of visual function, and to refer to self-reported losses as vision "problems" or "limitations." However, the NHIS questionnaire and datasets use the term "impairment" for such self-reported losses, so we have used it in that way in reference to NHIS data only.

TABLE 1-1 Rates of Visual Impairment (VI) and Blindness in Population-Based Studies

Authors	Population
Beaver Dam	White (one city in Wisconsin)
Baltimore:	White (inner city)
	Black (inner city)
Blue Mountain	White (Australian city)
Rotterdam	White (one district in city, Holland)
VER	Hispanic (2 cities, Arizona)
Salisbury Eye Evaluation	White (city in Maryland)
	Black (city in Maryland)

*This definition of visual impairment is more lenient than that of the other studies; it includes those with acuity of 20/40, whereas others defined impairment as acuity worse than 20/40.

Age Range	Definitions	Data
43+	VI *: ≤20/40 Blind: ≤20/200	VI: 5.2% Blind:0.5%
40+	VI: <20/40 Blind: ≤20/200	(white):2.2% (black): 3.9% (white): 0.76% (black): 1.75%
49+	VI: <20/40 Blind: ≤20/200	4% 0.7%
55+	VI: <20/40 Blind: ≤20/200	3.8% 0.75%
40+	VI: <20/40 Blind: (20/200	1.9% 0.3%
65+	VI: <20/40 Blind: ≤20/200	(white):2.7% (black): 5.3% (white): 0.5% (black): 1.7%

(LaPlante & Carlson, 1996). Visual impairment was estimated as the "main cause of activity limitation" for 558,000 people of all ages in the United States in 1992, with "blindness in both eyes" accounting for 189,000 of these. Reported visual impairments were the main condition causing work limitation for 256,000 people ages 18 to 69, and were one of "all conditions" causing work limitations for 580,000 people in this age range.

The employment and economic well-being of those reporting serious visual limitations is substantially affected, as the following section shows.

Visual Limitations and the Workplace

Unambiguous data on the prevalence of visual limitations among the population covered by the SSDI and SSI programs—working-age people ages 18-64, and children 0-17—do not exist. Nor do data on the employment and economic well-being of those populations.

Quite detailed objectively reported data on the visual limitations of subpopulations in the United States and other countries are available based on professional evaluations by clinicians, as reviewed above. But most of these studies have relatively small sample sizes and focus on older populations that contain a relatively large share of men and women age 65 and older who are not actively seeking employment, are not eligible for Social Security disability benefits, and are unlikely to be representative of the younger populations that these programs cover. We found no clinically based samples drawn from random samples of the children and the working-age populations eligible for SSI or SSDI benefits.

We were able to find nationally representative data on children and the working-age population, but these data, while rich in socioeconomic information, based all of their information about visual limitations on self-reports. Also, the questions asked were quite extreme in their attempt to identify visual limitations—for example, "Are you blind in both eyes?" Finally, because "blind in both eyes" and other serious visual limitations are relatively rare, even in quite large nationally representative samples, only a small number of people is actually identified, and hence it is difficult to obtain reliable estimates for subpopulations with these impairments—children, working-age population, men, women, etc.

An analysis of such self-reported data shows that there is substantial heterogeneity in the working-age population with disabilities. A study commissioned by the committee and included in Appendix A offers an approximation of the prevalence of visual limitations in the working-age population in the United States (ages 25-61) as well as their employment and economic well-being (Houtenville, 2001). Houtenville uses a random one-sixth sample of the working-age population reporting visual impairments (and other severe impairments), as well as a sample of the entire working-age population of the National Health Interview Survey (NHIS). Respondents were first asked if they had a health-based work limitation, and only then were they asked about the kind of impairment that limited their work (this procedure is referred to here as the choice-based sample). Because visual impairments are relatively rare in the working-age population, Houtenville pooled cross-sectional data from the NHIS for the years 1983-1996.

For the one-sixth random sample for all years, Houtenville found that 0.17 percent of working-age men and 0.17 percent of working-age women reported being "blind in both eyes." A larger percentage of men (4.89) and women (2.38) in this age range reported "some visual impairment." For the sample of working-age men and women who are asked about their impairments only if they first report that they have a work limitation, the percentage of men (0.10) and women (0.08) reporting being blind in both eyes fell dramatically. The same situation was found for men (0.67) and women (0.39) reporting some visual impairment. Houtenville shows that choice-based samples that ask only those who first report a work limitation about their impairment reported a significantly lower prevalence of these impairments in the working-age population. Nevertheless, his prevalence findings using the one-sixth random sample are still somewhat lower than those found in the population-based studies reported in Table 1-1. This is of course in large part likely to be caused by the much younger average working-age population he considered.

Using the random sample, Houtenville found that 49.4 percent of working-age men who report being blind in both eyes have worked over the past two weeks, but only 32.4 percent of a choice-based sample have done so. Of the other impairment categories he considered, only men with mental retardation or paraplegia, hemiplegia, or quadriplegia have significantly lower employment rates. In the choice-based sample, only those with paraplegia, hemiplegia, or quadriplegia have significantly lower employment rates. For women, no other group has significantly lower employment rates. In contrast, those with other visual impairments have significantly higher employment rates than do those who are blind in both eyes in both samples.

Overall, Houtenville (2001) found that men and women who are blind in both eyes are consistently less likely to be employed and more likely to receive SSDI or SSI and to live in lower-income households than those without visual impairment. In addition, he found that this is also true when those who are blind in both eyes are compared with all but the most serious impairment groups. However, he also found that those with vision impairments other than blindness in both eyes are significantly more connected to the labor force and live in higher-income households than those who are blind in both eyes.

Few studies have looked at the employment of working-age people with visual impairment from a national perspective. Houtenville (2001) compared his findings with those of Trupin et al. (1997) and Kirchner et al. (1999). While the definition of serious vision impairment varies across the three studies, the employment rates found in these studies are approximately the same for similarly defined populations.

In summary, Houtenville found considerable heterogeneity in the severity of impairments in the population with disabilities both across and within impairment groups. Those with severe visual impairments—that is, blindness in both eyes—have significantly lower employment rates and a higher prevalence of SSDI and SSI receipt than those with other visual impairments. While household income of those who are blind in both eyes is closer to that of the average household income of other impairment groups, it is still relatively low.

This suggests that those who are blind in both eyes and those with other serious visual impairments, as well as those with other serious impairments (e.g., mental retardation, paraplegia, hemiplegia, quadriplegia, cerebral palsy), are appropriate beneficiaries of SSDI and SSI benefits.

Houtenville's analysis of the NHIS data reported above is strongly suggestive of the importance of good vision for employment. The actual visual requirements in the workplace are extremely variable and not well documented. The committee turned to two major sources for information on the visual demands of the work environment: (1) O*NET, a job analysis database currently being developed by the U.S. Department of Labor and (2) the dataset associated with the Position Analysis Questionnaire (PAQ), a proprietary job analysis system. These are discussed in more detail in Chapter 3. Our analyses point out the importance of several key activities in the workplace for which visual input to performance is highly important: reading, mobility, social participation, and the use of tools. The committee specifically focused attention on these four activities to evaluate the possibilities for using performance-based tests of function in these domains to determine disability.

Children and Visual Impairments

Children, especially young children, present a special set of issues for disability determination because they often cannot be tested using the same methods used with adults. Moreover, it is difficult to find reliable information on the number of children with visual impairments in the United States. Because of the reporting requirements for federal programs mandating educational services for children with impairments, statistics are available on the number of children with various impairments served by programs funded under the federal Individuals with Disabilities Education Act (IDEA). The figures quoted here are taken from the 22nd annual report to Congress on the implementation of the Individuals with Disabilities Education Act by the Department of Education (U.S. Department of Education, Office of Special Education Programs, 2000).

Limitations of the Data

The 2000 IDEA report makes clear that, especially for infants and toddlers served by IDEA Part C and for preschoolers served under Part B, the proportion of children in the population served by these programs has not yet peaked and may vary widely from state to state. "Child-finding" efforts may be more successfully implemented in some areas than in others. In addition, in a few states, changes in methods of reporting have led to large year-to-year changes in the number of children reported as receiving services under IDEA. This report provides figures for children with visual impairments and for children categorized as deaf-blind. However, more children with visual impairments are served by these programs than are included in those two categories, since an unknown number of visually impaired children are included in the "multiple disabilities" category.

School-Age Children

Table 1-2 shows statistics for children with visual impairments taken from Table AA18 of the IDEA report (U.S. Department of Education, Office of Special Education Programs, 2000). Year-to-year changes could be the result of changes not only in the prevalence of visual impairments but also in the proportion of such children being deemed eligible and being served through these programs.

The table shows a slow but steady increase in the number of children with visual impairments served over the 10-year period, from 24,499 in 1989-1990 to 27,741 (a bit over 13 percent increase) in 1998-1999. The report estimates that the population of the United States and its territories for this age group grew from 56.5 to 63.35 million over the period 1988-1999 (no 1989 figures are given), an increase of about 12.1 percent. Thus the proportion of the population ages 6-21 served by the programs for visually impaired and deaf-blind children increased very slightly over the period of the report.

Infants, Toddlers, and Preschoolers

The statistical tables in the Department of Education 2000 report do not break out numbers by types of disabilities for children under age 6. Table AH5 of the report provides the number of infants and young children receiving services under Part C of IDEA, which serves infants and toddlers up to age 3. The table is sorted by type of services provided, as listed on the Individualized Family Service Plans developed for these youngest children. "Vision services" were provided to 8,846 infants and toddlers in 1997, the year reported in the 2000 report. This report does not provide figures for preschool children (ages 3-5) by type of services provided. The report includes some early findings from the National Early Intervention Longitudinal Study (NEILS), now under way, which should provide more detailed information on early childhood programs when it is completed.

Significant Public Health Problem

The SSA caseload under current program regulations suggests the magnitude of this problem. As of June 2001, there were 250,340 people receiving benefits on the basis either of blindness or of disability on the basis of visual impairment: 148,745 under Title II and 101,595 under Title XVI. Figure 1-1 shows an age-group breakdown for these beneficiaries. It is clear that the number of beneficiaries rises steeply with age within the working-age range. This is noteworthy, as the age distribution of the working-age population has already begun to shift toward older workers.

Over the past five years, SSA has received about 20,000 to 22,000 claims annually in the DI program and 17,000 to 20,000 in the SSI program from people claiming disability from visual impairments including blindness. In 2000, 57 percent of SSDI claims and 51 percent of SSI initial claims for visual impairments were allowed. Over the five years, the proportion of SSDI initial claims allowed has risen steadily from 49 percent in 1996 to 57 percent in 2000, with a growing number meeting the statutory blindness criteria, and

TABLE 1-2 Number of Children Served Under IDEA by Disability and Age Group, During the 1989-1990 Through 1998-1999 School Years

		Year			
Age Group	Category	1989-1990	1990-1991	1991-1992	1992-1993
6-11					
	Visual Impairments	10,956	11,347	11,635	11,210
	Deaf-Blind	684	651	608	554
	Total	11,640	11,998	12,243	11,764
12-17					
	Visual Impairments	9,980	10,350	10,530	10,641
	Deaf-Blind	624	587	594	599
	Total	10,604	10,937	11,124	11,240
18-21					
	Visual Impairments	1,930	1,985	1,918	1,693
	Deaf-Blind	325	286	225	241
	Total	2,255	2,271	2,143	1,934
All 6-21					
	Visual Impairments	22,866	23,682	24,083	23,544
	Deaf-Blind	1,633	1,524	1,427	1,394
	Total	24,499	25,206	25,510	24,938

Source: U.S. Department of Education, Office of Special Education Programs, (2000: Table AA18).

Year					
1993-1994	1994-1995	1995-1996	1996-1997	1997-1998	1998-1999
11,723	11,557	11,870	11,843	12,088	12,135
564	524	547	508	562	646
12,287	12,081	12,417	12,351	12,650	12,781
11,357	11,445	11,864	12,072	12,033	11,991
585	600	619	559	679	718
11,942	12,045	12,483	12,631	12,712	12,709
1,724	1,711	1,756	1,847	1,910	2,006
220	207	221	193	219	245
1,944	1,918	1,977	2,040	2,129	2,251
24,804	24,713	25,490	25,762	26,031	26,132
1,369	1,331	1,387	1,260	1,460	1,609
26,173	26,044	26,877	27,022	27,491	27,741

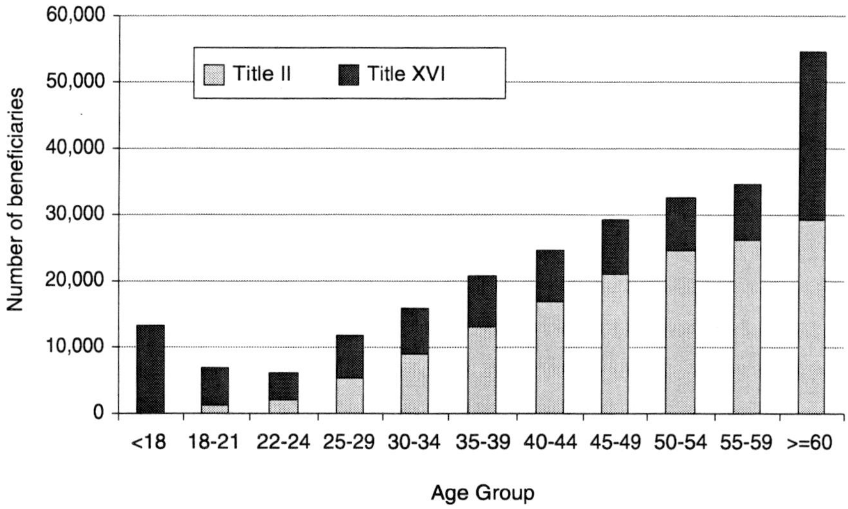

FIGURE 1-1. SSA Visually impaired and statutorily blind beneficiaries by age, June 2001.

declining numbers meeting the disability criteria without being statutorily blind.[2]

For SSI, the total percentage approved increased from 41 percent in 1997 to 51 percent in 1998 and has stayed at about that level. The 1998 figures show a large increase in the number of claims allowed for all categories of visual impairment, with much of the increase attributable to an increase in the number of claimants over 60 years of age. For this age group, the percentage of claims allowed ranges from 68 to 77 percent. In general, the proportion of claims allowed increases with the claimant's age, as would be expected when age is included as a vocational factor in the determination. The total number of claimants rose substantially between 1989 and 1996. Changes in eligibility rules in 1996 have resulted in slight declines thereafter.

[2]These figures are taken from various SSA data files and were prepared for the committee by staff of Social Security Administration Office of Disability, Division of Disability Program Information and Studies (DMAB1).

These data on the magnitude of the problem of blindness and visual impairment point to a significant public health issue in the United States, with evidence of a negative impact on the economic and employment status of the individuals affected. Good vision appears to be an important component of jobs in the workplace, although certainly people with visual loss are not irretrievably excluded from the labor force, especially if a supportive physical and social environment exists. Maximizing the abilities of those with visual impairments through rehabilitation and training can also influence performance and participation in the workplace.

Nevertheless, there are circumstances in which visual impairment can severely reduce the ability of an individual to obtain employment, resulting in the need for a humane society to provide an economic safety net. The criteria used for determining such disability will naturally shift with the acquisition of knowledge about the functioning of the visual system, new tests and procedures, and changes in the conceptual framework of disability. The issues raised in this section provide the context for the work the committee undertook in preparing this report.

THE SOCIAL SECURITY CONTEXT

When children and adults apply for disability benefits and claim that a visual impairment has limited their ability to function, SSA is required to determine their eligibility for blindness and disability benefits (see Appendix C for a glossary of terms used in reference to SSA disability programs). To ensure that these determinations are made fairly and consistently, SSA has developed criteria for eligibility and a process for assessing each claimant against the criteria. The criteria are designed to make the determination process as objective as possible, but to leave some room for considering individual circumstances. The criteria include duration and severity of the disabling condition, employment and income (and assets for SSI), "medical listings" of conditions that are presumptively disabling, and such vocational factors as age, education, and work experience.

In the case of people with visual impairments, SSA has medical listings criteria that parallel other federal and state agencies' definitions of statutory blindness, based on Snellen visual acuity and visual fields, with some allowance for combinations of less severe impairments. These criteria are identical for SSDI and SSI benefits. For people who do not meet the medical listings criteria, additional tests of vision may be used in the evaluation of functional capacity, but there are no clear guidelines at present for evaluating visual impairments that do not meet the medical listing criteria.

SSDI is funded by the same trust fund as the well-known SSA retirement program. It is a contributory plan; that is, one must have worked under and contributed to the Social Security tax program (FICA) to be eligible for these benefits. SSDI covers only working-age adults and their dependents. At retirement age, SSDI beneficiaries transition to the retirement benefits program.

SSI is a means-tested program for old-age assistance, aid to the blind, and aid to permanently and totally disabled adults. Blind and disabled children from families with limited income and resources are also covered under this program. The program considers both income and assets in its means-testing. SSI blindness and disability determinations are made using the same process and criteria as the SSDI program. SSI children who are 18 and under are evaluated using a different process and criteria. Funding for this program is not from the Social Security Trust Fund; SSI is primarily funded through congressional appropriations. Adult eligibility for entitlement under both the SSI and SSDI programs is based on demonstrating that a disabling, medically determinable impairment is present in an individual whose labor earnings capacity has fallen below a set limit, termed substantial gainful activity (SGA). This labor earnings limit is set higher for claimants with blindness than it is for claimants with disability. Neither SSDI nor SSI has provisions for variable benefits based on severity of impairment; the claimant either meets the disability criteria or does not.

SSI is the only SSA program that covers children with blindness or disability. Although the definition of blindness is the same for children, the definition of disability for children is somewhat different than that for adults. The definition of childhood disability has been changed more than once in recent years in response to court cases and legislation. Currently, if children do not meet the specifically listed medical criteria defining blindness and disability, they must be considered under an equivalence standard. The equivalence of their impairment to the specifically listed medical criteria must be evaluated by its medical or functional consequences; that is, it can medically equal a listed criterion or, using the functional domains cited in the SSA regulations, it can be judged functionally equivalent to the intent of the listings. The methodology used to make this decision is discussed below.

Procedures for Determining Disability

SSA reviews all claims for blindness and disability benefits using its sequential evaluation process. For adults, the process has five steps; for children, a three-step process is used.

Adults

For adults covered by SSDI and for adult SSI claimants, the disability determination process follows the steps shown in Figure 1-2. The first step of the sequential evaluation process requires that SSA determine whether the claimant is engaged in substantial gainful activity. Each year the SSA formally establishes an average monthly earnings level that serves to define SGA. The earnings limit is higher for blindness than it is for disability. For 2002, the monthly SGA limit is $780 for disabled claimants and $1,300 for blind claimants. If the claimant is determined not to be performing SGA, the case goes on to Step 2 of the sequential evaluation process. If the claimant is determined to be performing SGA, she or he is found ineligible for benefits at this step.

At Step 2, the claimant must document through a report or medical records provided by an acceptable medical source that a medically determinable impairment is present that significantly limits his or her

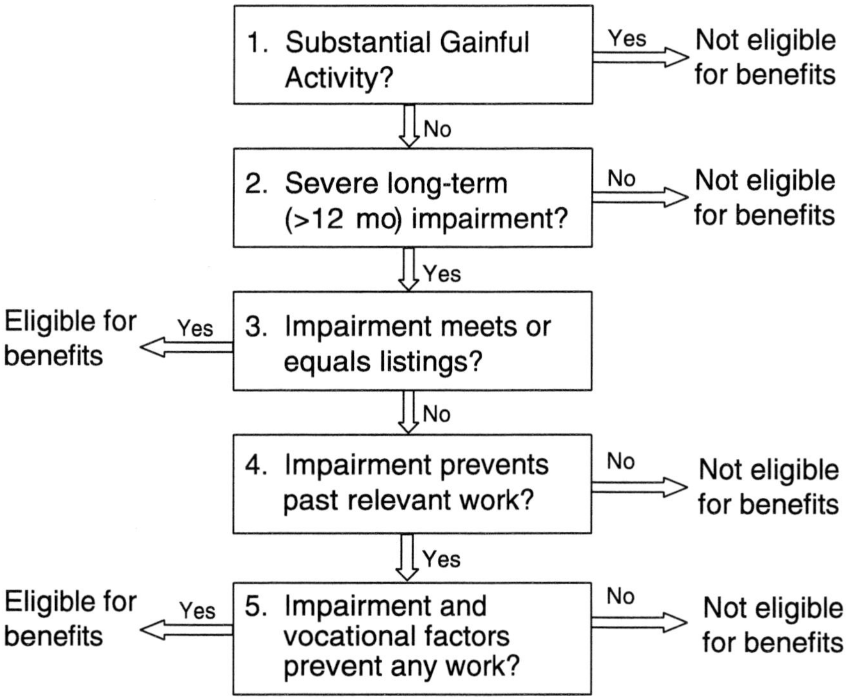

FIGURE 1-2. Disability decision flow for adults.

physical or mental ability to do basic work activities. Furthermore, medical evidence must support a judgment that the limitations imposed by the impairment have lasted or can be expected to last for at least 12 months or are expected to lead to the claimant's death. If these criteria are satisfied, the claim progresses to Step 3. If the criteria are not satisfied, the claimant is found ineligible for benefits at this step.

Step 3 of the sequential evaluation process uses medical criteria as a screening test to identify claimants who are obviously blind or disabled. In this step, SSA must decide whether the claimant's medically determinable impairment(s) meets or equals in severity the specific medical criteria listed in 20CFR Part 404, Subpart P, Appendix 1. This decision requires concurrence of a medical or psychological consultant. If the claimant has an impairment that is determined to meet or equal the listed criteria and that level of impairment severity has been demonstrated to have lasted or is expected to last for at least

12 months or to end in death, the claimant is found eligible for benefits. If not, the process continues to the consideration of vocational factors in Steps 4 and 5.

At this point in the process, the adjudicative team assesses the residual functional capacity of the claimant. Form SSA-4734-BK, called "Physical Residual Functional Capacity Assessment," is used for physical impairments, and Form SSA 4734 is used when a mental impairment has been identified. These are assessments of what the claimant can do in spite of any physical and mental impairment over a 12-month period of time. The forms require assessment of exertional, postural, manipulative, visual, communicative, and environmental limitations. The visual functions listed include near and far acuity, depth perception, accommodation, color vision, and field of vision.

In Step 4, the decision makers must determine whether any of the claimant's physical and mental limitations cited in the evaluations of residual functional capacity precludes the performance of "past relevant work." If the claimant is found able to perform past relevant work in spite of cited physical and mental limitations, he or she is found ineligible for benefits. If the claimant is found unable to perform past relevant work, the claim goes to Step 5.

In Step 5, the SSA uses a defined set of profiles and rules that consider the claimant's age, education, and work experience or skills. A decision is made whether the claimant is capable of performing any work in the U.S. economy. A so-called vocational grid is used as a decision aid, embodying the rules for determining disability. The grid combines the vocational factors and recommends findings for various combinations. Constructed in 1979 based on information from the *Dictionary of Occupational Titles* (Social Security Advisory Board, 2001b), it reflects SSA's evaluation of the existence of work in the national economy. It was designed to be used in cases of limitations of strength and stamina, for example, to consider whether a claimant is able to perform "sedentary," "light," "medium," or "heavy" work. It is not useful for other functional limitations, for which the assessment must be based on professional judgment.

If the claimant is found to have a disability under the rules of Step 5, he or she is eligible for benefits. If he or she is found not to have a disability, benefits are denied. If a claimant disagrees with SSA's decision, several levels of appeal are available.

Children

For children (covered under SSI only), a slightly different set of steps is followed, as shown in Figure 1-3.

Steps 1 and 2 are the same as for adults. Step 3 for children is initially the same as for adults. If a child is determined to have an impairment that meets or medically equals the criteria cited in the listings, and that impairment is expected to last for 12 months or to end in death, the child is eligible for SSI blindness or disability benefits. Since Steps 4 and 5 for adults are not appropriate for children, an additional

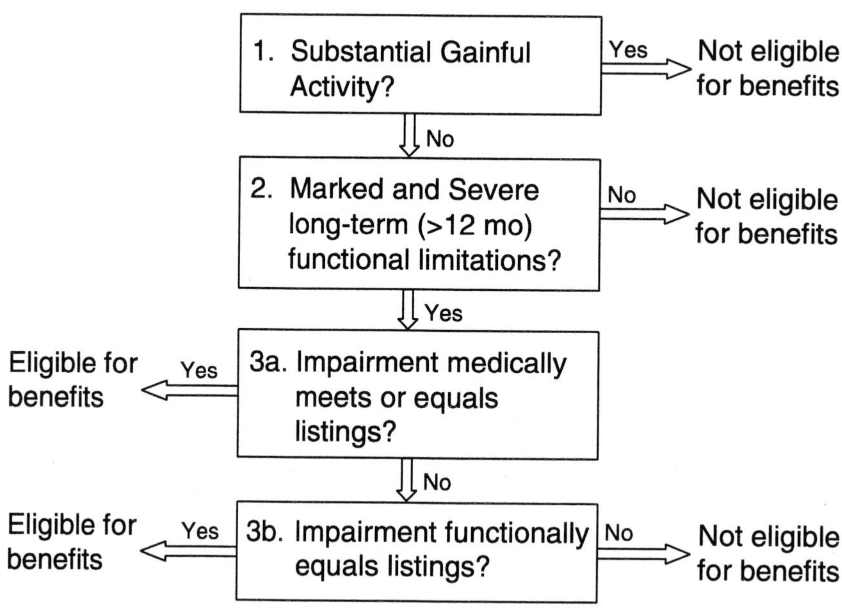

FIGURE 1-3. Disability decision flow for children.

decision point has been added to Step 3 of the process for children. Under new rules that took effect January 2, 2001, when a child is found to have a medically determinable impairment that does not meet or medically equal a listed criterion, SSA must make a determination of whether the child's impairment(s) *functionally* equals the intent of the listings.

The fundamental decision to be made is whether the effects of the impairment(s) are "marked and severe." This is judged mainly on the child's ability to perform in specific functional domains compared with normative data based on the ability of an unimpaired child of the same age, as discussed in Chapter 4. The new regulations specify the functional domains to be considered and give examples of age-appropriate levels of functioning for various age groups (20CFR §416.924-926a). The regulations state that "marked" limitation "is the equivalent of the functioning we would expect to find on standardized testing with scores that are at least two, but less than three standard deviations below the mean" (20 CFR §416.926a, (e) (ii)). "Extreme" limitation is described in a subsequent section as equivalent to at least three standard deviations below the mean.

If the child meets the functional equivalence criteria, which may be satisfied by showing marked limitations in two or more domains or extreme limitation in one domain, she or he is judged medically eligible for benefits. If not, she or he is ruled ineligible. All children who receive benefits must have their eligibility reviewed when they reach age 18, based on the adult SSI criteria.

Current Disability Criteria for Vision

In the discussion of Step 3 of the sequential evaluation process, we mentioned the listing of impairments found in Appendix 1 of subpart P of 20CFR Part 404. The vision listings deal principally with impairments of central visual acuity and visual fields. The vision listings are unique because the SSA statute includes a specific definition of blindness that is different from the definition of disability. People often refer to visual impairments that meet the legislative and SSA definition of blindness as "statutory blindness." We use the term here because it is important to understanding the SSA's determination process and criteria, although the committee recognizes that most people who meet the statutory definition of "blindness" have useful vision.

Statutory Blindness

A person is considered to be statutorily blind under the following conditions:

- Central visual acuity is 20/200 or worse in the better eye *or*
- The visual field extends to less than 10° from the fixation point, or its greatest diameter is less than 20°.

Some of the vision listings deal with blindness and some deal with disability. Listing 2.02 defines a visual acuity loss that meets the statutory definition of blindness. Listing 2.03 addresses visual field impairments and includes criteria that define statutory blindness and other criteria that define disability. Listing 2.04 provides for a finding of disability based on overall loss of visual efficiency resulting from both visual acuity and visual field impairments in the better eye.

Central Visual Acuity

Visual acuity is the capacity to distinguish fine detail. It is generally best in the center of the visual field, the region a person uses when reading, for example. The listing stipulates that acuity should be measured in this region of (normally) highest acuity. Reduced visual acuity may be caused by *refractive error* in the eye's optical system, which results in a blurred image on the retina. In most cases, reduced acuity is readily restored to normal by optical correction that compensates for the eye's refractive error. The determination of the appropriate correction, undertaken separately for each eye, is called *refraction*. Acuity measured after correction is the *best-corrected acuity*.

The listing stipulates that central visual acuity must be measured after best correction. Visual acuity loss that persists after best refractive correction can be a cause of blindness or disability under the SSA guidelines.

Most people without ocular pathology or amblyopia have best corrected visual acuities better than 20/20. The standard for blindness is a best-corrected central visual acuity in the eye with better acuity of 20/200 or worse.

Field of Vision

The visual field is the range of directions extending left, right, up, and down from the line of sight, over which the eye is sensitive to light. The normal field of vision can be reduced through contraction, resulting in the world's being seen as if through a tube, or through the development of a blind region or scotoma, leaving unimpaired vision surrounding the region. Sometimes sighted regions exist as islands in an otherwise blind visual field.

For the purpose of determining blindness or disability on the basis of visual field impairment, the SSA listings measure the size of the visual field in the better eye under specified conditions. The extent of the contracted visual field is represented by the sum of its angular extents along eight directions from the line of sight (up, down, left, right, and the intermediate diagonals). For the normal visual field, this sum is considered to be 500°. The definition of blindness on the basis of contraction of the visual field is a visual field that extends to less than 10° from the point of fixation or, alternatively, a field with its greatest diameter less than 20°.

Loss of Visual Efficiency

Impaired visual acuity or an impaired visual field, which alone would not be severe enough to meet the standard for blindness or disability, may nevertheless in combination be determined to be disabling. SSA

TABLE 1-3 Percentage of Central Visual Efficiency Corresponding to Central Visual Acuity Notations for Distance in the Phakic and Aphakic Eye (Better Eye)

Snellen		Percent Central Visual Efficiency		
English	Metric	Phakic	Aphakic Monocular	Aphakic Binocular
20/20	6/6	100	50	75
20/40	6/12	85	42	64
20/80	6/24	60	30	45
20/160	6/48	30	—	22
20/200	6/60	20	—	—

Source: Social Security Administration (2001: Table 1).

uses the term "visual efficiency" to represent the fraction of visual capacity that remains after losses are accounted for. It is derived by calculating "central visual efficiency" (acuity) and "visual field efficiency" separately, then combining them according to an SSA-provided algorithm. Listing 2.04 provides for the weighted combination of impairments, following the method set forth by Snell and Sterling (1925). Central visual efficiency for acuity is computed as

$$0.2^{(MAR-1)/9}$$

and expressed as a percentage (see the section on visual acuity in Chapter 2 for a definition of MAR). Table 1-3 shows how this measure of visual efficiency is related to Snellen acuity.

The standard for severe visual acuity listing-level impairment (20/200 or worse) is equivalent to a central visual efficiency of 20 percent or less in the better eye.

The visual field efficiency of the contracted field is calculated as:

(sum of extents [in degrees from fixation point] along 8 meridia)/500

and expressed as a percentage. The standard for disability based on visual field impairment is a visual field efficiency of 20 percent or less.

The aggregate measure of visual efficiency is calculated by combining the measurements of less-than-listing-level impairments of visual acuity and visual field that are present in the same eye. It is calculated as:

central visual efficiency × visual field efficiency

and expressed as a percentage. Listing-level impairment is met when the overall visual efficiency of the better eye is 20 percent or less. For example, a claimant with central visual acuity of 40 percent and visual field efficiency of 50 percent would just meet this criterion (40 percent times 50 percent = 20 percent).

A person is not considered statutorily blind if the standard for disability is met only through loss of visual efficiency.

Criteria for Children

The listings include special provisions for the evaluation of children. Visual acuity of listing-level severity is the same as for adults (20/200 or worse), but SSA recognizes that conventional Snellen charts may not be suitable for very young children and admits other "appropriate" methods of measurement.

Quoting from the SSA regulations, for children younger than 3 years, the standard is met if the child shows (Social Security Administration, 2001, p. 147):

1. Absence of accommodative reflex (except for infants under 6 months, plus any months of prematurity); or

2. Retrolental fibroplasia[3] with macular scarring or neovascularization; or

3. Bilateral congenital cataracts with visualization of the retinal red reflex only or when associated with other ocular pathology.

The visual field listing criteria are the same for children as for adults.

As noted above, a child's impairments are considered to be functionally equivalent to the intent of the listings if he or she has "marked" limitations in two broad domains of function—cognition/communication, social functioning, personal/behavioral functioning, and task completion—or an "extreme" limitation in one domain.

THE COMMITTEE'S APPROACH

The conceptual model underlying disability determination has been undergoing changes over the past several years, especially since the passage of the Americans with Disabilities Act (ADA) in 1990. The newer conceptualization follows a social model of disability, which postulates that factors both within the individual and in his or her physical and social/cultural environment combine to influence performance and participation in everyday life situations.

This model replaces the earlier stress on disability or handicap, and the negative aspects of an individual's situation, emphasizing instead the person's remaining capabilities and how they can best be supported to permit full economic and social participation. The ADA, based on the social model, represents a commitment in the United States to help individuals with disabilities to participate as fully as possible in the society and the economy.

[3]This is now more commonly referred to as retinopathy of prematurity. The *International Classification of Diseases, Ninth Revision* (ICD-9) allows for the use of either term.

The social model also underlies the approach now taken by the World Health Organization toward disability and handicap. Whereas the *International Classification of Impairment, Disability, and Handicap* (ICIDH) (World Health Organization, 1980) established definitions for these terms, the new *International Classification of Functioning, Disability and Health* (ICF) (World Health Organization, 2001) is an attempt to fully account for the interactions between the individual and the physical and social environment in determining the participation of an individual with a disability.

Generic Concepts and Terms as Applied to Vision

The committee carefully considered the social model as it applies to those with visual impairment, recognizing that a diagnosis of a visual disorder (or even the measured severity of visual impairment) does *not* inevitably predict a person's disability or handicap. However, this model does pose a dilemma for using the measurement of impairment as a surrogate for determining level of disability. In reviewing data on visual testing and functional status, the committee's paradigm was deceptively simple: visual loss, by some measure, is associated with increasing inability to carry out activities associated with employment or, in the case of children, age-appropriate activities. The data bearing on this issue present a more complicated picture, because the same level of visual loss can result in a wide spectrum of disability level, depending on such diverse factors as education, age, presence of other comorbid conditions, and social and environmental support. Thus, there is substantial variation in functional status for any given level of visual loss.

The committee also carefully evaluated the fourth and fifth editions of the American Medical Association's (AMA) *Guides to the Evaluation of Permanent Impairment: Vision* (American Medical Association, 1993, 2001). These guides are used in many workers' compensation disability determination procedures and represent a more traditional quantitative approach to evaluating the disability resulting from specific levels of impairment.

The committee has chosen a framework that recognizes a continuum from disorder to handicap: as one progresses from disease or disorder to impairment, and then to disability and to handicap, many variables within the individual and in his or her environment interact to determine the level of function. Figure 1-4, adapted from a document prepared as background for the 2001 AMA guides (International Society for Low Vision Research and Rehabilitation, 1999) illustrates this continuum. Instead of the term "functional vision," we use "visual task performance," which in our view more clearly expresses the intended meaning: performance of real-world tasks using vision.

At the left of the box are features of the organ (or organ system) and its function. *Diseases, disorders,* injuries, or other structural or physiological changes in an organ or organ system often lead to the outcomes we call *disabilities,* but they do not directly or unconditionally cause disabilities. Diseases or disorders affect the functioning of the organ system; in the case of the visual system, these are *visual functions.* Visual functions are measured using quantitative clinical tests, such as tests of acuity, visual fields, or contrast sensitivity. When we speak of visual functions we are referring to *the performance of the visual system, more or less in isolation, under standardized measurement conditions.*

An organ system function that fails to meet some agreed-on criterion of normal status is said to be impaired. *Impairment* refers to *a measurable deficit in what the organ system is able to do, compared with its normal function.* It may be expressed in such terms as "systolic blood pressure of 180 mmHg" or "visual acuity of less than 20/60 on a Snellen chart."[4]

The right side of Figure 1-4 describes the capabilities and performance of the whole person in the environment. It starts with skills and *abilities,* meaningful things the person can do, like reading, driving,

[4]The ICIDH (World Health Organization, 1980) definition: "In the context of health experience, an impairment is any loss or abnormality of psychological, physiological, or anatomical structure or function" (p. 27).

	The Organ		The Person	
Aspects:	**Structural change, anatomical change**	**Functional change at the organ level**	**Skills, abilities of the individual**	**Social, economic consequences**
Neutral Terms:	Health condition	Organ function	Skills, abilities	Social participation
Loss, limitation:	Disorder, injury	Impairment	Disability	Handicap
ICIDH—80:	Disorder	Impairment	Disability	Handicap
ICF:	Structural change	Functional change, impairment	Activity + performance code	Participation + performance code
Application to Vision:		Visual functions --Measured quantitatively, e.g, visual acuity	Functional vision * --Described qualitatively,e.g., reading ability	

*Visual task performance in our framework

FIGURE 1-4. Aspects of vision loss.

Source: Adapted from International Society for Low Vision Research and Rehabilitation (1999).

keyboarding, crossing the street, or identifying birds. Generally, abilities are described more qualitatively than the raw visual functions, although this report examines some quantitative measures of visual task performance that might be considered by SSA. From the concept of ability, it is a short step to the concept of *disability, a reduction in or loss of an ability*. Examples of visual disabilities include difficulty reading normal size print and using tools or small machinery. As noted above, disability is recognized as a complex interplay between the individual, the complexity of the task, and the surrounding environmental and social supports.[5]

The term *handicap,* in modern practice, refers to the result of an interaction between a person and the environment. We use it only to refer to *the negative result of the interaction between a person's impaired abilities and the environment in which she or he is attempting to function.* Thus a *disability* that prevents a person from climbing stairs imposes a *handicap* when that person must live, work, or otherwise participate or obtain services in a structure that has stairs and lacks wheelchair ramps, elevators, or other assistive devices. Although the disability may be real and permanent, it need not result in a handicap if the person has a suitably designed supportive environment in which to live and work or is able to use assistive technology.[6]

SSA uses "disability" or "disabled" as a term that applies to those who are deemed eligible for disability benefits as a result of the formal determination process. The agency uses the terms to describe the relationship of the person to the criteria for its programs, not

---

[5]The ICIDH (World Health Organization, 1980) definition: "In the context of health experience, a disability is any restriction or lack (resulting from an impairment) of ability to perform an activity in the manner or within the range considered normal for a human being" (p. 28).

[6]The ICIDH (World Health Organization, 1980) definition: "In the context of health experience, a handicap is a disadvantage for a given individual, resulting from an impairment or a disability, that limits or prevents the fulfillment of a role that is normal (depending on age, sex, and social and cultural factors) for that individual" (p. 29).

necessarily as a description of his or her personal functional status. The SSA disability determination process (already described) follows a path starting with a medical model, embodied in the listings of impairments, through Step 3 of the decision process; it then proceeds to a model that implicitly accounts for some social and physical environmental factors in the later steps, in which vocational factors are considered. The listed medical conditions are assumed to produce impairments so severe that individuals are disabled by the mere presence of the condition, as determined by physical diagnostic markers. For persons whose conditions meet or equal the listings and who are not engaged in substantial gainful activity, SSA does not require that functional capacity be evaluated to determine eligibility for benefits.

For those whose conditions do not meet or equal the medical listings, SSA switches to an evaluation of functional capacity in relation to the work environment (based on a simplistic model of work). The process evaluates the claimant's ability first to perform recent relevant employment and then to perform any work in the U.S. economy. The vocational grids mentioned earlier are used as decision aids when the impairment is in the ability to perform physical labor, but for other work, the guidance is sparse at best. The decision maker considers the claimant's age, education, and work experience, and, by implication, transferable skills. At this time, SSA prescribes no formal tests or evaluation protocols to determine what the claimant actually can do, no formal method for determining what disability might result from an individual's impairments in the living and work environments, nor what the mitigating effects of environmental accommodations or assistive technology might be.

Vision-Specific Concepts and Terms

As explained above, visual functions are measured using quantitative clinical tests. When we speak of *visual functions* we are referring to the performance of the visual system, more or less in isolation, under standardized measurement conditions. The specific visual functions considered in this study are:

- visual acuity,
- visual fields,
- contrast sensitivity,
- color vision,
- binocular function,
- visual search.

The committee also examined environmental conditions that may exacerbate visual impairments, chiefly extremes of lighting (glare, high or low luminance) and transitions between high and low luminance conditions. Full definitions of these visual functions are given in Chapter 2, which treats each of them in detail.

The committee selected four task or activity domains as exemplars of everyday and work functions in which vision is an important contributor to performance capability. The committee sought to identify categories of tasks that are important across a wide range of daily life and work situations, that may be reasonable surrogates for visually intensive job tasks, that are of moderate complexity, and for which data are available in the research literature. The selection process is discussed in more detail in Chapter 3. After considerable discussion of candidate task domains, the committee chose the following:

- Reading and other sustained near tasks (e.g., computer use);
- Mobility, including both ambulatory and driving situations;
- Social participation, including visual communication;
- Tool use and manipulation, including hand-eye coordination.

These domains were used as organizing concepts in our examination of the scientific evidence on relationships between visual functions and visual task performance.

Lines of Inquiry

For the purposes of the SSA benefit programs, disability is defined by "the inability to engage in any substantial gainful activity, by reason of any medically determinable physical or mental impairment(s)" (Social Security Administration, 2001). SSA is required to document the disability of each claimant in the process of deciding whether he or she is eligible for disability benefits. Because disability represents the outcome of interactions between the person and his or her environment (both physical and social), there are many possible avenues for determining whether any individual claimant has a disability.

The first and most obvious variable is the measurement of the physical (in this case, visual) impairment. The committee examined how this is now done by SSA and also examined evidence on best practices for current tests and on new or emerging ways to test visual functions. We established psychometric and other criteria that vision tests should meet if they are to be recommended for use in SSA disability determination. We also gave careful consideration to what visual functions should be measured, evaluating evidence both for the importance of the functions for task performance and for the availability of tests that met our criteria. Finally, the committee reviewed ways in which to combine test results into a composite index of visual impairment.

Because disability occurs at the interface of visual ability and task demands, the next obvious area of inquiry was the determination of whether disability from visual causes could be determined by judging performance on a set of standardized tasks. In order to approach this issue, the committee selected a set of tasks or activity domains that represent common, visually intensive, job tasks. The committee pursued research on available survey-based job task taxonomies and datasets that include information on the visual requirements of jobs or job categories, which may serve to inform SSA policies or practices.

The committee considered the utility of directly measuring performance on these surrogate tasks, seeking information on instruments available for this purpose. Other information sources were questionnaire instruments that gather self-reports of performance abilities from individuals, notably health-related quality of life instruments. Such instruments that have been developed specifically for people with visual disorders have been used to demonstrate a relationship between visual impairment and task performance limitations, and we examined these carefully.

The committee's final line of inquiry was the examination of data on the employment and economic consequences of visual impairment. We commissioned studies of datasets generated by the National Health Interview Survey and the National Health and Nutrition Evaluation Survey, both nationally representative surveys conducted by the federal government that include information on self-reported disabilities and economic and employment status.

Information Sources and Standards

The committee and staff conducted literature searches in the peer-reviewed and technical literature (e.g., government-sponsored reports) on vision-related topics, testing, disability determination, disability programs, and other topics. For vision and vision testing, the peer-reviewed research and clinical literature was the predominant source, although many other sources were also tapped.

Standards for Evidence

Peer-reviewed scientific literature was the most desirable source of information for this study, and when it was available it was used. Committee members applied their professional judgment in evaluating the methodology of studies they reviewed, rejecting studies that appeared to be poorly designed, executed, or analyzed. Technical reports and other information sources, such as analyses of survey datasets, were evaluated for acceptability, with special attention to the data sources used in preparing the reports and to the methodology used. The committee often discussed the strengths and weaknesses of particular evidence in its deliberations.

When weaknesses were found but a report or study was deemed worthy of inclusion, the weaknesses are discussed along with the evidence in this report. The committee is especially careful to note the limitations of epidemiological and survey-based studies that could be used to infer characteristics of populations. Often the findings are worth discussing, but only limited inferences can be drawn because of the size or other characteristics of the study sample. In some cases, the committee commissioned specialists to perform data analyses, to ensure that the analyses were done by people who knew well the idiosyncrasies and limitations of the source data.

Public Forum

In the committee's view, it was important to obtain input for this study from organizations providing services to people with visual impairments and advocating for their interests. The committee therefore organized a public forum to gather input from these communities. Representatives of national and regional organizations and others were invited to make presentations. A list of organizations invited to nominate speakers and a list of speakers and major topics appear in Appendix B.

ORGANIZATION OF THE REPORT

Three chapters follow this introduction. Chapter 2 lays out the committee's findings on tests of visual function. Each function is examined in detail, and tests of the function are evaluated for their potential value in disability determination, with detailed rationale for the conclusions that we reached and the recommendations we made. Chapter 3 presents our findings on the relationships between visual functions and the tasks of everyday life. It discusses the four task domains found to be important, as well as evaluations of health-related quality of life studies and occupational analysis methods and datasets. Chapter 4 covers the special issues that affect how children's visual function can and should be tested.

Each of these chapters includes recommendations for SSA actions on visual disability determination, as well as for research that will improve visual disability determination. The recommendations cover what aspects of vision should be tested, how the tests should be conducted, and how to combine results of tests if warranted. Suggestions are provided for future research to address issues that remain unresolved.

Appendixes A through D provide the full text of one commissioned paper, the details of the public forum, a glossary of SSA terms, and brief biographical sketches of the committee members.

2

TESTS OF VISUAL FUNCTIONS

Tests of visual functions are at the core of current disability determination practices for visually impaired claimants at the Social Security Administration (SSA), and the committee's task required us to carefully review and evaluate these tests. This chapter presents the results of that review. Each fundamental function is discussed, beginning with acuity and visual fields, the functions currently tested by SSA for disability determination. Next we present the evidence on the testing of contrast sensitivity, followed by other visual functions that the committee judged worthy of consideration as candidates for testing by SSA—most of which were mentioned in the earlier NRC report (National Research Council, 1994). Some closely related functions are grouped in a single section.

For each function, we considered evidence on why the function is important in the evaluation of visual disability and reviewed and evaluated evidence of the relationships between that function and performance in the four daily living and work task domains selected (see Chapter 1). The committee established criteria for acceptable tests and then reviewed and evaluated currently available and emerging new tests of each function against these criteria. Each section describes the strengths and weaknesses of available and emerging tests for a particular function. Finally, each section presents, with rationale, our recommendations for or against SSA's testing that function for disability determination and describes further research required to improve testing or otherwise support better disability determination practices.

A separate section discusses ways in which scores on tests of visual function could be mathematically combined to yield a single index of visual impairment for a claimant. The committee's recommendations for the testing of visual functions are summarized in the final section.

VISUAL ACUITY

Description

Visual acuity is a measure of the spatial resolving power of the visual system; it indicates the angular size of the smallest detail that can be resolved. Clinical tests of visual acuity determine a size threshold for a recognition task. The targets to be recognized are called "optotypes," and typically they are letters, Landolt rings, or "tumbling E's" designed so the width of the strokes and the gaps are one fifth of the height of the optotype character. An individual's visual acuity is determined by measuring the angular size of the smallest optotypes whose identity (letters) or orientation (Landolt rings and tumbling E's) can be recognized.

Visual acuity is typically measured under conditions of high contrast, using printed or projected charts with optotypes like those described above. The results of visual acuity testing are usually expressed in Snellen notation, which is the ratio of the test distance to the distance at which the critical detail of the smallest optotype resolved would subtend 1 minute of visual angle. Thus, a minimum angle of resolution (MAR) of 1 minute of visual angle (or arc, sometimes abbreviated as "min arc") when tested at 20 feet (6 meters) is expressed as 20/20 (6/6), whereas an MAR of 10 minutes of arc if tested at 20 feet is expressed as 20/200 (6/60). Alternative means of expressing visual acuity are the decimal notation (the reciprocal of the MAR or the

Snellen fraction), logMAR notation (the common logarithm of the MAR), the visual acuity rating, VAR, where VAR = 100 – 50 (logMAR), and the Snell-Sterling visual efficiency (VE = $0.2^{(MAR-1)/9}$). Table 2-1 presents these alternative forms of measurement as a conversion table. The standard for normal acuity has traditionally been considered to be 20/20. However, individuals with normal, disease-free eyes often have acuity better than 20/20, provided that refractive error has been corrected (Elliott et al., 1995).

Evaluation

Why the Measurement Is Useful

Ophthalmologists and optometrists routinely measure visual acuity for various purposes. In the measurement of refractive error, the lens power that permits the best visual acuity is often an important criterion. In the diagnosis and monitoring of eye diseases that may affect vision, changes of visual acuity are often taken to indicate the presence and magnitude of change in the medical condition. Ocular diseases and disorders that affect the transparency and optical regularity of the cornea, lens, or vitreous will degrade the optical image, with adverse effects on visual acuity. Diseases affecting the central region of the retina or the associated optic nerve pathways are likely to cause reductions in visual acuity. Visual acuity measurements are also used by some licensing authorities and employers as eligibility criteria for some occupations (e.g., airline pilot, police officer) and activities (e.g., driving). Visual acuity has traditionally been used as the primary indicator of the magnitude of functional impairment due to vision loss.

Good spatial resolution is important for a variety of everyday tasks in the workplace, but probably most critically for reading text and interpreting symbols, key components of many jobs. Visual acuity also plays a central role in discriminating and recognizing small objects or the detailed features of objects. The visual acuity demand for a given task depends on the size of the critical detail in the task and the observation distance. For example, a person with good visual acuity might be expected to recognize faces at about 20 meters. To

TABLE 2-1 Conversion Table for Visual Acuity Notations

Distance Vision

LogMAR notation	MAR exact	MAR notation*	Decimal notation*	VE% notation	VAR notation
–0.30	0.501	0.50	2.00	109.4%	115
–0.20	0.631	0.63	1.60	106.8%	110
–0.10	0.794	0.80	1.25	103.6%	105
0.00	1.000	1.00	1.00	100.0%	100
0.10	1.259	1.25	0.80	95.6%	95
0.20	1.585	1.60	0.63	89.8%	90
0.30	1.995	2.0	0.50	83.6%	85
0.40	2.512	2.5	0.40	76.5%	80
0.50	3.162	3.2	0.32	67.5%	75
0.60	3.981	4.0	0.25	58.5%	70
0.70	5.012	5.0	0.20	48.9%	65
0.80	6.310	6.3	0.160	38.8%	60
0.90	7.943	8.0	0.125	28.6%	55
1.00	10.00	10.0	0.100	20.0%	50
1.10	12.59	12.5	0.080	12.8%	45
1.20	15.85	16	0.063	6.8%	40
1.30	19.95	20	0.050	3.3%	35
1.40	25.12	25	0.040	1.4%	30
1.50	31.62	32	0.032	0.4%	25
1.60	39.81	40	0.025		20
1.70	50.12	50	0.020		15
1.80	63.10	63	0.016		10
1.90	79.43	80	0.013		5
2.00	100.0	100	0.010		0

*Note: Numbers rounded to simplify sequences. Rounding errors do not exceed 1.2 percent.

Source: Ian Bailey, personal communication.

Snellen Fractions			Near Vision At 40 centimeters			
Based on 20 ft.*	Based on 6 m.*	Based on 4 m.*	Snellen notation 0.40 meters*	M Units *	Points *	x-height (mm)
20/10	6/3	4/2	0.40/0.20	0.20	1.6	0.29
20/12.5	6/3.8	4/2.5	0.40/0.25	0.25	2.0	0.36
20/16	6/4.8	4/3.2	0.40/0.32	0.32	2.5	0.47
20/20	6/6	4/4	0.40/0.40	0.40	3.2	0.58
20/25	6/7.5	4/5	0.40/0.50	0.50	4.0	0.73
20/32	6/9.5	4/6.3	0.40/0.63	0.63	5.0	0.92
20/40	6/12	4/8	0.40/0.80	0.80	6.3	1.16
20/50	6/15	4/10	0.40/1.00	1.00	8.0	1.45
20/63	6/19	4/12.5	0.40/1.25	1.25	10.0	1.82
20/80	6/24	4/16	0.40/1.60	1.60	12.5	2.33
20/100	6/30	4/20	0.40/2.0	2.0	16	2.91
20/125	6/38	4/25	0.40/2.5	2.5	20	3.64
20/160	6/48	4/32	0.40/3.2	3.2	25	4.65
20/200	6/60	4/40	0.40/4.0	4.0	32	5.82
20/250	6/75	4/50	0.40/5.0	5.0	40	7.27
20/320	6/95	4/63	0.40/6.3	6.3	50	9.16
20/400	6/120	4/80	0.40/8.0	8.0	63	11.6
20/500	6/150	4/100	0.40/10.0	10.0	80	14.5
20/630	6/190	4/125	0.40/12.5	12.5	100	18.2
20/800	6/240	4/160	0.40/16	16	125	23.3
20/1000	6/300	4/200	0.40/20	20	160	29.1
20/1250	6/380	4/250	0.40/25	25	200	36.4
20/1600	6/480	4/320	0.40/32	32	250	46.5
20/2000	6/600	4/400	0.40/40	40	320	58.2

recognize the same faces, a person with poor visual acuity would have to get significantly closer.

In the workplace, there is a multitude of tasks in which it is important to see fine details. Some examples are reading labels, gauges, and dials; inspecting products for cracks, scratches, and foreign material; and visually guided manipulation, as in needle-threading, surgery, and fine assembly tasks. In mobility, acuity is important for recognizing environmental landmarks, avoiding small obstacles, and reading highway signs during driving (Hofstetter, 1976). Acuity is also a strong predictor of self-reported vision-related quality of life.

Value as a Practical Measure

In 1865, Hermann Snellen designed the first letter chart for the clinical measurement of visual acuity. It had a large letter at the top, and below it there were 6 rows of letters and numbers in progressively smaller sizes. The chart was viewed from a standard distance, and the size of the smallest letters that could be read provided the measure of visual acuity. Since then, numerous modifications have been made to Snellen's original chart design, with changes being made to the selection and design of the letters or symbols, the range of sizes, the progression of sizes, the number of letters in the rows, and the spacing between letters and between rows (see Figure 2-1 for a sample chart). While the design has evolved to improve the validity and reliability of visual acuity measurement, Snellen's letter chart approach has prevailed for more than a century. Letter charts are used almost universally for visual acuity testing of literate adults and school-age children in clinical and research settings. Alternative charts and other test procedures are sometimes necessary for testing infants and preschool children and other individuals who are unable to identify or respond appropriately to the letters or symbols on the chart. While there may be some further modifications to chart design or test procedures, it can be expected that letter chart testing will remain the standard means of measuring visual acuity.

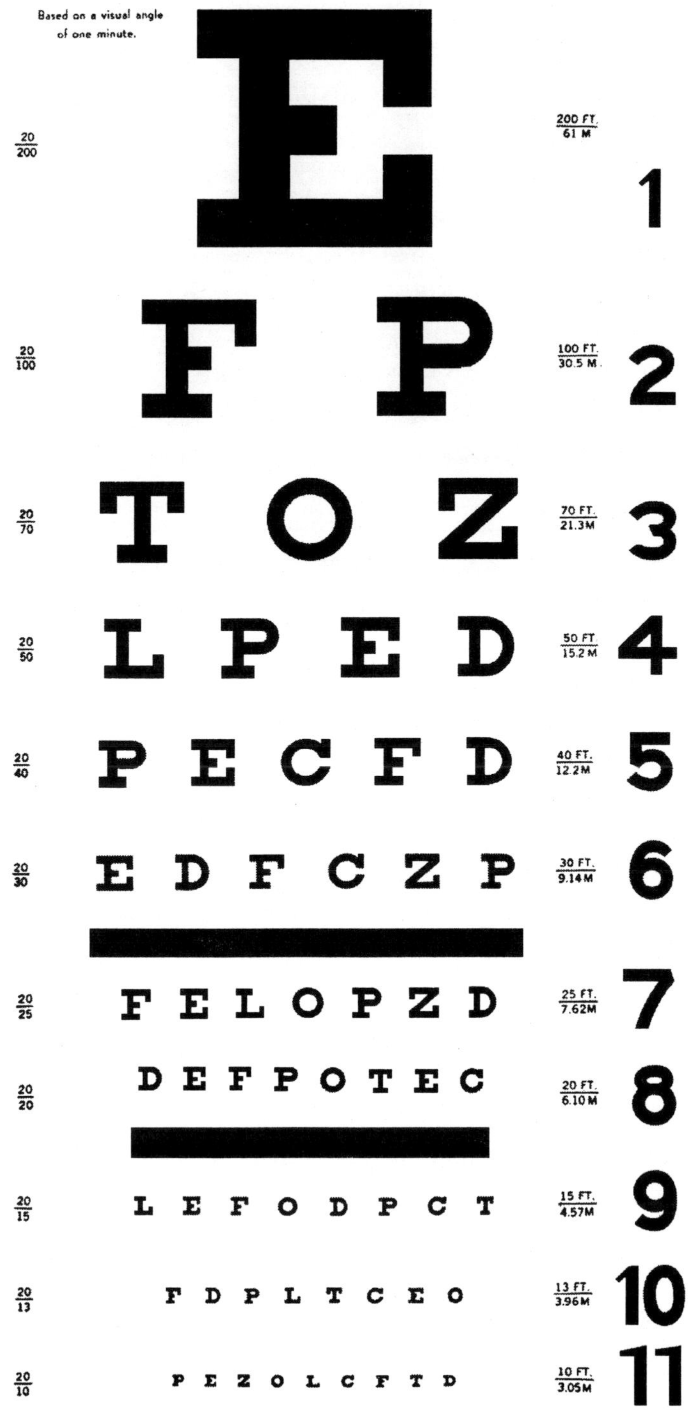

FIGURE 2-1. Snellen-type acuity chart. Source: National Eye Institute, National Institutes of Health.

Quantifying Performance

The current SSA standard defines Impairment of Central Visual Acuity as best-corrected Snellen acuity of 20/200 or worse in the better eye, measured with a distance visual acuity chart (Social Security Administration, 1999). Specific recommendations for visual acuity chart design and testing conditions have been made by several bodies (American National Standards Institute International Standards, 1986a, 1986b; Consilium Ophthalmologicum Universale Visual Functions Committee, 1988; National Research Council, 1980, 1994). On the basis of these recommendations, we identify four weaknesses in the current SSA standard:

1. In the SSA standard, the type of chart(s) to be used for testing visual acuity is specified only as "Snellen." There is no standardized Snellen chart. The most commonly used projector charts and panel charts differ significantly from Snellen's original chart design, but they are still referred to as Snellen charts. Commonly these charts have few letters at the larger sizes, the size progression varies from one chart to the next, and there is a pattern of having more letters and relatively closer spacings at the smaller sizes.

As emphasized by the 1980 report of the Committee on Vision (National Research Council, 1980), the design of the chart used (including optotype, the number and spacing of optotypes on a line, the range and progression of optotype sizes, the chart luminance, and the nominal contrast between the optotypes and their background) has an important influence on the results of visual acuity measurement. The present standard does not specify chart design requirements and permits the use of charts that may produce very different visual acuity scores. For example, the standard is met when someone fails to read any optotypes that are smaller than the 20/200 optotype. On the most commonly used Snellen charts, the next smallest size optotype is in a 20/100 row, but on others it may be 20/160 or even 20/180. Applying the SSA criterion of "20/200 or worse distance acuity" to such different charts has the functional effect of making the cutoff less than 20/100, less than 20/160, or less than 20/180, according to the chart being used.

The current SSA criterion cannot be applied consistently unless there are specific constraints on the design of the test charts. In particular, the optotype size that is next smallest to 20/200 should be specified. The recommended visual acuity chart design has two steps of size 20/125 and 20/160 between the 20/100 and 20/200 levels, and it is also recommend that credit be given for partial success in reading the sample of letters at each size. The SSA standard for Impairment of Central Visual Acuity is that the visual acuity should be 20/200 or worse. With charts of the recommended and more modern design, the literal application of the SSA criterion is that the standard is met when no letters at all can be read at the 20/160 level or smaller. However, the common practice has been and remains testing acuity with charts that have no intermediate sizes between 20/100 and 20/200. As it has been most commonly applied, this means that the SSA standard is met when no letters at all can be read at the 20/100 size or smaller. We are not recommending a change from the criterion for Impairment of Central Visual Acuity. We do, however, recommend standardization of chart design, which would raise policy issues for SSA.

The literal application of the 20/200 or worse criterion with a recommended chart would mean that a sizable group of people who currently qualify would be no longer classified as having Impairment of Central Visual Acuity. These are the people who would be able to read all or some of the letters at the 20/160 or 20/125 sizes while being unable to read any at the 20/100 level. Alternatively, SSA could choose to continue allowing the most commonly applied criterion: no letters can be read at the 20/100 size. This would lead to a sizable group of people's meeting the criterion, even though their visual acuities could be anywhere in the range from 20/125 to one letter better than 20/200.

2. The standard does not specify the conditions under which visual acuity should be tested. The level of illumination and the testing environment are important factors affecting performance. Inadequate illumination leads to poor performance, as does glare from extraneous light sources. The standard *does* specify that visual acuity should be tested with best correction; thus, care should be taken to ensure that refractive error is properly corrected prior to visual acuity testing.

3. The standard does not specify the use of standardized testing procedures. There is no universal standard procedure for measuring performance on different lines of a chart, and there are no standard procedures for scoring performance; for example, what should be done when a subject is correct for some elements on each of two adjacent lines? It is common clinical practice to assign a score that indicates the smallest size at which a certain proportion of the optotypes can be read (often the required proportion is "greater than 50 percent"). Scores can depend on whether guessing is encouraged or is obligatory when letters are difficult to read. The absence of standard testing and scoring methods reduces the reliability of measurements.

4. The standard deals only with the performance of the better eye. Everyday vision, however, is based on simultaneous viewing of the world with *both* eyes. Monocular acuity of the better eye may sometimes underestimate binocular acuity, for example, under conditions in which binocular summation occurs (Cagenello et al., 1993; Home, 1978; Pardhan, 1993) or in subjects with latent nystagmus, a condition in which rhythmic eye movements occur in the unoccluded eye when the other eye is occluded (Helveston & Ellis, 1984). Alternatively, monocular acuity of the better eye may sometimes overestimate binocular acuity, for example, under conditions in which inhibition is produced by the worse eye (Pardhan, 1993; Taylor et al., 1991). Thus, monocular acuity of the better eye is not always an adequate predictor of binocular acuity and therefore of visual resolution in everyday life.

Standardizing Visual Acuity Measurement

Chart Design

There is general agreement that the design of a visual acuity chart should be such that the visual task is the same at each size level, so that size remains the only significant variable from one size level to the next (Bailey & Lovie, 1976). For this principle to be satisfied, the size progression should be logarithmic, there should be the same number of optotypes at each size level, the spacings between optotypes within a row and between rows should be proportional to the size of the optotype, and the average recognition difficulty should be approximately the same for each row of optotypes.

The Committee on Vision (National Research Council, 1980) recommended the Landolt ring as the reference standard for optotypes, and it considered the Sloan family of 10 nonserif letters (**CDHKNORSVZ**) designed on a 5 × 5 grid (Sloan, 1959) to be acceptable. Another widely accepted family of optotypes is the British Standards family of 10 nonserif letters (**DEFHNPRUVZ**), which are designed on a 5 × 4 grid (British Standards Institution, 1968). Both of these charts use letters with a stroke width (critical detail) equal to 1/5 of the letter height. In clinical research today, there is almost universal use of the Early Treatment for Diabetic Retinopathy Study (ETDRS) chart (Figure 2-2) (Ferris et al., 1982), which uses Sloan letters, and the Bailey-Lovie (1976) chart, which uses the British family of letters. These two charts were found acceptable in the 1994 Committee on Vision report (National Research Council, 1994). Both charts have five letters per row, one letter width separating adjacent letters, with the spacing between adjacent rows equal to the height of the letters in the smaller row. Both charts have 14 rows covering a 20-fold range of letter sizes, and both follow a logarithmic (geometric) size progression with a ratio of 0.1 log unit (1.2589×) between each row and the next.

Observation Conditions

For assessment of distance visual acuity, test distance should be 3 meters (10 feet) or more, to minimize the need for the use of accommodation to bring the optotypes into focus. The traditional test distance is 6 meters (20 feet); however, the Committee on Vision (National Research Council, 1980) recommended that the standard test distance be changed to 4 meters because this distance presents an accommodation demand of exactly 0.25 D; it is also conveniently 10 times longer than 40 cm, which is a commonly used distance for testing near vision (Hofstetter, 1973). The ETDRS clinical research protocols use a 4-meter standard test distance, with a recommendation

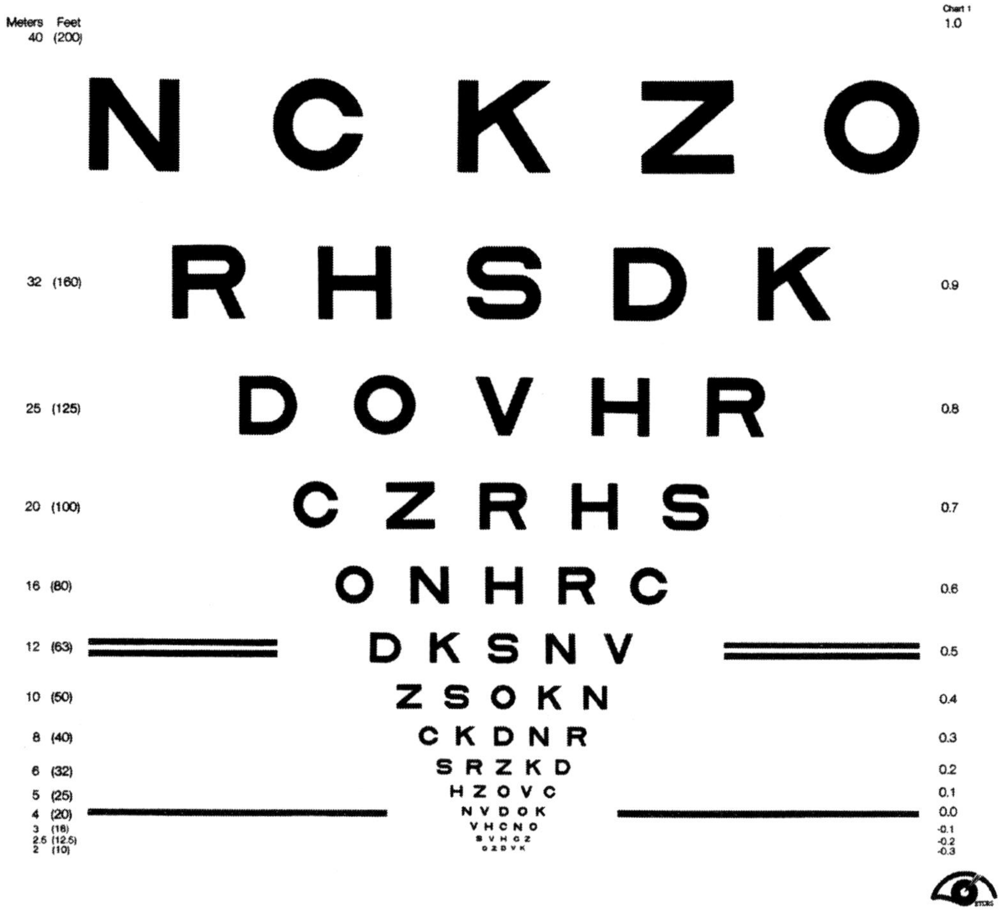

FIGURE 2-2. ETDRS "Chart 1" acuity chart. Source: National Eye Institute, National Institutes of Health.

for shortening of the viewing distance to 1 meter when a visual acuity of 4/40 (equivalent to 20/200) cannot be achieved.

On some charts, the print size is labeled in units of angular size that assume a certain presentation distance. If the testing is performed at some other distance, it is important to use care in scoring and in interpreting the score, to ensure that the nonstandard distance is correctly taken into account. For charts that carry labels in other units that express angular size in logarithmic units (logMAR or VAR), using the chart at nonstandard distances requires a constant number to be added or subtracted from the score indicated by the size label on the chart.

The charts should be presented in high contrast at moderate photopic luminance. The Committee on Vision (National Research Council, 1980) recommended that the luminance of the chart background be 85+/–5 cd/m^2, and that the general room illumination should be low enough that it does not reduce the contrast of the optotypes below 0.85. The 1994 Committee on Vision report recommended 160 cd/m^2 background luminance, with a minimum of 80 cd/m^2 (National Research Council, 1994). Most common clinical projectors are designed to produce a background luminance of 85 cd/m^2, but higher luminances of about 300 cd/m^2 are used in many modern projectors, particularly those from Europe. For normally sighted subjects, a twofold change in photopic luminance produces a change of about 5 percent (0.02 log unit) in the acuity score (Sheedy et al., 1984). Tighter tolerances for luminance (of about +/–10 percent or +/–0.04 log units) are recommended for clinical research or for clinical testing when it is important to standardize the luminance conditions (Ferris & Bailey, 1996). Many people with visual impairment can be extraordinarily sensitive to lighting levels (Lie, 1977; Lovie-Kitchin & Bowman, 1985; Sloan, 1969) and, if the goal is to assess functional disability, it may be appropriate to take additional measures of visual acuity at nonstandard luminance levels.

Glare conditions should be avoided. The luminance of the objects and surface surrounding the test chart should not exceed the luminance of the test chart. Care should be taken to avoid reflections from the surface of the chart. Any bright light source or bright reflection in the subject's field of vision has the potential to be a source of disability glare, which can have the effect of reducing the contrast in the retinal image.

Testing Procedures

Normally, visual acuity is measured when the optimal optical correction (eyeglasses or contact lenses) is being worn. For disability determination, it is logically most appropriate to test binocular acuity. The older algorithm of the American Medical Association (AMA) (American Medical Association, 1993; American Medical Association & the Committee on Medical Rating of Physical Impairment, 1958) for calculating binocular visual efficiency took the monocular acuity of the better eye and added a negative weighting dependent on the visual acuity in the worse eye. The algorithm given in the 1993 AMA guide is

$$\frac{3 \times \text{impairment value of better eye} + \text{impairment value of worse eye}}{4}$$

(American Medical Association, 1993). The 2001 AMA guide now recommends using a weighted combination of binocular, right eye, and left eye acuity scores to calculate an acuity-related impairment rating: "Visual impairment ratings are calculated using the formula $(3OU + OD + OS)/5$ instead of the prior formula $(3 \times \text{better eye} + 1 \times \text{lesser eye})/4$. The new formula better accounts for situations where the binocular function is not identical to the function of the better eye" (American Medical Association, 2001, p.278).

Under section 12.2b.4, on monocular versus binocular acuity, the new AMA guide states: "Because binocular viewing represents the most common viewing condition in daily life, the impairment rating should consider the best-corrected binocular visual acuity as well as the best-corrected acuity for each eye separately" (American Medical Association, 2001, p.282).

In the committee's view, measurement of binocular visual acuity is the most appropriate method for evaluating disability. The AMA's recent inclusion of binocular acuity in their new formula for scoring visual acuity impairment provides similar recognition of the appropriateness of binocular visual acuity testing.

When being tested, the subject should be encouraged to guess at the letters in a row if 40 percent or more of the letters have been read correctly in the previous row. This procedure does not force the subject to guess, but encourages him or her to persist as the letters are becoming difficult to recognize with full confidence. It also does not oblige guessing when the subject feels that letter identification is impossible. If the subject cannot read all letters in the top (largest) row, then the chart should be moved to a closer distance. Should the subject be able to read the smallest letters, the chart should be moved farther from the subject.

Scoring Method

The Committee on Vision (National Research Council, 1980) recommended defining visual acuity as the smallest size at which at least 7 out of 10 optotypes are read correctly. The committee indicated that acuity could alternatively be specified as the last optotype size at which all letters were read, plus the number of optotypes read at the next smaller size (e.g., 20/30+3), or as the number of optotypes missed at the smallest line read (e.g., 20/30–2).

A number of studies have shown that, for logarithmically spaced charts with a constant number of letters per line, such as the Bailey-Lovie (1976) and ETDRS (Ferris et al., 1982) charts, there is greater accuracy in the acuity measurement (i.e., less deviation from the true acuity score) and less variation in test-retest scores when using letter-by-letter scoring rather than assigning a score on a row-by-row basis (Arditi & Cagenello, 1993; Bailey et al., 1991). The 1994 report of the Committee on Vision (National Research Council, 1994) recommended this scoring method. With the Bailey-Lovie and ETDRS charts, there are five letters per row and, given the size progression ratio of 0.1 log units, each letter read correctly can be assigned a value of 0.02 logMAR. Thus there is a total value of 0.1 logMAR per row. The VAR method of designating visual acuity operates similarly, with 1 point assigned for each letter read correctly, so there are 5 points per row. For any chart design, a logMAR value can be assigned to the letters in a given line by subtracting the logMAR value for that letter size from the logMAR value of the next largest size and dividing that difference by the number of letters in that row.

Measurement reliability may be further increased by taking repeated measurements, but care must be taken to avoid subjects' memorizing the letter sequences. Some letter charts are produced in multiple forms with different letter sequences that aid in preventing memorization.

Near Visual Acuity

Near visual acuity is measured with hand-held charts, typically at a distance of 40 cm. If the near vision test chart has the same or similar design features as the letter chart used for distance visual acuity, if other test conditions (luminance, contrast, etc.) are the same, and if the subject is wearing appropriate refractive error correction, then the distance and near visual acuity scores should be equivalent to each other. Lovie-Kitchin and Brown (2000) reported a difference of approximately one-half line (two letters) between distance and near visual acuity measured with Bailey-Lovie charts in 24 individuals between 25 and 77 years of age. Lovie-Kitchin attributed the slightly worse near acuity to variations in accommodation, pupil size, and/or depth of focus. In a more recent study of 78 individuals between 21 and 68 years of age, Lovie-Kitchin and Brown (2000) found a difference of one line between distance and near acuity, which they attributed largely to inadequate correction of near vision in older, presbyopic subjects who were tested with their habitual correction rather than the best correction.

Recommendations

Our recommendations concerning assessment of visual acuity are similar to those of the Committee on Vision in its 1980 and 1994 reports (National Research Council, 1980, 1994). We therefore recommend that visual acuity charts should contain the same number of optotypes in each row, the space between optotypes in a row should be at least as wide as the optotypes in that row, and the size of the optotypes should decrease in 0.1 log unit steps from row to row. The recommended chart luminance is 160 cd/m^2, and it should not be less than 80 cd/m^2. Viewing should be free from glare, with a level of contrast between optotypes and background that is above 80 percent. The person being tested should be encouraged to read as many optotypes on the chart as possible and to guess at an optotype if he or she is unsure. Acuity results should be scored on an optotype-by-optotype basis, since this scoring procedure produces lower test-retest variability than does row-by-row scoring.

For disability determination, visual acuity should be tested under binocular conditions, since this provides the most representative measure of an individual's everyday vision. The common clinical practice is to measure the two monocular visual acuities and not test acuity under binocular viewing. The AMA Guide to the Evaluation of Permanent Visual Impairment has used algorithms for combining the two monocular acuities using an averaging procedure that gives a weighting factor of 3:1 to the better eye, and more recently they have proposed an algorithm that combines the two monocular acuities and the binocular acuity. Rubin et al. (2000) found that neither of the AMA algorithms predicted binocular visual acuity as well as taking the visual acuity in the better of the two eyes. We recommend that if binocular vision is not tested, the acuity of the better eye should be used for disability determination.

SSA has need of a cutoff criterion for deciding whether or not an individual has a functional disability. We conclude that currently the scientific evidence does not support a particular visual acuity criterion as a determinant of visual disability. (Chapter 3 provides discussions of the evidence we considered.) Given the history and legislation behind the current SSA standard of "20/200 or worse distance acuity" as the principal criterion for visual disability, we recommend continued use of the 20/200 criterion. Since we recommend a visual acuity chart design that would include optotypes at the 20/160 level, applying the "20/200 or worse" criterion literally to scores obtained with such a chart would set the effective criterion to "worse than 20/160 distance acuity." The scoring of the charts currently used in disability determination sets the effective criterion at "worse than 20/100."

The recommended charts have a 20/100 line that would allow SSA to maintain the effective criterion at its current position, but SSA must make the decision on whether this should be done.

It is important to acknowledge the arbitrary nature of selecting a single criterion of visual acuity loss for automatically classifying an individual as having a disability. Visual loss, however it is measured, is associated with decreasing ability to carry out activities associated with employment or (in the case of children) age-appropriate activities. In choosing a visual acuity criterion for determining who is visually disabled, there are some complexities that must be recognized.

It is becoming increasingly clear that the relationships between deficits in visual acuity and deficits in functional status, whether involving mobility, face recognition, or performance of various motor tasks, are monotonic functions with considerable "noise." This means that an individual's disability level cannot be confidently predicted from his or her visual acuity alone. Smooth monotonic relationships between acuity and the various functional abilities mean that there will be no clear critical threshold point or sharp inflection above which there is a sharp increase in disability. For any arbitrary cutoff point, there will be substantial numbers of people with better vision who will have more difficulty than expected when performing the given task, and a similar number of people with poorer vision who will have less difficulty than expected when performing the task.

From the published relationships between acuity and functional abilities, it might be predicted that an individual with reduced visual acuity would have certain deficits in functional abilities in several different functional tasks. However, the individual is likely to function better than expected at some tasks and worse at others. Overall disability depends not only on the extent of functional deficits at specific tasks, but also on the relative importance that each of those tasks has in the individual's regular day-to-day activities.

In conclusion, because available scientific evidence does not justify any criterion for disability, further research is warranted that relates scores on tests of visual impairment to self-report, performance of tasks of everyday life, and performance in the workplace. Such research would provide urgently needed information on possible disability criteria.

VISUAL FIELDS

Description

The visual field refers to the spatial extent over which the visual system is sensitive to light. The size of the visual field is expressed in terms of visual angle, which is simply the angle subtended at the eye. Visual field *eccentricity* is the angular distance from the point of fixation, known as the fovea, out to peripheral visual field locations. In normal eyes, the total monocular visual field extent is approximately 160° horizontally and 100° vertically. The visual fields of the two eyes overlap, except for the far temporal visual field of each eye. The binocular visual field thus extends slightly farther horizontally to approximately 180-200°. By convention in clinical perimetry, the *macular region* extends out to 5° radius (10° diameter) from fixation, the *central* visual field refers to peripheral eccentricities out to 30° radius (60° diameter), and the *peripheral* visual field refers to eccentricities that are beyond 30° radius (60° diameter). Throughout this section on visual fields, these definitions of macular, central, and peripheral visual fields are employed.[1]

For normal illumination in the work environment, visual function and visual sensitivity are not uniform over the entire visual field. Under typical illumination conditions for the workplace, the point of fixation has the best visual function and highest sensitivity. Visual sensitivity and other visual functions systematically decline with increasing peripheral eccentricity.

---

[1]In other sections of this report, the term "central" generally refers to macular vision, since this is the definition commonly used in the research literature, e.g., in studies on effects of central or peripheral vision impairments on task function.

The visual field is typically measured by one of several methods of perimetry, which in its most conventional form involves the detection of a small spot of light projected onto a uniform background. The 1994 report of the Committee on Vision (National Research Council, 1994) provides an overview of visual field measurement techniques and important factors relevant to visual field testing. Currently, the most common form of visual field testing is automated static perimetry. For the most commonly used test procedure, the sensitivity for detecting a small spot of light projected onto a uniform white background (the minimum amount of light needed to detect the spot of light) is measured for 76 locations on an evenly spaced grid (6° spacing) throughout the central 30° radius of the visual field.

Evaluation

Why the Measure Is Useful

Perimetry and visual field testing are methods commonly used in clinical ophthalmic settings to provide a quantitative assessment of the integrity of the field of view. Visual field testing is important because it is the only clinical test that evaluates vision outside the macula. All other tests of visual function that are performed in a clinical ophthalmic setting evaluate foveal vision (vision at the point of fixation). Thus, measurement of the visual field provides information that does not overlap with other procedures. Peripheral and central vision have been found to be important for performing many daily activities, and people with significantly restricted visual fields experience many difficulties with occupational demands and other activities (Gutierrez et al., 1997; Johnson & Keltner, 1983; Lovie-Kitchin, Mainstone, et al., 1990; Lovie-Kitchin, Woods, et al., 2001; Marron & Bailey, 1982). As mentioned earlier, visual field measurements are currently used by SSA as part of their visual disability determination procedures. This section provides a summary of the relationship between visual fields and four tasks that are important with respect to the work environment: reading, orientation/mobility, social participation, and tool use.

Reading. Most of the research on reading has been concerned with factors related to foveal vision capabilities. The relationship between reading and nonfoveal visual fields has mainly been centered on two areas: (1) the residual reading capabilities of the remaining visual field in people with central visual loss and (2) reading problems in people with homonymous hemianopsia, which is complete loss of either the right or left side of the visual field, usually due to stroke. When foveal vision is degraded, reading speed and comprehension are reduced (Chung et al., 1998; Rayner & Bertera, 1979; Rubin & Turano, 1994). Some of this loss is due to inaccurate eye movements, and some is due to the limited rate at which the remaining visual field can perform the pattern decoding required for reading (Rubin & Turano, 1994). In subjects with simulated central scotomas (blind spots or areas of nonseeing surrounded by areas of seeing), reading rates are faster when the material is presented to the inferior visual field than for other visual field locations (Petre et al., 2000).

During reading, people with right homonymous hemianopsias make a greater number of refixation saccades that are smaller in amplitude than for normally sighted individuals (DeLuca et al., 1996; Trauzettel-Klosinski & Brendler, 1998). People with left homonymous hemianopsias make a greater number of refixations on the return sweep to begin reading a new line (Trauzettel-Klosinski & Brendler, 1998). Although both types of hemianopsias reduce reading speed, right homonymous hemianopsias have been reported to produce greater deficits than left homonymous hemianopsias (Trauzettel-Klosinski & Brendler, 1998).

Orientation/Mobility. Much is known about the relationship between visual field status and mobility, particularly for driving. Marron and Bailey (1982) found that the visual field was an important predictor of success in mobility training for people with low vision. Turano and colleagues have reported that people with either central or peripheral visual field loss exhibit a deficit in the visual stabilization of body sway (Turano, Dagnelie, & Herdman, 1996; Turano, Herdman, & Dagnelie, 1993). In addition, they have reported deficits in mobility performance in people with restricted visual fields due to glaucoma or retinitis pigmentosa (Geruschat et al., 1998; Turano et al., 1999).

Lovie-Kitchen et al. (1990) evaluated the relationship between visual field size and orientation and mobility performance in nine people with low vision and nine age-matched normal controls, using an indoor obstacle course. They found that mobility performance (time taken to traverse the course and number of errors) was significantly influenced by total visual field extent. Individuals with smaller visual field extents had poorer mobility performance. Although both time to traverse the course and errors were affected by visual field size, errors were more highly correlated with visual field extent. The central 37° radius and the right, left, and inferior zones in the midperiphery were the most important visual field locations for mobility performance. Horizontal objects at head height and large objects on or suspended just above the floor were the most difficult for people with low vision to distinguish. A recent follow-up study of 79 people with low vision and 20 age-matched controls (Lovie-Kitchin et al., 2001) confirmed these findings. In addition, they reported that mobility performance became impaired when the visual field extent was smaller than 85°, and that mobility training would be required at some point when an individual's visual field was between 20° and 85°.

The visual field requirements for a driver's license vary considerably from one country to another (Charman, 1985) and from one state to another in this country (Keltner & Johnson, 1987). For those entities that have a visual field requirement for driving, the horizontal extent varies from about 20° to about 140°. A number of investigators have found statistically significant relationships between visual field size and driving accident and conviction records (Burg, 1967, 1968; North, 1985; Shinar, 1977; Shinar et al., 1975). However, although these relationships are statistically significant, the correlations are quite low, and visual field extent typically accounts for only about 5 percent of the variance for accident and conviction records.

Council and Allen (1974) found no relationship between the visual field size and accident and conviction records, although their peripheral vision test procedure was not validated and was likely to have rather high false positive and false negative rates. Johnson and Keltner (1983) found that accidents and convictions were more than twice as high in drivers with visual field loss in both eyes, compared with age- and sex-matched controls with normal peripheral vision.

There was no difference in accident and conviction records of drivers with visual field loss in only one eye compared with age- and sex-matched controls with normal peripheral vision.

Evaluation of the driving performance of people with various ocular and neurological disorders has been performed with the use of driving simulators (Hedin & Lovsund, 1986; Szlyk & Brigell, 1992). Although people with visual field loss tended to demonstrate deficits in driving performance, there were large individual differences. Some individuals appeared to be able to compensate for their visual field loss while others did not, even though they may have had equivalent visual field damage.

Wood and Troutbeck (1992) evaluated the influence of restricting the binocular visual field of drivers using a closed road track. They found that restricted visual fields impaired several driving tasks, including identification of road signs, efficiency in traversing the course, obstacle avoidance, and maneuvering through limited spaces. However, these deficits were not significant until the binocular visual field had been reduced to 40° or less.

Ball, Owsley, and colleagues have developed an alternative method of evaluating the central visual field (Owsley et al., 1991). Their test procedure evaluates visual search, localization, and divided attention tasks and is known as the useful field of view. Deficits in the useful field of view are more prevalent in older drivers than is traditionally measured visual field loss. Their findings suggest that the useful field of view may be a better predictor of accidents than visual fields or any other vision test. Chapter 3 presents a more detailed discussion of this research in the section on driving mobility.

Social Participation. There is only sparse information in the literature concerning the relationship between visual fields and social participation. Gutierrez et al. (1997) reported a statistically significant relationship ($p < .001$) between the visual field status of the better eye and the VF-14 social function scale ($r = -0.29$) and the emotion/well-being scale ($r = -0.28$) for people with glaucoma. From a practical standpoint, extensive visual field loss can impair an individual's ability to be aware of the presence and location of others, which can affect social interactions.

Tool Use/Manipulation. There is little or no formal literature on the role of the peripheral visual field and tool use/manipulation. Most tasks involving the use of tools are primarily dependent on central vision. However, any activity concerned with tool use/manipulation that incorporates a visual search task (e.g., detection of warning lights on a panel display, localization of objects to reach) may be affected by visual field loss, particularly if it is severe loss in both eyes.

Value as a Practical Measure

For nearly 200 years, perimetry and visual field testing procedures have been used clinically to assess the status of the peripheral visual field. Although there are a small number of individuals who are unable to perform perimetry because of significant physical or mental limitations, most adults can be tested with some form of perimetry. Automated static perimetry is currently a standard clinical ophthalmic diagnostic procedure that is used by the majority of eye care practitioners.

Quantifying Performance

The current visual field requirement for legal blindness is defined in terms of the size of the isopter generated by a Goldmann III/4e stimulus along eight principal meridians (0, 45, 90, 135, 180, 225, 270 and 315°). Figure 2-3 illustrates the plotting of an isopter. The chart represents the visual field of a normal right eye, with the greatest measured extent of vision, in degrees from the point of fixation (center of the diagram), marked on each of the eight meridians. The heavy dotted line connecting these points is the isopter. The Goldmann III/4e stimulus consists of a 0.43° target of 318 cd/m^2 luminance (1,000 apostilbs) projected onto a 10 cd/m^2 background luminance (31.5 apostilbs). A visual field is considered to be normal if the sum of the radii of the eight principal meridians is equal to or greater than 500°. Total visual disability (0 percent efficiency) is defined as a contraction of the visual field of the better eye to less than or

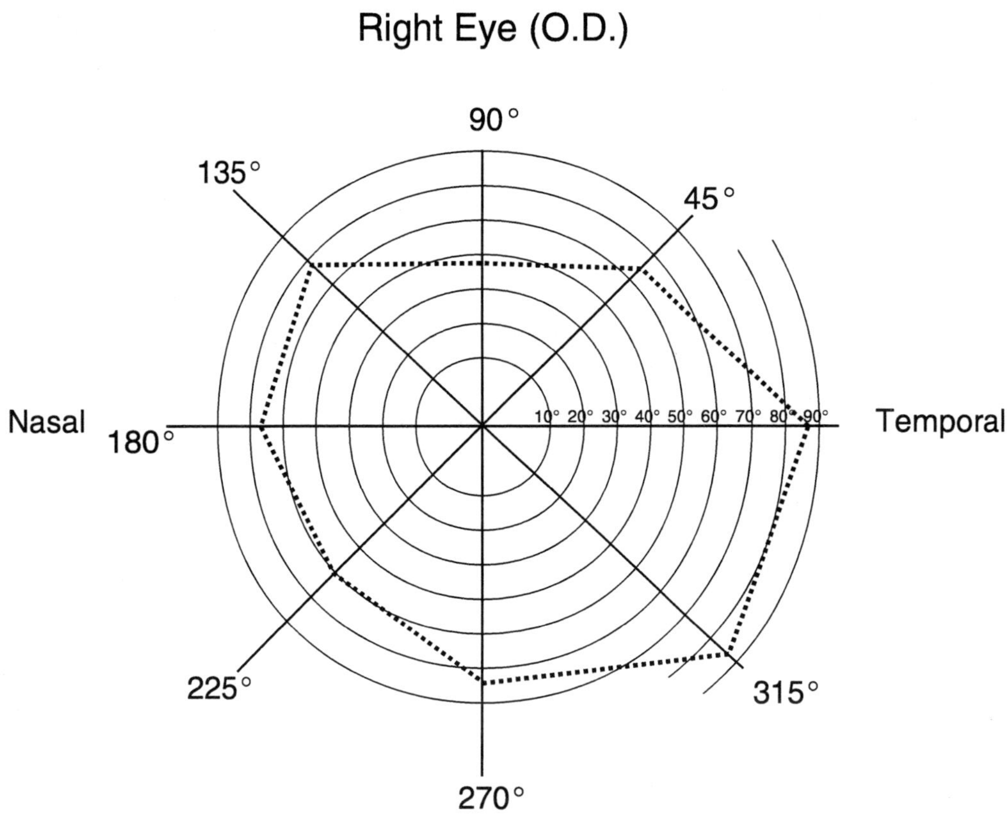

Meridian	Extent
0/360°	87°
45°	57°
90°	37°
135°	60°
180°	56°
225°	52°
270°	64°
315°	87°
Total	500°

FIGURE 2-3. Plotting of an isopter for visual field determination, adapted from Social Security Administration (2001).

equal to 10° from fixation, or less than or equal to 20° maximum diameter. For less than total disability, the percentage of visual efficiency is calculated as the sum of the radii of the eight principal meridians divided by 500° multiplied by 100.

There are several problems associated with the current method of making disability determinations for visual field loss. First, there is the very practical issue that Goldmann perimeters are becoming increasingly scarce, and fewer individuals have the proper training for performing kinetic testing on the Goldmann perimeter (Anderson & Patella, 1999). It is estimated that more than 95 percent of all eye care practitioners in the United States use an automated device to perform visual field testing. Second, with Goldmann perimetry a single isopter is used to define the outer limit of peripheral vision. This ignores scotomas, which could represent a large portion of the visual field.

For example, an individual with retinitis pigmentosa could have an extensive "ring" scotoma extending from approximately 3° from fixation out to more than 50°. However, with a rim of seeing beyond the ring scotoma, it is possible that the individual could show a normal or nearly normal Goldmann III/4e isopter despite having a scotoma encompassing a major portion of the visual field. Third, kinetic testing on the Goldmann perimeter can vary considerably from one examiner to another, whereas automated perimetric test strategies are conducted in the same manner every time. Fourth, Goldmann perimetric testing does not provide a standard means of assessing the reliability of the individual being tested or the accuracy and reliability of fixation, whereas automated perimetry does. Fifth, the Goldmann testing protocol evaluates the visual field extent along only eight meridians; intermediate areas between these meridians are not evaluated. Finally, the current standards are based on monocular visual field characteristics, whereas performance in real life is dependent on the binocular visual field. Because areas of nonseeing in the two eyes do not always overlap, the visual field of the better eye does not necessarily provide the best indication of the functional binocular visual field. However, there is currently no simple procedure available commercially for determining the binocular visual field from monocular data. Until such procedures become available, the visual field of the better eye should be used for disability determination. Many of these issues were pointed out previously by the Committee on Vision (National Research Council, 1994).

We conclude from our study of available perimetry methods that automated threshold static perimetry procedures should be employed as the method of performing visual field disability determinations. To ensure that accurate, reliable and valid results are obtained, we also recommend that an automated static perimeter meet the following criteria to be considered as an approved visual field device for SSA disability determinations:

1. The automated static perimeter should be capable of performing threshold testing using a white size III Goldmann target and a 31.5 apostilb (10 cd/m^2) white background.

2. The perimeter should be capable of measuring sensitivity for the central 30° radius of the visual field with equal numbers of target locations in each quadrant of the field, and target locations no more than 6° apart.

3. The perimeter should be a projection perimeter or should produce measures that are equal to those obtained on a projection perimeter.

4. The perimeter should have an internal normative database for automatically comparing an individual's performance with that of the general population.

5. The perimeter should have a statistical analysis package that is able to calculate visual field indices, particularly mean deviation or mean defect (MD), which is the average deviation of visual field sensitivity in comparison to normal values for the central 30° radius of the visual field.

6. The perimeter should demonstrate high sensitivity (ability to correctly detect visual field loss) and specificity (ability to correctly identify normal visual fields).

7. The perimeter should demonstrate good test-retest reliability.

8. The perimeter should have undergone clinical validation studies by three or more independent laboratories with results published in peer-reviewed ophthalmic journals.

At the present time, two perimeters are known to meet these criteria: the Humphrey Field Analyzer and the Octopus. Several studies have shown that the results obtained by the Humphrey Field Analyzer and the Octopus are highly correlated (Funkhouser & Funkhouser, 1991; Johnson et al., 1987b; Papp et al., 2001).

Mean deviation (MD) on the Humphrey Field Analyzer and mean defect (MD) on the Octopus perimeter represent the average overall deviation of visual field sensitivity from normal for the central 30° radius of the visual field. MD is a suitable marker of visual field status that takes into account both the size and depth (severity) of sensitivity losses. MD is automatically calculated by a statistical analysis program provided in the perimeter software that compares individual results to a database, and is printed out in hard copy. The normative databases include people of different ages, gender, and ethnicity. For each visual field location, the subject's sensitivity is compared with the average sensitivity for people of the same age, using the values in the database. For each visual field location, a "deviation from average normal" value in decibels (dB), a logarithmic scale, is determined. If the subject's sensitivity is better than the average normal individual of the same age, then the deviation value is positive. If the subject's sensitivity is lower, then the deviation is negative. Mean deviation or mean defect is thus the average sensitivity deviation from the normal values for all measured visual field locations.

There are several advantages to using these values as a means of determining visual field loss. First, MD represents a direct comparison of the subject's sensitivity with that of the normal population. Second, it automatically takes normal aging changes of the visual field into account, comparing the subject's results to normal individuals of the same age. Third, it is a quantitative measurement. Fourth, it not only takes into account the extent of the visual field, but it also evaluates the density of sensitivity loss. It therefore represents a better indicator of the individual's overall visual field capabilities. Finally, it serves as the best overall quantitative indicator of the amount of visual field damage.

There are two minor disadvantages. MD does not provide an indication of the spatial extent of visual field loss, and it is derived from evaluations of only the central visual field (60° diameter or 30° radius). The advantages greatly outweigh the disadvantages for disability determinations, however. If an individual had complete peripheral visual field loss and normal vision within the central 10° radius (the current SSA visual field standard), this would correspond to an MD of approximately –22 dB, which is considered to represent extensive visual field loss.

Relation to Other Measures

Visual field measures can be somewhat independent of visual acuity, contrast sensitivity, color vision, stereopsis, and other central visual function measures. For some disorders, visual field loss can be present when visual acuity and contrast sensitivity are normal. In other cases, visual field loss can occur in conjunction with visual acuity or contrast sensitivity deficits. Thus, it is important that the visual field and visual acuity be considered together for disability determinations. A method of combining visual field and visual acuity values to derive an aggregate disability score is presented later in this chapter.

Quality of Information Available

Automated threshold static perimetry using a projection perimeter is the current gold standard for ophthalmic visual field testing. The threshold procedures for those perimeters meeting our proposed criteria have been shown to produce accurate and reliable information concerning visual field sensitivity. Recently, new threshold test strategies for the Humphrey Field Analyzer, SITA-standard and SITA-fast, have been able to reduce testing time by 35 to 50 percent (Bengtsson & Heijl, 1998a, 1998b, 1999a, 1999b; Bengtsson, Heijl, et al., 1998; Bengtsson, Olsson, et al., 1997; Wild et al., 1999), while maintaining the same accuracy and reliability as previous staircase threshold procedures. A similar efficient test strategy, Tendency Oriented Perimetry (TOP), has been introduced for the Octopus perimeter (Morales et al., 2000). Automated threshold testing of the central 30° radius seems to be the most appropriate means of obtaining the best visual field information for disability determinations.

Recently, there was an investigation of an experimental automated kinetic perimetry procedure implemented on the Humphrey Field Analyzer (Odom et al., 1998). Based on their findings, those authors recommend that this new custom automated kinetic perimetry procedure be used for disability determinations. The committee disagrees with these recommendations for several reasons. First, kinetic perimetry is more variable than static perimetry, even when the procedure is automated (Lynn et al., 1991; Keltner et al., 1999). Second, there have been numerous attempts over the past 25 years to develop and validate an automated procedure for performing kinetic perimetry (Johnson et al., 1987a; Lynn et al., 1991; Miller et al., 1989; Schiefer et al., 2001; Zingirian et al., 1991). To date, all of these attempts have failed to produce a valid kinetic visual field test, in spite of the fact that some of these utilized much more sophisticated algorithms than those described in the Odom et al. (1998) report. Examples of the many problems encountered for automated kinetic perimetry can be found in Lynn et al. (1991). In the committee's view, automated kinetic perimetry affords no clear advantages over automated static perimetry and has a number of drawbacks. It should be noted that Humphrey Systems has recently released an automated kinetic perimetry program that it is promoting for disability determinations. However, no clinical validation studies of this procedure have been performed to date, and therefore its performance characteristics are unknown at the present time. In our judgment, automated threshold static perimetry should be used as the basis for establishing visual field status for disability determinations.

Recommendations

The committee recommends that the current SSA standard should be revised so that disability determinations are based on the results of automated static projection perimetry rather than Goldmann (kinetic, nonautomated) visual fields. At present, the Humphrey Field Analyzer and the Octopus perimeters are known to meet the criteria that we propose for automated perimeters that are to be used for disability determination. (Previous recommended methodology and scoring procedures for manual kinetic perimetry using the Goldmann perimetry were not based on empirical data. No validation study of the Goldmann disability determination procedure was performed.)

For both devices, we recommend that a threshold procedure should be employed for visual field determinations (for example, Full Threshold, Fastpac, SITA, and SITA Fast are all suitable alternatives for the Humphrey; Threshold, TOPS, and TOPS Plus are suitable alternatives for the Octopus). We recommend using a target presentation pattern that can measure sensitivity for the central 30° radius of the visual field with equal numbers of target locations in each quadrant of the field, and target locations no more than 6° apart.

We recommend that suprathreshold screening procedures should not be used because the techniques have not been validated, the results from them are not quantitative, and they generally do not provide a good indication of the amount of visual field damage that is present. We also recommend not using the visual field scoring procedures recently published by the American Medical Association (1993). The AMA guidelines are not based on empirical data, the procedures have not been validated, and their properties are largely unknown.

To account for scotomas and normal visual field locations between major meridians, we recommend that an index of the overall visual field status be used for disability determinations. MD provides the best overall indication of visual field status, taking into account both the spatial extent and the localized sensitivity variations that are present in the visual field. An MD of –22 dB approximately corresponds to a visual field extent of less than 10° radius (the current SSA standard). Mean deviation and Advanced Glaucoma Intervention

Study (AGIS) scores (which are highly correlated with mean deviation because both are derived from individual total deviation values) have been shown to be related to quality of life indicators and mobility skills (Gutierrez et al., 1997; Sumi et al., 2000). For this reason, MD represents an excellent measure on which to base disability determinations.

Ideally, one would have a measure of the binocular visual field serve as the basis for disability determinations because the binocular visual field is what people use for daily activities. However, simple procedures for determining the binocular visual field empirically, or deriving it from monocular visual field results, are not currently available. Current automated perimeters are not designed to perform binocular testing. Neither is an easy procedure for calculating the binocular visual field currently available. We recommend further research to be directed toward developing such procedures. Until such procedures can be implemented, we recommend that the visual field results for the better eye should be used for disability determinations. Thus, the recommended visual field criterion for SSA disability determinations would be an MD in the better eye of –22 dB or worse.

Issues Needing Further Study

Aside from studies of driving and a few investigations of mobility performance in people with low vision, there is currently very little information on the relationship between the status of the visual field and performance of daily activities, occupational demands, and task performance. Several validation studies have been performed for occupational vision requirements of correctional officers, youth counselors, and a group of California supervisors, parole agents, game wardens, park rangers, driver's license examiners, and youth authority academic teachers (Johnson, 1993; Johnson & Brintz, 1994, 1996, 1997; Johnson & Day, 1994a, 1994b; Johnson et al., 1992). The specific tasks that were performed in these studies were different for each occupation and were designed to simulate activities that were an essential part of the job. However, in each instance, performance deficits were found for visual field sizes below 60° in diameter. This is similar to the findings by Lovie-Kitchen and colleagues (2001) that mobility performance became impaired for those with visual field sizes less than 85° in diameter. For some demanding surveillance and search tasks, a visual field of 120° or more in diameter was necessary for maintaining adequate task performance. However, very little is known about the impact of reduced visual fields on activities of daily living and occupational requirements. Another area in need of future research is the development of techniques for providing valid and reliable measures of binocular visual field sensitivity.

CONTRAST SENSITIVITY

Description

Contrast is a measure of the differences in luminance (brightness) across borders. For example, typical text, consisting of black print on a white background, has very high contrast. Figure 2-4 (Pelli et al., 1988) illustrates letters with high contrast (about 100 percent) at the top left, becoming lower contrast as one reads down the chart. Contrast sensitivity is a measure of the lowest contrast that an observer can detect. A subject's contrast sensitivity on such a chart is expressed as a measure of the lowest contrast letters he or she can read correctly.

Evaluation

Why the Measure Might Be Useful

Contrast provides critical information about edges, borders, and variations in luminance. Thus, the normal visual system has high contrast sensitivity. While it has long been realized that measurements of contrast sensitivity might be particularly informative about visual disability, it is only in the past decade or so that it has become possible to measure contrast sensitivity simply and accurately in clinical practice or to use measures of contrast sensitivity in screening conducted by lay people.

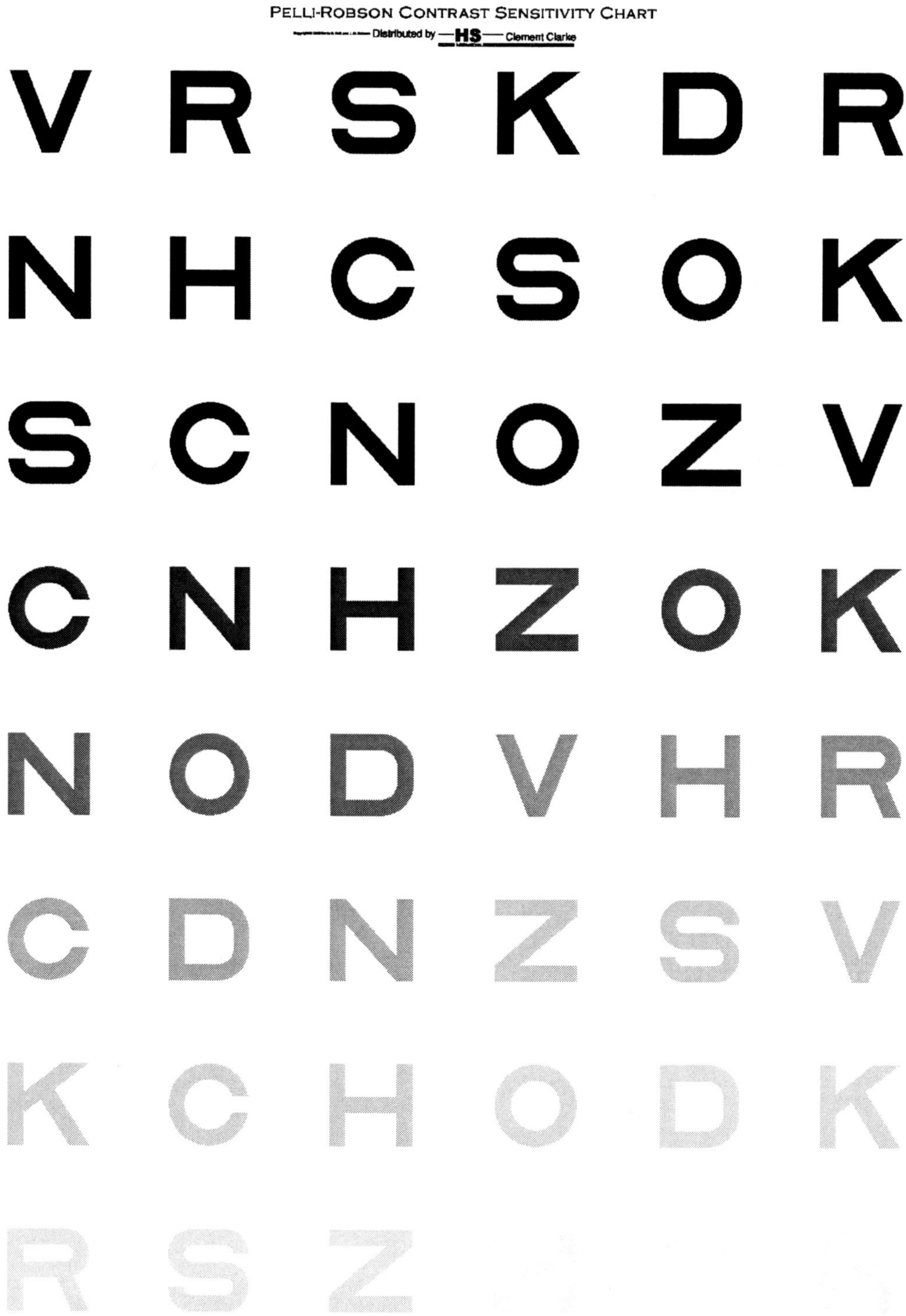

FIGURE 2-4. Pelli-Robson contrast sensitivity chart (Pelli, Robson, & Wilkins, 1988). Reproduced by permission of Denis Pelli.

Current disability assessment for vision involves primarily high-contrast letters; however, the world is not always seen in high contrast. The standard high-contrast visual acuity chart measures the ability to see black letters (about 1 or 2 percent reflectance) on a white background (close to 100 percent reflectance) giving close to 100 percent contrast.[2] Furthermore, the measurement is conducted in excellent lighting. The real world, however, is very far from this ideal. It consists of objects with an average reflectance of 18 percent, and the contrast between objects of interest and their backgrounds is usually much less than 100 percent. For example, the contrast between the pavement and the sidewalk, which is the main cue that defines the edge of a curb, may typically be just a few percent.

Contrast sensitivity tests can pick up losses that are not evident from measuring visual acuity. For example, contrast sensitivity tests may be sensitive to visual loss caused by cataracts, glaucoma, and multiple sclerosis (diseases in which impairment in contrast sensitivity is common), in subjects with little or no loss in visual acuity (Regan, 1991b). These people may fail to see large, low-contrast objects under conditions of poor visibility (such as fog) despite normal or near normal visual acuity. Elliott (1998) lists additional situations in which contrast sensitivity testing may be useful. In addition, several chapters in the Spatial Vision volume of Cronly-Dillon (Cronly-Dillon, 1991; Regan, 1991a) discuss contrast sensitivity in normal vision and in disease.

As Regan (1991b) points out, these losses are "hidden to the Snellen test." Moreover, as documented below, contrast sensitivity may predict performance for both reading and mobility in persons with low vision and makes strong predictions related to driving. Similarly, contrast sensitivity may be an important predictor of performance in individuals with cerebral lesions (Regan, 1991b). Although contrast sensitivity may not be very helpful in diagnosis, it is very useful in predicting disability.

---

[2]There are at least two conventions for expressing luminance contrast. The one used here is the Weber contrast ratio, in which the difference between the maximum and minimum luminances is divided by the maximum luminance: $(L\text{max} - L\text{min}) / L\text{max}$.

Reading. Reading is remarkably robust to contrast variations in normally sighted readers (Legge, Rubin, & Luebker, 1987; Legge, Rubin, Pelli, & Schleske, 1985). However, in one small-sample study it was estimated that the "critical contrast" (i.e., the contrast at which the reading rate drops to half of its maximum value) is, on average, four times higher in persons with low vision than in normally sighted persons, and this critical contrast is strongly correlated with the person's contrast sensitivity (Rubin & Legge, 1989). Indeed, Rubin and Legge suggest that there is a subset of individuals with low vision (with cataract and cloudy media) who are essentially normal readers, except for an early stage of reduction in retinal image contrast. Based on this and other evidence, Leat et al. (1999) suggest that a Pelli-Robson contrast sensitivity score of less than 1.5 would result in visual impairment and a score of less than 1.05 would result in disability. (The Pelli-Robson test is described in detail below. It measures contrast sensitivity using a single large letter size, with contrast varying across groups of letters.) In a recent large-scale study, West et al. (in press) found that more than 50 percent of people with a Pelli-Robson score of lower than 1.4 read fewer than 90 words per minute (wpm) (defined as disabling).

The Pelli-Robson score represents the logarithm of the subject's contrast sensitivity. Thus a score of 2, indicating a contrast sensitivity of 100 percent, means that the lowest contrast letters the observer can read correctly have a contrast of 1 percent (i.e., 1/100).

Whittaker and Lovie-Kitchin (1993) surveyed the literature on the effects of various parameters, including contrast, on reading speed. They defined the "contrast reserve" as the ratio of print contrast to threshold contrast. From their survey of the published data on low and normal reading rates versus text contrast, they concluded that the contrast reserve had to be at least 10:1 for reading at a low normal speed of 174 wpm; a 4:1 reserve to read at 88 wpm, and a 3:1 reserve for "spot reading," i.e., 44 wpm. These were upper-bound values, and many subjects who had contrast reserves of, say, 10:1 did not reach 174 wpm.

For text contrast of 100 percent, a person would require a contrast threshold of 10 percent or lower in order to achieve the 10:1 contrast reserve necessary for the low normal rate of 174 wpm. If the text itself is lower contrast, for example, newsprint with a contrast of 70 percent, then the reader's contrast threshold would have to be lower than 7 percent to achieve the desired 10:1 reserve. A contrast threshold of 10 percent corresponds to a Pelli-Robson score of 1.0. Based on the analysis of Whittaker and Lovie-Kitchin, we can conclude that a contrast sensitivity of 1.0 or better is required to read high-contrast print at a low normal speed. Although the details of the Whittaker and Lovie-Kitchin and the Leat et al. (1999) studies differ, their conclusions are rather close.

To summarize, it seems reasonable to conclude that a person with a contrast sensitivity of 1.0 might sometimes be able to achieve a low normal reading speed (174 wpm), but most will read more slowly. If text contrast is lower or contrast sensitivity is poorer, reading will be slower. Thus, setting a Pelli-Robson boundary of about 1.0 almost certainly guarantees that everyone below this line will have functionally significant contrast limitation in reading.

Although standard letter chart acuity and contrast sensitivity are highly correlated in the overall population, it is not possible on an individual (clinical) basis to predict contrast sensitivity accurately from acuity (Haegerstrom-Portnoy, et al., 2000). It is therefore necessary to measure both, because measuring contrast sensitivity provides new information related to visual disability.

Mobility. For normally sighted people, mobility is remarkably robust to contrast, at least under controlled conditions. Pelli (1987) found that in normally sighted subjects mobility is only slightly impaired when the contrast is reduced to 2 to 4 percent of the normal level. However, these studies were performed in a relatively safe shopping mall environment, with few of the typical low-contrast hazards, such as step-ups. Poor contrast sensitivity (a Pelli-Robson score of 0.9 or lower) is disabling with regard to walking speed (West et al., in press).

In contrast, for those with visual impairments, a number of studies have shown an association between contrast sensitivity and mobility (Geruschat et al., 1998; Kuyk & Elliott, 1999; Kuyk, et al., 1998; Marron & Bailey, 1982; Rubin, et al., 1994; Turano et al., 1999). As noted in the section on ambulatory mobility (in Chapter 3), in nearly all cases, contrast sensitivity was a far better predictor of mobility performance than acuity (and often the only predictor). For example, Marron and Bailey (1982) reported a strong correlation between mobility and contrast sensitivity in a group of people with low vision. Contrast sensitivity was a better predictor of mobility performance than visual acuity. Combining visual field measures with contrast sensitivity provided the best predictor of mobility performance.

Contrast sensitivity is a better predictor of driving performance than visual acuity. Reduced contrast sensitivity is associated with older persons' reports of difficulty in mobility and driving (Rubin et al., 1994). Closed road driving with simulated cataracts produces decrements in driving performance, and the overall driving score is correlated with Pelli-Robson contrast sensitivity (Wood & Troutbeck, 1995; Wood, et al., 1993). There have also been several reports that suggest a relationship between contrast sensitivity and number of (at-fault) crashes (Ball et al., 1993; Owsley, Ball, et al., 1998). As noted in Chapter 3, contrast sensitivity impairment in older drivers, especially those with cataracts, is associated with crash involvement, when visual acuity shows no association (Owsley, McGwin, et al., 2001).

Social Participation and Tool Use/Manipulation. Not much is known about the relationship between contrast sensitivity and social participation or tool use. Contrast sensitivity has been related to face recognition (Owsley & Sloane, 1987). West et al. (in press) showed that subjects with 1.3 log contrast would be unable to recognize more than 50 percent of faces in a face recognition test. Contrast sensitivity loss has been associated with difficulty with everyday tasks, both self-reported difficulty (Rubin et al., 2001) and difficulty based on performance measures (Rubin et al., 1994; West et al., in press); however, these areas require additional study. It is clear from observations of typical manual tasks (e.g., sewing with a dark thread on dark cloth, doing woodwork and joinery) that the contrasts between different crucial parts of the task materials can be very low, as can the luminances of the materials. It is likely that if one's ability to see under such reduced contrast (and luminance) is impaired, task performance will be adversely affected.

Potential Value as a Practical Measure

The importance of measuring contrast sensitivity is that it can provide information that cannot be obtained from visual acuity measures, and it is often a better predictor of performance than visual acuity, as discussed above.

Quantifying Performance

In the laboratory, contrast sensitivity is usually measured psychophysically, using patches of grating (bars) that vary over a wide range of sizes (spatial frequencies). Typically, the gratings are computer generated and displayed on a computer screen or cathode ray tube. This allows the experimenter to construct a contrast sensitivity function. However, for clinical, screening, or disability determination purposes the contrast sensitivity function is inefficient and difficult to interpret. Moreover, the typical laboratory test for it requires sophisticated and specialized equipment.

Ideally, a contrast sensitivity test for disability determination should satisfy several criteria. It should be simple to administer, requiring no sophisticated electronic or computer equipment, well standardized, reliable, valid, sensitive to visual loss, and relatively insensitive to changes in focus, viewing distance, and illumination. It should provide a single score that is meaningful and can easily be compared with extensive normative data and should provide information about visual function not captured by other tests (such as high contrast acuity).

Several clinical tests of contrast sensitivity have been developed over the last two decades. One of the first was the Vistech charts, which measure contrast sensitivity for gratings of several spatial frequencies. One difficulty with these charts is that the result is a contrast sensitivity function rather than a single number. Another difficulty is that test-retest reliability for the Vistech charts has been shown to be lower than for some other contrast sensitivity tests (Rubin, 1988). Reliability is a critical requirement for disability determination. The

Vistech test is not suitable for individuals with significant degrees of astigmatism, because the gratings are oriented. Finally, there is only a single target at each contrast level, so there is effectively one trial per level. In addition to the Vistech, there are also several low (fixed) contrast letter charts available, as well as CRT-based contrast sensitivity tests.

The currently available test that best meets the requirements laid out above is the recently developed Pelli-Robson chart (Pelli et al., 1988). This test measures contrast sensitivity for a single (large) letter size. Specifically, the chart uses Sloan letters (6 per line), arranged in groups whose contrast varies from high to low. The chart is simple to use, because the subject simply reads the letters, starting with the highest contrast, until she or he misses two or three letters in a single group. Each group has three letters of the same contrast level, so there are three trials per contrast level. The subject is assigned a score based on the contrast of the last group in which two or three letters were correctly read. The score, a single number, is a measure of the subject's log contrast sensitivity. Thus a score of 2 means that the subject was able to read at least two of the three letters with a contrast of 1 percent (contrast sensitivity = 100 percent or log 2). The single score facilitates combining scores across visual functions to obtain an aggregate visual impairment score for use in determining disability.

The Pelli-Robson chart is quick and easy to administer. Because it is based on reading letters, it can be easily administered to anyone who is literate; however, it is not useful with nonverbal individuals or those who are unfamiliar with the alphabet. It is robust to changes in viewing distance, defocus, and to some degree illumination level. Also, since letters contain many orientations, it is not strongly dependent on a particular orientation, as the Vistech chart is. It is simple, efficient, and provides user-friendly information by providing a single number to describe the observer's contrast sensitivity. The chart has been extensively normed and validated, and there is now an extensive literature on the reliability and validity of the test.

The Pelli-Robson chart reflects contrast sensitivity near the peak of the contrast sensitivity function (Rohaly & Owsley, 1993). It is actually a measure of the height of the contrast sensitivity function, similar to measuring contrast sensitivity for a luminance edge. Thus, it should be sensitive to losses that affect low and medium spatial frequencies, losses that might not be evident for high-contrast acuity, thus providing information not captured by acuity testing. The Pelli-Robson chart is now widely used in clinical trials and is being considered for use by some state departments of motor vehicles as part of their driving test battery.

The Pelli-Robson chart provides a graded index of performance (log contrast sensitivity), and the score appears to reasonably reflect degree of ability or disability. As noted above, Leat et al. (1999) argue that a score of less than about 1.5 reflects visual impairment, and they estimated that a score of less than 1.05 would result in disability. This score represents an approximately 10-fold loss of contrast sensitivity. That is, the person requires 10 times as much contrast to see the target letters as a person with normal vision (e.g., 10 percent contrast versus the normal 1 percent). A loss of this magnitude would have a huge impact on one's ability to drive or read. In short, a 10-fold loss of letter contrast sensitivity would be quite disabling.

Relation to Other Measures

Contrast sensitivity measures provide information that is related to, but is also distinct from, high-contrast visual acuity measures. For example, a number of studies have reported that the correlation between high-contrast acuity and contrast sensitivity is on the order of 0.5 to 0.6 (Rubin, Bandeen-Roche, et al., 1994; Rubin, West, et al., 1997). It is widely believed that letter contrast sensitivity (as assessed by Pelli-Robson) reflects the contrast sensitivity near the peak of the contrast sensitivity function, while high-contrast letter acuity probably reflects sensitivity at high spatial frequencies.

Does contrast sensitivity provide a unique measure of disability? It subsumes visual acuity. Thus an individual with visual acuity poorer than 20/200 is likely to have reduced contrast sensitivity, and one with a visual acuity of 20/40 or better is unlikely to have significantly reduced contrast sensitivity. However, between those limits (acuity between about 20/50 and 20/100), contrast sensitivity may distinguish individuals with visual impairment from those with no impairment; in other words, some individuals whose visual acuity is better than the current SSA disability standard have genuine visual impairment that is evident in their contrast sensitivity scores. For example, people with multiple sclerosis (Regan, 1991b) or visual pathway disorders (Elliott, 1998) may show significant contrast sensitivity loss with little visual acuity loss and, as discussed in Chapter 3, contrast sensitivity is a better predictor of mobility and reading performance than visual acuity.

Quality of Information Available

A number of different contrast sensitivity tests are available. As noted above, contrast sensitivity is the standard laboratory measure of spatial vision. There are now a number of commercially available charts for testing contrast sensitivity, the most widely used of which are the Vistech charts and the Pelli-Robson card. The latter is very well standardized, and both have been widely used and tested in clinical populations. In a group of 66 normally sighted subjects and 64 patients ranging from 16 to 83 years of age, the Pelli-Robson chart had higher test-retest reliability (0.98 for normal subjects and 0.86 for patients) than either the Vistech charts or lab-based measurements (Rubin, 1988). The coefficient of repeatability (95 percent confidence interval) of Pelli-Robson contrast sensitivity scores is ±0.15 log units (Elliott, Hurst, & Weatherill, 1990). The Elliott et al. study suggests that a score of 1.65 log units for young subjects and 1.5 log units for older subjects corresponds to the lower limit for normal performance (based on the 95 percent confidence limits). For older adults, a contrast sensitivity score less than about 1.3 is associated with an increased risk of driving accidents relative to those with normal contrast sensitivity (Owsley & McGwin, 1999).

Recommendations

Currently SSA does not test contrast sensitivity to determine a person's visual disability. It is possible for individuals to have relatively good visual acuity and/or fields and have reduced contrast sensitivity that is disabling. Therefore, we recommend adding contrast sensitivity as an additional basis for disability determination for individuals with visual acuity between a lower limit of 20/50 and an upper limit of 20/200. It is not necessary to measure contrast sensitivity in individuals who meet the SSA medical listings criteria for visual acuity or visual fields, but it is recommended for those with visual acuity between 20/50 and 20/200 and other indications or self-report of serious visual impairment. This idea is illustrated in Figure 2-5.

The test used should be simple to administer, require no sophisticated equipment, and be well-standardized, reliable, valid, sensitive to visual loss, and relatively insensitive to changes in focus, viewing distance, and illumination. It should provide a single score that can be compared with normative data. One currently available test, the Pelli-Robson, is known to meet these criteria, and other tests now available or to be developed in the future may do so as well. We recommend that if the Pelli Robson test is used, testing should be done at 160 cd/m^2, the same luminance used for acuity testing. A score of less than 1.05 on the Pelli-Robson test would be a reasonably conservative boundary for disability.

Issues Needing Further Study

The relationships of contrast sensitivity to performance on tests of mobility, social participation, and tool use/manipulation are areas clearly in need of further study. Glare is an exacerbating factor for seeing low-contrast objects. There is no standard, widely available test for glare; however, it should be noted that people who perform poorly under low-contrast conditions usually perform even more poorly under glare, due to light scatter. Thus glare testing is an area requiring further study.

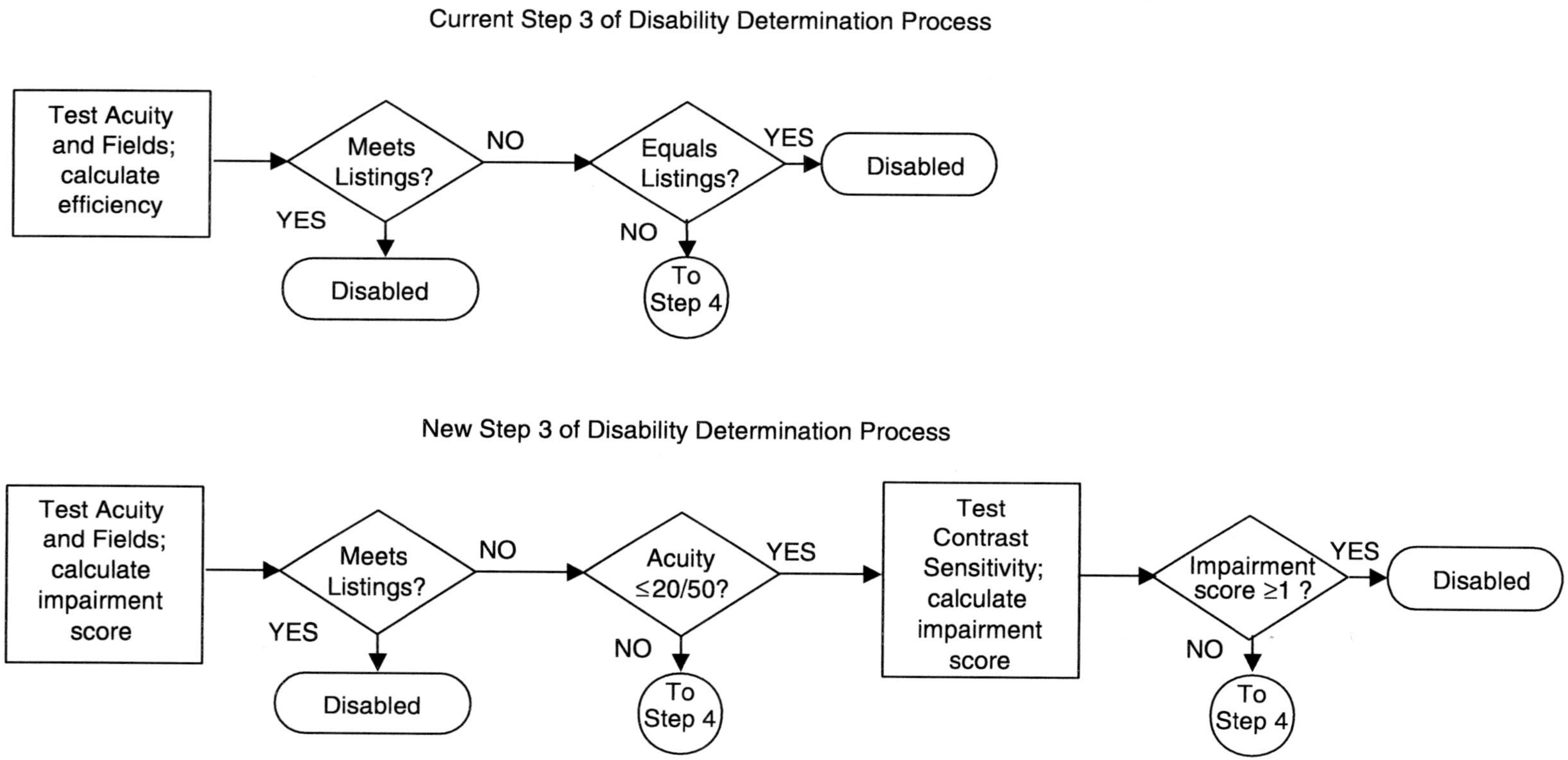

FIGURE 2-5. Incorporating contrast sensitivity testing into the SSA disability determination process.

It is also well known that low light levels are a serious exacerbating factor in one's ability to see low-contrast objects, particularly for older and visually impaired persons. New tests such as the SKILL Card (Haegerstrom-Portnoy et al., 1997) exist for this condition, but they have not been extensively used with working-age visually impaired subjects and therefore require further study. Another area requiring further study is the contrast sensitivity testing of young children (see Chapter 4).

COLOR VISION

Description

The color of a surface is determined by how it reflects light and is generally a stable property of the surface. This makes color a reliable cue for distinguishing and identifying objects, and normal color vision permits us to distinguish a rich range of naturally occurring surfaces. Inability to distinguish colors may make objects less distinguishable. Impaired capacity to distinguish colors can be congenital or acquired.

Congenital deficits occur in approximately 8 percent of Northern European men, perhaps less in other ethnic groups, and less than 0.5 percent of women (Hsia & Graham, 1965). Mild deficit results when an individual has the usual three kinds of cone photoreceptors but with one or more of these being most sensitive in an unusual part of the visible spectrum. This happens in about 5 percent of men. Severe deficit results from the absence of one of the normal three classes of cone photoreceptor; about 2 percent of men lack either the long-wavelength (L) or middle-wavelength (M) cone receptor. This leads to very poor color discrimination in the red-green part of the spectrum. Loss of the short-wavelength (S) cone, which affects men and women equally and leads to a severe impairment of discrimination in the blue region of the spectrum, is very rare. Even in cases of severe color vision deficiency, color confusion occurs for only some portions of the color spectrum, and many colors can still be distinguished.

Acquired color vision deficiencies are produced by pathological changes to the visual system. Yellowing of the lens and cataract development produce blue (tritan) deficiencies. Most diseases of the retina tend to produce color vision deficits in the short-wavelength (blue) part of the spectrum, whereas optic nerve diseases tend to produce red-green deficits. In some cases, nonspecific color deficits are found for certain eye diseases, in which color discrimination is poor throughout the color spectrum. Pokorny et al. (1979) and Adams et al. (1998) provide comprehensive discussions of congenital and acquired color vision deficiencies.

A variety of tests is available for evaluating color discrimination. Rapid screening procedures include pseudoisochromatic plate tests, such as the Ishihara, Dvorine, H-R-R, and others (which are able to distinguish between persons with normal color vision and those with any type of color vision deficiency) and the Farnsworth panel D-15 test (which distinguishes individuals with severe color vision deficiencies from those with normal color vision or only mild color vision losses). These tests are good for screening and classifying color vision abnormalities, but they do not accurately quantify the extent of color vision deficiency. More sophisticated test procedures, such as the Farnsworth-Munsell 100 Hues test and the Nagel and Pickford-Nicholson anomaloscopes, are able to classify both the type of color vision deficiency and its severity. All of these test procedures, with the exception of the anomaloscope, are available in most eye clinics, as well as for testing general populations. Specialized color vision testing can be undertaken in the laboratory, but this requires the construction of custom equipment that is not generally available to others. A description of the commonly used color vision tests is available in Pokorny et al. (1979).

Evaluation

Why the Measure Might Be Useful

Impairments of color vision make objects harder to distinguish and identify. In some instances, a difference in color may be the predominant or only cue available to distinguish objects. People who suffer from one form of congenital color vision loss (protanopia) may also find it hard to see lights of long wavelength. Well-established tests are available to characterize impaired color vision, and some of these are relatively easily administered.

Potential Value as a Practical Measure

Most of the work on predicting real-world performance from color vision tests has been concerned with tasks involving transportation (vehicle driving, aviation, etc.) and tasks of specific occupations in which color discrimination is crucial (appraisers of precious stones, quality control specialists for paint and dye samples, etc.). For example, Lakowski and Oliver (1978) found that color-defective individuals could not identify different grades of fuel oil, which are instilled with a dye to provide unique tints for different fuel oil grades. Similarly, they also reported that normal color vision was essential for the accurate grading of diamonds. An excellent comprehensive review of the importance of color vision for the transportation industry is found in Vingrys and Cole (1988). Pokorny et al. (1979) also provide a review of the implications of color vision deficiencies for various occupations. North (1993) includes an appendix table by Voke that lists occupations in which defective color vision may impair performance. This list represents a very small subset of the total number of occupations in the general workforce.

Quantifying Performance

Several varieties of color vision tests are used for clinical and occupational purposes. An excellent review of these can be found in Pokorny et al. (1979). The simplest tests are those used for screening purposes; various forms of pseudoisochromatic plate tests (Ishihara, Dvorine, H-R-R, etc.) have been developed and validated for rapid screening. They consist of a series of plates containing dots of various sizes and colors. Persons with normal (trichromatic) color vision are able to distinguish from its background an object or number defined by similarly colored dots, whereas a person with impaired color vision will not be able to distinguish the object from the background. In some versions, a larger series of plates is used to determine the type (red/green/blue) and severity (mild/moderate/severe) of color deficiency. In general, properly designed and administered pseudoisochromatic plates have been found to do an excellent job of distinguishing persons with normal color vision from those with color deficiencies. However, their ability to accurately determine the type and severity of color vision deficit is quite limited.

The Farnsworth panel D-15 is another screening test. It consists of a series of 15 color chips that are to be arranged in order of their color similarity. The D-15 test clearly distinguishes persons with severe color vision deficiencies and those with normal color vision or only mild to moderate deficit. It also is able to accurately determine the type of color vision deficiency (red/green/blue). The D-15 was designed as an occupational color vision test procedure because it is a good predictor of whether a person will have difficulties for those occupations in which color discrimination is routinely performed as part of the job. The Farnsworth-Munsell 100 Hues test is an extended form of the D-15 test. It consists of 85 color chips in 4 boxes that must be arranged in order of their color similarity. Arrangement errors are recorded on a polar coordinate chart that has the color spectrum arranged in a circle. The spectral locations at which color arrangement errors occur define the type of color deficiency, and the magnitude of the arrangement errors measures the severity of the deficit. For occupational purposes, it provides the best quantitative information about the severity of color vision deficiency, and it has often been used as the color vision measure to correlate with task performance.

Finally, anomaloscopes provide an accurate and precise measurement of color vision deficiency, although they are not commonly used for occupational purposes.

Relation to Other Measures

Unlike visual function measures that demonstrate some degree of correlation with each other, such as visual acuity and contrast sensitivity, which to some extent tap the same underlying capabilities, color vision is a relatively independent dimension of vision.

Quality of Information Available

A number of investigations have examined the relationship between color vision deficits and task performance in controlled studies, many of which are reviewed in Vingrys and Cole (1988) and Pokorny et al. (1979).

Recommendations

To the extent that normal color discrimination is a critical factor for specific jobs, color deficient individuals may be unable to perform them or may require a longer time to perform them. Only a limited number of tasks (e.g., quality control of paint and dye samples, grading of precious gems, identification of plant and animal species) depend significantly on normal color vision. In some others (e.g., law enforcement, firefighting, civil aviation, the military) color-blind people may have restrictions placed on them or be excluded from certain positions. Color vision has a minor or negligible role for most jobs, and we recommend that it not be considered further with regard to visual disability determination.

BINOCULAR FUNCTION

Description

Binocular vision (seeing with two eyes) is normal and confers three benefits: it makes hard-to-see objects easier to detect, it enlarges the total field of view, and it improves a person's capacity to distinguish small differences in depth.

Visual performance is normally slightly but reliably better when people undertake tasks using two eyes rather than one. In studies of *binocular summation* tasks that have examined this explicitly, the contrast required to detect a grating pattern binocularly is lower by a factor of about 1.4 than the contrast required to detect it monocularly (Campbell & Green, 1965; Legge, 1984a; Pardhan, 1993). The benefits of binocular vision are smaller when the task is to discriminate small differences in the contrast of clearly visible patterns (Legge, 1984b). Binocular acuity is slightly better than monocular acuity (Blake & Fox, 1973; Cagenello et al., 1993; Rubin et al., 2000). For this reason, we recommend that, for the purposes of determining disability, acuity be tested binocularly. A similar small advantage of binocular vision has been shown in more complex perceptual-motor tasks, such as finding objects in camouflage, controlling posture, pointing, and reading (Jones & Lee, 1981; Sheedy et al., 1986).

The normal field of view is comprised of regions contributed by the two eyes. Because the eyes face forward, these regions overlap substantially, although not completely. With the eyes looking ahead, each eye's field extends about 95° toward the temple and about 55° toward the nose in Caucasians (Fischer & Wagenaar, 1954). The overlapping region is known as the binocular visual field and normally spans horizontally the central 110°. To either side of it is a region, about 40° wide at its maximum, seen by one or the other eye alone. Thus using two eyes extends the width of the field that can be seen at any one time. When one eye has an impaired visual field in the region of binocular overlap, the other eye may provide normal vision.

The most distinctive benefit of using two eyes derives from the fact that, because they are horizontally separated, they do not have exactly the same view of the visual world. The small differences between the images in the two eyes are systematically related to the arrangement of objects in depth, providing information from which the visual system is able to distinguish small differences in the distances at which objects lie. This capability, known as *stereopsis,* is most beneficial for making fine depth judgments, especially when objects are nearby (i.e., within arm's reach) (Howard & Rogers, 1995).

For all three of these capabilities, enhanced acuity, field of view, and stereopsis, the brain must properly combine information from the two eyes. If vision in the two eyes differs substantially, the brain may be unable to combine the information into a unified view *(binocular single vision)* or may be unable to use the differences between the images to distinguish small differences in depth. Binocular vision can also be disturbed even though each eye alone is functioning normally. Abnormalities in the brain, or improperly coordinated movements of the eyes, or misalignment of them, can disrupt normal binocular vision. When the brain is unable to combine information from the two eyes, a person may experience double vision *(diplopia)* or *binocular rivalry,* a sometimes haphazard switching of vision from one eye to the other.

Binocular function is unusually sensitive to visual experience during development. If early in life the eyes are misaligned (*strabismus*) or the images in the two eyes differ substantially (as might occur when one is well focused but the other not), one eye tends to become dominant, stereopsis often does not develop, and the weaker eye may never become capable of seeing well, even after appropriate refraction. About 3 percent of the population lacks stereopsis (Richards, 1970), and 2-5 percent of the population has some visual abnormality that leaves them with uncorrectable poor vision in one eye but not the other (Cross, 1985; Ehrlich et al., 1983; Flom & Neumaier, 1966; Thompson et al., 1991). Richards (1970) reports that up to 30 percent of the adult population has some deficiency of stereopsis.

Evaluation

Why the Measure Might Be Useful

Failure to combine information from the two eyes can lead to a reduced ability to see small differences in depth. Moreover, under some circumstances, the vision of the two eyes might conflict, making vision poorer than if one eye alone was used.

Potential Value as a Practical Measure

Binocular vision has very little effect on reading (Jones & Lee, 1981; Legge, Pelli, et al., 1985; Sheedy et al., 1986), but at least one study (Ivers et al., 2000) showed that impaired stereopsis is associated with hip fractures among older people. Ivers et al. reported a significant trend toward elevated odds ratios for hip fracture as stereopsis impairment increased, compared with those whose stereopsis was in the normal range.

Loss of vision in one eye does not appear to affect the performance of drivers in test maneuvers (McKnight et al., 1991; Wood & Troutbeck, 1992; Wood et al., 1993), but it has been found in some studies to elevate crash risk (Laberge-Nadeau et al., 1996; Maag et al., 1997; Rogers, Ratz, & Janke, 1987). Depth perception, for which stereopsis is helpful under some circumstances, is frequently considered moderately important, although seldom essential, in using tools. In the workplace overall, depth perception is rated as being of moderate or high importance in only 15 percent of jobs, as discussed in the occupational analysis section of Chapter 3 (see Table 3-1 for PAQ ratings).

Quantifying Performance

Several simple tests exist to characterize stereopsis. This is usually done through the measurement of *stereoacuity,* the smallest discernible separation in depth that a person can detect, based on the geometry of the images in the two eyes. These include the Randot stereo test, the TNO stereo test, the Lang stereo test, and others. The Randot stereo test uses images produced on polarization film. The viewer wears a pair of polarizing glasses so that one image is viewed by one eye and the other image is viewed by the other eye. A slight difference in the position of the image between the two eyes creates a small *retinal disparity*, which serves as the stereopsis cue and causes the image to "stand out" from the page. The test contains some images that do not stand out, and the subject's task is to select the ones that do stand out. The test has a graded series of images to determine the minimal retinal disparity at which stereoacuity is present. The TNO stereo test is similar, except that it uses a series of red and green dots to create images, and the subject views the test through a pair of glasses with a red filter over one eye and a green filter over the other. The Lang stereo test is also similar, except that it uses a Fresnel lens above the test plate to produce slightly different images to the two eyes, while avoiding the need for special glasses.

Recommendations

Our recommendations here concern impairments of binocular function and are distinct from our recommendations in other sections that other visual functions should be tested binocularly. Abnormalities of binocular function are relatively common, and for most people intrude little on everyday life. Few, if any, tasks depend on the visual capability that requires the two eyes to work in partnership (stereopsis), and people with only monocular vision are seldom circumscribed in what they can do. When disrupted binocular function interferes with binocular single vision (via diplopia or rivalry) this can generally be circumvented by patching one eye. We therefore recommend that abnormalities of binocular function not be considered in the determination of disability.

VISUAL SEARCH

Visual search is a crucial ability in everyday life and consists of localizing or finding an object of interest among other objects or "distractors." We live in a visually cluttered world with a myriad of objects and ongoing events. Thus, visual search is essential to the performance of tasks typical of the workplace, such as reading, mobility, social participation, and the manipulation of objects. Although visual search is not a basic visual sensory function, it is a function of the visual system and can therefore be considered a visual function as defined in Chapter 1.

Previous research on normally sighted persons has demonstrated that it is possible to predict visual search performance in laboratory tasks on the basis of visual sensory factors, such as visual acuity, contrast sensitivity, and visual field sensitivity (Carrasco & Chang, 1995; Carrasco & Frieder, 1997; Geisler & Chou, 1995; Verghese & Nakayama, 1994). However, there is little research on whether visual sensory factors correctly predict the visual search abilities of people with low vision, either in laboratory tasks or, more relevant to our discussion here, tasks performed in the real world. Given that visual search is a fundamental part of seeing, future research should consider whether a visual search screening test would be useful in disability determination screening batteries in order to validly capture task performance problems experienced by visually impaired persons, or whether visual sensory tests (e.g., visual acuity, visual field) are alone sufficient.

Evaluation

Driving is a task for which it is already clear that visual sensory tests by themselves are inadequate for predicting performance problems (see Chapter 3). As mentioned earlier, a visual search task called the useful field of view test (Ball et al., 1990) has been used extensively to study driving. It consists of a radial localization task performed under divided attention conditions, wherein targets are presented briefly (<250 msec) among distracting stimuli. Those persons who have slow visual processing speed and divided and selective attention problems perform poorly on the test. Research has shown that poor scores on the useful field of view test are better predictors of crash involvement and driving performance problems among older drivers than are visual sensory tests like visual acuity (Ball et al., 1993; Cushman, 1996;

Duchek et al., 1998; Hunt et al., 1993; Owsley, Ball, et al., 1998; Rizzo et al., 1997; Rubin et al., 1999; Wood et al., 1993). Research using other tests of visual search further confirms the critical nature of visual search in safe driving (Barrett et al., 1977; Duchek et al., 1998; Goode et al., 1998; Kahneman et al., 1973; Mihal & Barrett, 1976). Test features that appear to be most critical in identifying crash-prone drivers are those that embody divided attention components and place high demands on rapid visual processing (Owsley, Ball, et al., 1998). The critical nature of visual search abilities in driving is not surprising since controlling a vehicle is a complex visual task not only involving the sensory registration of events, but also requiring the simultaneous monitoring of central and peripheral vision and the filtering out of irrelevant stimuli, all performed under time-limited conditions. Research has demonstrated that the vast majority of crash-involved older drivers have excellent visual sensory ability (Ball et al., 1993; Owsley, Ball, et al., 1998), so crash-prone drivers would remain largely undetected by a visual sensory screening test.

There is some evidence that visual search ability is also independently related to the performance of other types of tasks, such as locating objects of interest in the environment, reading text on objects, and using tools (Owsley, McGwin, et al., 2001; Owsley, Sloane, et al., 2001). However, research in this area is relatively sparse.

Recommendations

Given the available evidence to date, the committee recommends at this time that a test of visual search ability not be used in the visual disability determination process. Since visual search is a fundamental aspect of seeing, further work is needed to clarify the relationship between visual search impairments and the performance of work-related tasks. However, it is already clear that deficits in visual search ability are associated with an increased risk for motor vehicle collision and impaired driving performance. Thus, for jobs involving driving, a useful addition to a driving fitness evaluation would be a test of visual search ability. The most effective design of this test needs to be determined by further research.

GLARE AND LIGHT/DARK ADAPTATION

Measurement of visual function in the clinic or the laboratory is usually performed under ideal conditions of daytime ("photopic") lighting and the absence of extraneous light sources. Recommended lighting for acuity testing is on the order of 160 cd/m^2 (National Research Council, 1994). In the real world, however, levels encountered in bright sunlight can be up to 400 times greater than this, and in night driving typically 500 times dimmer (Pitts, 1993). Strong extraneous light sources such as oncoming headlights or a bright sky often surround a visual target, creating glare problems. Also, a person may have to adapt to rapidly changing lighting conditions (as when coming into a dimly lit room from bright sunlight).

Conditions of glare and low lighting arise in the course of many workplace tasks (e.g., driving, construction work, computer use). They are only a minor annoyance to most people, who can quickly compensate, but they can be disabling for those with certain eye conditions. Conversely, individuals with rod monochromacy or cone dystrophies may experience substantially impaired vision at high light intensities (Elliott et al., 1989; National Research Council, 1994; Zadnik et al., 2000).

The committee examined the impacts of low and changing light levels and glare on vision impairment to determine whether special tests should be included for identification and assessment of individuals unduly affected by these conditions.

Vision at Low Light Levels

The normal visual system can adapt to a wide range of light levels, although acuity and contrast sensitivity are reduced as light level is reduced. However, ability to function in low light is dramatically disrupted in aging (Adams et al., 1988; Sloane et al., 1988), macular disease (Jacobson et al., 1986; Owsley, Jackson, et al., 2001), congenital stationary night blindness, retinitis pigmentosa (Brown et al., 1984), diabetes (Wolfe & Sadun, 1991), optic neuritis (Schneck et al., 1993), fundus albi punctatis, and glaucoma (Glovinsky et al., 1992). Large changes in visual acuity can occur with relatively modest changes in illumination in many people with impaired vision (Lie, 1977; Lovie-Kitchin & Bowman, 1985; Sloan, 1969).

In studies of vision in macular degeneration, Bullimore and colleagues have found that changes in illumination could produce substantial decrements in reading acuity, maximum reading speed, and reading eye movement patterns, as well as in face recognition ability (Bullimore et al., 1991). The measured size of scotomas and field constrictions can often be dependent on luminance levels in macular degeneration and retinitis pigmentosa (Bullimore & Bailey, 1995).

Studies demonstrate that mobility problems in visually impaired people are exacerbated under low illumination (Kuyk et al., 1996; Turano et al., 1999), particularly in those with age-related maculopathy (Brown et al., 1986). Surveys indicate that the most frequent complaint of older people about their vision is the inability to read fine print under poor lighting conditions (Brabyn et al., 1995; Kosnik et al., 1988). Inability to see well in low light conditions would clearly be disabling for many employees, such as movie theater personnel and darkroom technicians, who perform their work in a dimly lit environment.

Low luminance testing in the clinic is not often performed due to problems in producing calibrated light levels. An alternative method, the SKILL card (Haegerstrom-Portnoy et al., 1997) uses a dark gray acuity card with black letters to measure acuity under low-contrast, low-luminance conditions without turning down the lights. Although norms and an increasing body of data on this test exist, to date it is used mainly in research settings. Light sensitivity under scotopic (low luminance) conditions has also been tested using specially modified automated perimeters in studies designed to improve understanding of retinal degenerations (e.g., Jacobson et al., 1986). However, these devices are not commercially available.

Adaptation to Rapidly Changing Light Conditions

Retinal diseases can cause a slowing in the rate of adaptation to low or medium light after exposure to bright light, a process referred to as dark adaptation, which depends mainly on the dynamics of the retina's response to light (Barlow, 1972). The magnitude and duration of the temporary vision impairment depends on such test conditions as the intensity and duration of the initial "bleaching" light and the wavelength of the test target. The return to normal visual function is a gradual process; it may take many seconds but sometimes extends to over 30 minutes.

Difficulty adapting to poor or changing light levels is widely acknowledged to have a serious impact on the mobility of many visually impaired persons (Geruschat & Smith, 1997; Szlyk et al., 1990). Even if vision returns to normal after a period of adaptation, an extended period of adaptation may expose such an individual to such dangers as tripping and falling when going from bright sun to indoors or being temporarily blinded by oncoming headlights. Problems with visual adaptation in older adults have been linked to involvement in motor vehicle collisions and falls that result in injuries (Massie et al., 1995; McMurdo & Gaskell, 1991; Mortimer & Fell, 1989). Severe deficits in adaptation could have disabling effects on any task performed under changing lighting conditions.

Although dark adaptometry is an accepted clinical tool, especially in the diagnosis of retinal disorders, there are few instruments designed to carry out this assessment. The Goldmann-Weekers Adaptometer is the most common instrument; however, its test protocol is vulnerable to examiner and subject biases, similar to those discussed in the context of Goldmann visual fields. Custom-made dark adaptometers have been used to measure dark adaptation in research (Jackson et al., 1998; Jacobson et al., 1986; Steinmetz et al., 1993) but these devices are not commercially available.

Recovery of vision after a drastic change in luminance is often referred to as "glare recovery." In the macular photostress test (Glaser et al., 1977), the subject is presented with a bright light (e.g., an ordinary penlight held an inch from the eye) for a short time (e.g., 10 seconds).

The time taken for vision to recover to some predetermined endpoint is measured. There is no agreed-on standardization of glare recovery testing in terms of such factors as glare intensity, time, and type and size of target used.

Glare Disability

Glare disability is a reduction of the contrast of the retinal image caused by extraneous bright light sources present in the visual field. People with conditions that increase light scatter within the eye experience exaggerated impairments under conditions of glare (Rubin et al., 1993). Glare resulting from light scatter may be due to optical irregularities in the ocular media, such as cataract, corneal opacification, and keratoconus, or it might have origins external to the eye, such as scatter from airborne particles or irregularities on otherwise transparent surfaces, such as windows and spectacle lenses. The intensity of the scattered light depends on the area and luminance of the glare source and its angular proximity to the line of sight. Disability glare can also be of retinal origin, when strong stimulation of one large region of the retina affects the sensitivity of other regions of the retina.

The impact of veiling glare depends on the contrast and acuity demands of the visual task. For example, when looking at a person silhouetted against a window or a very bright sky, contrast reduction can make it difficult to discern features in the face. In driving, detecting pedestrians, the edge of the roadway, or reading signs against a bright sky, sun, or headlights is likely to be difficult if ability to see in the presence of glare is impaired. Disability glare has been associated with the occurrence of motor vehicle collisions (Brabyn et al., 1994), although not all studies agree (Owsley, Jackson, et al., 2001), and with self-reported difficulty in performing night driving and near vision tasks (Rubin et al., 2001). People with retinitis pigmentosa have particularly severe problems with glare in mobility tasks (Turano et al., 1998). Severe glare disability is likely to affect aspects of mobility, such as reading street signs against a bright sky, detecting low-contrast curbs, or seeing objects on white pavement when walking into the sun, although research has not comprehensively addressed these issues.

In tests of disability glare, the subject is usually required to perform a visual task (visual acuity, low-contrast visual acuity, and contrast sensitivity tests) in the presence of the glare source. Some tests use small, bright glare sources at a fixed location relative to the test task, while others use a more extensive glare source surrounding the task. The intensity of the scattered light depends on the angle from the glare source. Glare testers have been commercially available since the predecessors of the Miller Nadler test (1990), which used a slide projector viewer that provided the surround glare for Landolt ring targets of various contrasts. The Brightness Acuity Tester (BAT) (Holladay et al., 1987) is a hemispherical bowl with a controlled glare source held close to the eye, with a 12 mm aperture that allows the viewing of test targets. The clinician chooses the specific test task (e.g., ETDRS chart, Pelli-Robson chart, Bailey-Lovie low-contrast visual acuity chart) (Elliott & Bullimore, 1993). The Berkeley Glare Test (Bailey & Bullimore, 1991) uses low-contrast acuity charts against a large, bright background and can assess disability glare under binocular viewing conditions. Van den Berg and colleagues (de Waard et al., 1992) describe a test to measure intraocular light scatter in which an annulus (or ring) of flickering light is the glare source, and a small spot inside the annulus, flickering in counterphase to the glare source, is the test target whose modulation is adjusted until it appears that there is no flicker.

Today, none of these glare tests is widely used apart from research applications, except for the BAT, which is somewhat popular clinically in cataract surgery evaluation. Other disability glare tests that have not been widely discussed or studied in the literature are the InnoMed true vision analyzer (TVA), the VisTech VCT 8000, the EyeCon 5 (Neumann et al., 1988), the Humphrey Automatic Refractor Model 570 (Beckman et al., 1992), and the Opthimus glare test (Martin, 1999). Each is different in its visual stimulus parameters, and no standardized method of measurement has been widely agreed on. A phenomenon known as "glare discomfort" has also been described in the clinical literature, referring to a subjective feeling of unpleasantness from exposure to bright light. Its functional impact is poorly understood, and there are no standard and accepted tests.

Recommendations

There is a growing body of evidence that low luminance and conditions of glare can significantly accentuate visual disability and even elicit impaired function in a person whose vision may be normal under ideal conditions. Because of the relative lack of standardization in test procedures, the committee recommends not adopting low luminance, glare, dark adaptation, or glare recovery tests as part of the disability determination procedure at this time, but further research should be encouraged on the impact of these exacerbating factors on task performance and on methods for documenting these problems. Meanwhile, the inclusion of contrast sensitivity testing should at least partly address the need for testing under less than ideal viewing conditions that are closer to those encountered in the real world.

VISUAL EFFICIENCY

SSA recognizes that impaired central acuity and impaired visual fields, neither of which alone would meet the disability standard in the listings, can in combination result in an overall impairment that is disabling. Impairment is characterized by a composite measure of the *visual efficiency* of the better eye, derived from component measures of central visual efficiency (from measured acuity) and visual field efficiency (from measured fields).

We examined the computation of central visual efficiency and visual field efficiency, considering how well each index characterizes impairments and how an appropriate composite index of performance might best be calculated in the context of our recommended methods for measuring visual function. This composite measure would also need to accommodate measurements of contrast sensitivity, when these had been made as part of the disability assessment.

In addition to examining the measure of efficiency, we examined the criterion for disability, to establish whether the relationships between performance on tests of visual function and performance on everyday tasks suggest any natural criterion. Given our recommended changes to the procedures for measuring visual acuity and fields and changes to the ways in which performance is scored, we also considered what level of efficiency would correspond to the current criterion for disability.

Central Visual Efficiency

Following an investigation of how glasses that diffused light to varying degrees impaired visual acuity and considering perceptual scaling issues generally, Snell and Sterling (1925) proposed that as the minimum angle of resolution increased linearly (from a standard 1 minute of arc) a person's visual efficiency (*E*) decreased geometrically:

$$E = k^{(1\text{-MAR})}$$

where k is a constant of proportionality. Snell and Sterling found experimentally that to reduce normal (20/20) acuity to "qualitative vision" (no useful resolving power) required six times the diffusing strength needed to reduce 20/20 acuity to 20/40, so they proposed that 20/40 vision represented a one-sixth (16.7 percent) loss of visual efficiency. An acuity of 20/200 would represent an 83 percent loss of efficiency; Snell and Sterling defined 20/200 to represent 80 percent loss of efficiency and thereby established *k* to be 0.83625. The resulting visual efficiency scale is that still used by SSA. The current standard offers alternative efficiency scales for use when one or both eyes lack a lens (aphakia). Table 1-3 illustrates these scales.

The available evidence on the real-world consequences of different degrees of impaired acuity (Rubin et al., 2001; West et al., in press) endorses the principle embodied in the current standard that (as with many visual functions) there is a logarithmic relationship between visual acuity and overall performance. Thus, for example, an acuity of 20/80 is as much worse than 20/40 as an acuity of 20/200 is worse than 20/100. Nevertheless, the efficiency scale has weaknesses. First, it provides little room to distinguish individuals whose impairments range from severe low vision (represented by the current 20/200 criterion for statutory blindness) through complete blindness. The difference between 20/200 and 20/277 represents a decrease in efficiency of 0.1 (0.2 – 0.1), and the difference between 20/277 and no useful vision represents an efficiency change of the same magnitude. Second, the prescribed adjustment for aphakia is no longer appropriate. An allowance for aphakia might have been reasonable when a person whose lens had been removed in cataract surgery had to wear powerful glasses, which magnified the image and created a significant reduction in visual field. Nowadays, correction is almost always provided by a surgically implanted intraocular lens, usually supplemented by spectacles and less often by contact lenses. Acuity should always be tested with the best tolerable correction.

The procedure and measure we have recommended for characterizing acuity gives rise to a logarithmic measure (logMAR, see the acuity section) that provides a simple proportional indicator of visual performance. This measure directly expresses visual impairment (as performance declines, the score rises): a score of 1.0 corresponds to the current acuity criterion of 20/200. Because of this, the committee recommends that the logMAR score be used directly in the computation of an overall measure of visual performance for disability determination, as described in the section on combining measures, below. There is no need to compute any index of central visual efficiency.

Visual Field Efficiency

The SSA standard computes visual field efficiency as the sum of the field extents measured along eight directions from the line of sight (up, down, left, right, and the intermediate diagonals), divided by 500, the sum considered to represent the normal field. This ratio is expressed as a percentage. The standard for severe impairment is a visual field efficiency of 20 percent or less. The standard for statutory blindness is a visual field extent of 10° or less from the fixation point, or a greatest diameter of 20° or less.

The prescribed method of estimating visual field efficiency ignores scotomas within the outer bound of the measured visual field, and it provides no means to estimate the visual field available by using both eyes. A better measure of efficiency would make use of the richer and more reliable characterization of the visual field now possible with modern instruments, and it would be based on the effective binocular visual field rather than the monocular field of the better eye.

Our recommended method for expressing impairment is the mean deviation (MD, see the visual fields section). It characterizes the aggregate loss of sensitivity within the central 60° of visual field on a logarithmic scale. The MD score captures performance over a range that extends to 30 dB mean loss of sensitivity, which is essentially complete blindness. Like the proposed measure of acuity, the MD score is a logarithmic measure that provides a direct proportional indicator of impairment that can be used in disability determination. The current disability criterion (a field restricted to the central 20° or less) would correspond to an MD of –22 dB, assuming an intact field in the central 20° and complete loss beyond. Given the directness and simplicity of MD as measure of performance, it can be used without modification in the computation of an overall measure of visual impairment for disability determination, as described in the section on combining measures below. There is no need to compute an index of percentage remaining visual field efficiency.

Contrast Sensitivity

We have recommended that contrast sensitivity be measured when a claimant has a best corrected acuity of 20/50 (logMAR 0.4) or worse but does not meet the SSA listing criterion of 20/200 or worse. Our recommended instrument for measuring contrast sensitivity is scored in a way that provides a direct expression of log contrast sensitivity (based on the Weber contrast ratio, $L\text{max} - L\text{min}/L\text{max}$). Taking normal log contrast sensitivity as 2.0, an expression of impairment that is commensurate with those obtained from the recommended measurements of visual acuity and visual fields would be $2 - CS$. As discussed earlier, there is considerable evidence that a threefold loss of sensitivity (impairment score 1.5) represents consequentially impaired vision, and a tenfold loss (impairment score 1.0) represents severely impaired vision.

Combining Measures

SSA regulations prescribe a method for computing the overall loss of visual function that might result from impairments of both acuity and visual fields. Overall efficiency (visual efficiency) is calculated as

$$\text{Visual efficiency} = \text{central visual efficiency} \times \text{visual field efficiency.}$$

This measure gives equal weight to the component scores. The standard for severe impairment is an overall efficiency in the better eye of 20 percent or less. Two important issues arise: Is the equal weighting of component scores reasonable, and do the impairments act multiplicatively?

Because impairments of acuity and fields limit performance in quite different ways and generally in different domains of activity, their relative importance is likely to be task-dependent. One approach to understanding their relative importance would be to establish what levels of impairment on each have equivalent effects on higher-level performance indicators, such as quality of life measures. At present there is insufficient evidence on what might be the appropriate weightings of acuity and fields in any composite measure to be used for disability determination. We recommend that research be done on this question. In the meantime, we recommend that SSA continue its current practice of giving equal weight to the measures of visual acuity and visual fields.

Recommendations

Beyond establishing commensurate scales for characterizing acuity, visual fields, and contrast sensitivity, we need to be able to compute an aggregate indicator of impairment. We know too little about the interactions between multiple visual impairments to recommend a change in SSA's current practice of deriving an overall measure by multiplicative combination of component measures. Some recent evidence (Rubin et al., 2001) suggests that impairments act independently in affecting overall visual performance. We recommend that further research be undertaken to examine directly how different kinds of impairments interact in determining overall visual performance.

In the meantime, the committee recommends that, with the modification noted below, SSA continue its current practice of computing an overall measure of performance as the product of the component measures. This principle implies that different tests measure independent aspects of visual function, which cannot be completely true. For example, a central scotoma will be reflected in both an acuity score and a visual field score, but its weight in the visual field score will be slight. The problem is consequential for acuity scores and contrast sensitivity scores, which are generally well correlated. For this reason, we recommend that when contrast sensitivity has been measured (which would be done only when a loss is suspected beyond that captured by an acuity score), the contrast sensitivity score should supplant the acuity score in the calculation.

Because our recommended measures of acuity, visual fields, and contrast sensitivity are already logarithmic measures of impairment, we need only add the scores to compute an overall measure in order to achieve a combined multiplicative score. Recognizing that we must give equal weight to visual fields and to visual acuity (or contrast sensitivity), but that we use either a measure of acuity or a measure of contrast sensitivity, we recommend that the overall measure of impairment should be computed as:

$$\text{aggregate impairment} = \text{logMAR} + |MD|/22$$

when the scores to be combined are visual acuity and visual field and

$$\text{aggregate impairment} = (2 - \text{CS}) + |MD|/22$$

when the scores to be combined are contrast sensitivity and visual field. The current standard for disability would be met when the aggregate impairment equals or exceeds 1.0.

Disability Criteria

The acuity standard for statutory blindness (central acuity of 20/200 or worse) appears to have resulted from an examination (Snell, 1925) of the fitness for work of individuals with varying degrees of visual impairment. Snell found that the "threshold for incapacity" lay between 20/200 and 20/400. There is little evidence that this criterion reflects current employment rates of people with visual impairments or that it provides a reliable characterization of their visual capabilities in the workplace.

The studies we have reviewed and also clinical consensus (American Medical Association, 1993, 2001) suggest that the current acuity standard and the current visual field standard represent severely impaired vision. Nevertheless, the evidence also shows that overall visual performance varies continuously, and roughly linearly, with the measures of visual acuity, visual fields, and contrast sensitivity that we have recommended. Evidence about *visual function* therefore provides no guidance on where it might be appropriate to place a criterion for eligibility for disability benefits. While recognizing that a criterion is required, we make no recommendation about where it should be placed.

A decision about where to place the criterion involves many policy factors, including considerations of overall cost. At present, it is not possible to estimate the cost increases or savings that would result from changing the disability criteria now in place, for we do not know how the measures of acuity, fields, and contrast sensitivity are distributed among the population of working age. We therefore recommend that research be undertaken to establish the distributions of our recommended measures of acuity, fields, and contrast sensitivity in the working-age population.

Should SSA implement our recommendations for testing and scoring acuity, fields, and contrast sensitivity and at the same time retain a disability standard equivalent to the current one, we make these observations:

1. From measurement of visual acuity, a logMAR score of 1.0 or greater meets the current standard.

2. From measurement of visual fields, an *MD* score of –22db or worse meets the current standard.

3. It is not necessary to recommend a criterion for contrast sensitivity alone, because such a score will be used only in combination with a visual field score when visual acuity is 20/50 or worse.

4. An aggregate impairment score of 1.0 or more corresponds to the current standard of 20 percent visual efficiency.

Children

An aggregate impairment score may be calculated for children who are old enough to be tested using the instruments designed for adults.

RECOMMENDATIONS FOR TESTS OF VISUAL FUNCTIONS

The committee's recommendations for the testing of visual functions for determination of disability focus on strengthening the testing of visual acuity and visual fields and adding one additional test, of contrast sensitivity, under certain circumstances. Another important recommendation is to consider establishing formal methods to ensure the quality of test administration and to evaluate new tests as they are proposed for use. In addition, the committee recommends that SSA support specific research efforts that will provide a firm scientific basis for future decisions about disability determination for people with visual impairments.

Acuity Testing

Our recommendations concerning assessment of visual acuity are similar to those of the Committee on Vision in its 1980 and 1994 reports (National Research Council, 1980, 1994). We therefore recommend that visual acuity charts should contain the same number of optotypes in each row; the space between optotypes in a row should be at least as wide as the optotypes in that row; and the size of the optotypes should decrease in 0.1 log unit steps from row to row. Chart luminance should be at least 80 cd/m^2, with 160 cd/m^2 optimal, free from glare, with a level of contrast between optotypes and background that is above 80 percent. The person being tested should be encouraged to read as many optotypes on the chart as possible and to guess at an optotype if he or she is unsure. Acuity results should be scored on an optotype-by-optotype basis, since this scoring procedure produces lower test-retest variability than does row-by-row scoring.

For disability determination, visual acuity should be tested under binocular conditions, since this provides the most representative measure of an individual's everyday vision. However, if monocular acuity is tested rather than binocular acuity, the acuity of the better eye should be used for disability determination. Testing should be performed with the subject wearing the best tolerable refractive correction.

Given the history and legislation behind the current SSA standard of "20/200 or worse distance acuity" as the principal criterion for visual disability, the committee recommends continuation of the 20/200 cutoff criterion. Since we recommend a visual acuity chart design that would include optotypes at the 20/160 level, applying the "20/200 or worse" criterion literally to scores obtained with such a chart would set the effective criterion to "worse than 20/160 distance acuity." The scoring of the charts currently used in disability determination sets the effective criterion at "worse than 20/100." The recommended charts have a 20/100 line that would allow SSA to maintain the criterion at the current effective acuity level, but SSA must make the decision on whether this should be done.

Visual Field Testing

The committee recommends that the current SSA standard should be revised so that disability determinations are based on the results of automated static projection perimetry rather than Goldmann (kinetic, nonautomated) visual fields.

We propose the following criteria for any perimeter to be used by SSA for disability determination:

1. The automated static perimeter should be capable of performing threshold testing using a white size III Goldmann target and a 31.5 apostilb (10 cd/m^2) white background.

2. The perimeter should be capable of measuring sensitivity for the central 30° radius of the visual field with equal numbers of target locations in each quadrant of the field, and target locations no more than 6° apart.

3. The perimeter should be a projection perimeter or should produce measures that are equal to those obtained on a projection perimeter.

4. The perimeter should have an internal normative database for automatically comparing an individual's performance with that of the general population.

5. The perimeter should have a statistical analysis package that is able to calculate visual field indices, particularly mean deviation or mean defect (*MD*), which is the average deviation of visual field sensitivity in comparison to normal values for the central 30° radius of the visual field.

6. The perimeter should demonstrate high sensitivity (ability to correctly detect visual field loss) and specificity (ability to correctly identify normal visual fields).

7. The perimeter should demonstrate good test-retest reliability.

8. The perimeter should have undergone clinical validation studies by three or more independent laboratories with results published in peer-reviewed ophthalmic journals.

At present, the Humphrey Field Analyzer and the Octopus perimeters are known to meet these criteria.

For qualified devices, we recommend that a threshold procedure should be employed for visual field determinations (for example, Full Threshold, Fastpac, SITA, and SITA Fast are all suitable alternatives for the Humphrey; Threshold, TOPS, and TOPS Plus are suitable alternatives for the Octopus).

Ideally, one would have a measure of the binocular visual field serve as the basis for disability determinations because the binocular visual field is what people use for daily activities. However, simple procedures for determining the binocular visual field empirically, or deriving it from monocular visual field results, are not currently available. Until such procedures can be implemented, we recommend that the visual field results for the better eye should be used for disability determinations.

To account for scotomas and normal visual field locations between major meridians, we recommend that an index of the overall visual field status, such as mean deviation or mean defect, should be used for disability determinations. *MD* provides the best overall indication of visual field status, taking into account both the spatial extent and the localized sensitivity variations that are present in the visual field. An *MD* of –22 dB approximately corresponds to a visual field extent of less than 10° radius (the current SSA standard) and would serve as a reasonable criterion for disability determination.

Contrast Sensitivity Testing

The committee recommends that contrast sensitivity be assessed as an additional basis for disability determination for claimants who do not meet the current medical listing criteria for disability, but who have acuity between 20/50 and 20/200 and show other evidence or self-report of serious visual impairment. Contrast sensitivity testing of this subset of claimants can provide useful information not captured by high-contrast acuity testing.

A contrast sensitivity test should be simple to administer, requiring no sophisticated electronic or computer equipment, well-standardized, reliable, valid, sensitive to visual loss, and relatively insensitive to changes in focus, viewing distance, and illumination. It should provide a single score that is meaningful and can easily be compared with extensive normative data, and it should provide information about visual function not captured by other tests (such as high contrast acuity).

One available test, the Pelli-Robson, is known to meet these criteria for a satisfactory test, as may others now available or emerging in the future.

Testing of Other Visual Functions

The committee recommends not testing visual functions other than acuity, fields, and contrast sensitivity at this time. Our review of the evidence has not shown that testing of color vision is justified by the additional information it would provide. Testing of binocularity, visual search, and adaptation to glare and luminance change, although worthy of further study because of their potential importance to visual task performance, are not recommended with the tests now available. Well-documented severe impairments of visual functions other than acuity, fields, or contrast sensitivity could be taken into account as "adjustments" in the disability determination process.

Combining Scores to Derive a Measure of Impairment

We know too little about the interactions between multiple visual impairments to recommend a change in SSA's current practice of deriving an overall measure by multiplicative combination of component measures. We recommend that research be undertaken to examine directly how different kinds of impairments interact in determining overall visual performance, so that the appropriate rule may be developed for combining component measures.

In the meantime, the committee recommends that, with the modification noted below, SSA continue its current practice of computing an overall measure of performance as the product of the component measures. For reasons fully explained in the chapter, we recommend that when contrast sensitivity has been measured (which would be done only when a loss is suspected beyond that captured by an acuity score), the contrast sensitivity score should supplant the acuity score in the calculation.

Because our recommended measures of acuity, visual fields, and contrast sensitivity are already logarithmic measures of impairment, it is not necessary to calculate central visual efficiency and visual field efficiency. We need only add the scores to compute an overall measure. Recognizing that we must give equal weight to visual fields and to visual acuity (or contrast sensitivity), but that we use either a measure of acuity or a measure of contrast sensitivity, we recommend that the overall measure of impairment should be computed as:

$$\text{aggregate impairment} = \text{logMAR} + |MD|/22$$

when the scores to be combined are visual acuity and visual field and

$$\text{aggregate impairment} = (2 - \text{CS}) + |MD|/22$$

when the scores to be combined are contrast sensitivity and visual field. The current standard for disability would be met when this aggregate impairment equals or exceeds 1.0.

Assurance of Test Quality

The committee recommends that SSA should develop standards for the selection of tests to be used in disability determination and consider establishing a formal body of experts on vision testing to implement these standards. This could take the form of a standing advisory board or a panel of consultants with both clinical and scientific expertise; it would review proposed new tests and changes to tests now used, approving those that meet the standards.

The committee also recommends that SSA consider developing standards for test administration, in consultation with the ophthalmological and optometric communities, exploring ways to ensure that such standards are met by professionals testing SSA claimants, while respecting the value of practitioners' clinical judgment. This could greatly improve the reliability of testing. Implementation possibilities range from initiating an accreditation or certification system for providers and their test facilities to establishing dedicated test centers that would operate under SSA supervision.

These quality assurance recommendations apply to tests of visual task performance (discussed in Chapter 3) as well as to tests of basic visual functions.

Research Recommendations

Research is needed relating the outcome of visual assessment using such tools as visual acuity charts to an individual's ability to function in the workplace and in society. The results of such studies would allow future evaluation of the adequacy of the traditional cutoff of 20/200.

There is currently very little information available on the relationship between the status of the peripheral visual field and the performance of daily activities, occupational demands, and task performance. This area merits further research to support the validity of using visual field measurements as predictors of functional capabilities. Another important area is the development of techniques for providing valid and reliable measures of binocular visual field sensitivity.

The relationships of contrast sensitivity to performance on tests of mobility, social participation, and tool use/manipulation are areas clearly in need of further study, as is the contrast sensitivity testing of young children (see Chapter 4).

Glare and vision in poor and changing lighting are exacerbating factors for seeing low-contrast objects. There is no standard, widely available test for glare. Thus research is needed on glare testing and on the impact of exacerbating factors, including glare, on task performance, and methods for documenting these problems. New tests are available to test low luminance, low-contrast acuity, but they have not been extensively used among working-age visually impaired people and therefore require further study, which would also be useful for tests of binocularity and of visual search and related functions.

3

VISUAL TASK PERFORMANCE

This chapter is concerned with the relationship of vision to the performance of everyday life and work tasks. In approaching the question of how to determine if a worker has a disability for visual reasons the Social Security Administration (SSA) currently relies primarily on tests of basic, objectively testable visual functions—namely, acuity and visual fields—with the implicit assumption that these measures can predict ability to perform visually intensive work and daily life tasks. As understanding of the complexity of the relationship between the traditional measures of visual function and an individual's actual abilities to perform important tasks has grown, SSA has become concerned about the predictive validity of such tests and specifically requested the committee to explore the possibility of using measures that more directly test the ability to perform daily life and work tasks.

The use of such measures would be contingent on meeting several challenges. First is the need to select a manageable set of surrogate tasks that adequately represent important vision-related tasks of everyday life and work. Second, SSA would have to ensure that tests of such tasks proposed for use in disability determination demonstrate construct validity and are reliable and well normed. The tests also must show a robust relationship to the requirements of jobs in the U.S. economy (i.e., must demonstrate strong predictive validity) as demonstrated in rigorous peer-reviewed research. The development of such tests is thus dependent on knowledge of the vision-related task requirements of the immense variety of jobs in the economy—jobs that are not stable but change over time.

The committee conducted several interrelated inquiries in its effort to assess (1) the relationships between visual function measures and performance of everyday life and job tasks and (2) the possibility of using tests of vision-related tasks in disability determination. First, an iterative process was used to select a limited number of task domains to represent the broad range of vision-related everyday life and work tasks. Many candidate task domains were discussed, and a short list was developed, based on the collective expertise of committee members. In a concurrent effort described below, the relationships of the most common standard vision measures to actual performance on various jobs and tasks were analyzed. The information gathered in this review, when fed back to the selection of task domains, supported the committee's selection of four task domains as representative and inclusive of the important tasks of everyday life and work:

- *reading* and related close work, such as use of a computer display,
- *mobility*, both ambulatory and driving,
- *social participation*, and
- *tool use* and manipulative tasks.

The committee sought evidence to demonstrate (through both direct observation and self-report) the nature of the relationships between visual function measures such as acuity, visual fields, contrast sensitivity, and others and the actual ability of individuals in a community setting to perform important daily life tasks and other vision-related tasks that would be of importance in a job setting. Such evidence would scientifically support the claim that the testing of visual functions can predict job performance abilities—a predictive relationship that has not to our knowledge been rigorously demonstrated for the tests now used by SSA. We surveyed and evaluated the experimental literature on these relationships. In addition, we conducted a concurrent literature review and analysis of the relationship of the vision measures now used by SSA—visual acuity and visual field loss—to individual self-reported functioning and health-related quality of life (HRQOL), in part because SSA requested that we evaluate the usefulness of HRQOL measures in disability determination methodology. This work provided valuable information for the committee's task domain selection.

An important goal of this work was to characterize the form of any relationships that were found between specific vision test results and task performance. For example, is there a step function or threshold in acuity or visual field scores at which performance on particular tasks deteriorates significantly, or is the relationship relatively continuous and uninflected, meaning that a "natural" cutoff point for disability could not be derived from the relationship?

Finally, we assessed job analysis databases, two of them in depth, to determine the availability and quality of information about how important vision functions are related to the performance of job tasks, using current Department of Labor job taxonomies. In addition, we analyzed the importance of vision to specific job tasks or skills independent of the job categories. This effort was designed to evaluate the evidence available to support more specific and tailored job disability assessments that would require determination of which visual measures should be weighed in determining vision-related disability for specific job categories and the underlying job tasks in each category.

This chapter discusses the committee's findings from this set of investigations and analyses. First we present the findings on the importance and relationships to visual functions of each of the four task domains: reading, mobility, social participation, and tool use and manipulative tasks. These sections include reviews of available tests for these task domains and recommendations on the use of such tests for disability determination. Next we present findings on health-related quality of life measures, followed by a review of the evidence from occupational analysis databases. Finally, we summarize our recommendations regarding use of tests of visual task performance in disability determinations.

READING

Description

The Case for Including Reading Performance in Disability Determination

Disability is one of the four levels of evaluation in the widely used classification of vision outlined by Colenbrander (International Society for Low Vision Research and Rehabilitation, 1999): disorder, impairment, disability, and handicap. Reading difficulty is the primary exemplar of a disability. Reading is a skill or ability possessed by a person rather than a characteristic of an eye or visual system per se.

Like other important abilities of daily life, reading performance depends in complex ways on the interaction of visual input, cognitive proficiency, oculomotor control, and probably other factors. Two people with identical eye disorders and levels of impairment (as measured by such clinical tests as acuity) might easily perform differently in reading. The same person with no change in eye disorder or measured impairment might improve his or her reading performance as a result of rehabilitation. Reading also differs from clinical tests of visual impairment in being dynamic in character. Reading, like driving and hand-eye coordination, involves rapid visual information processing and online integration of vision with other processes. As described below, impairments in acuity, contrast sensitivity, and field status (especially central field loss) affect reading performance in characteristic ways, but they do not provide accurate predictions of reading ability.

Agencies concerned with assessing disability in relation to work seek to determine whether individuals possess the capacities or skills to perform jobs. If reading is essential for a job, then a necessary condition for employment is the ability to read, with measured values of acuity or field being of only indirect relevance. Since reading is an essential component of many jobs in the modern American economy, a person with reduced reading ability is certainly disadvantaged. In this case, direct measurement of reading performance would be valuable in disability determination.

Reading is only one of many possible skills that might figure in disability assessment. How important is reading? Throughout the world, reading is one of the most highly valued activities in human culture. The United Nations and other international bodies use literacy rates as one of the primary indicators of social and economic development. To quote from Hamadache (1990): "The struggle for literacy is also a struggle for justice, for access to knowledge, and for equality. Literacy is an essential precondition for the effective exercise of human rights." When eye disorders deprive or limit people's access to the printed word, the issue is vision disability, not literacy, but the individual consequences may be just as severe. Because of the fundamental importance of reading, low vision is sometimes defined as the inability to read a newspaper at a normal distance with best correction (glasses or contact lenses).

Reading difficulty is often cited as the most common presenting symptom in low vision clinics. For instance, Elliott et al. (1997) reported that reading was the primary objective for 75 percent of elderly patients seeking low vision rehabilitation and the secondary objective for 21 percent. Leat et al. (1999) reported that surveyed patients had a priority for reading medicine bottles and bank statements over reading the newspaper.

During the public forum held by the committee as part of its information-gathering activities, most of the presenters noted the limitations of impairment measures for assessing disability in skills of daily life, including reading. This concern with reading is consistent with our analysis, based on the Position Analysis Questionnaire, a proprietary job analysis system, that indicated that written communication is important in 47 percent of jobs.

Given the importance of reading to employment and other activities of daily life and the imprecision of estimating reading disability from traditional measures of visual impairment, a strong case can be made for including evaluation of reading performance in disability assessment. As described below, although reading performance is related to measures of visual impairment (acuity, contrast sensitivity, and field), a direct measurement of reading performance on a well-standardized test would provide additional information that may be relevant to disability determination.

Before presenting a recommendation about the inclusion of a test of reading in disability assessment, we address several questions: What is the range of reading tasks under consideration? What aspects of reading have been measured? What clinical tests of reading vision already exist? What are the desirable characteristics of a suitable reading test for disability assessment? After addressing these questions, we turn to an evaluation of reading tests for assessing disability.

The Range of Reading Tasks

Reading is a cluster of different tasks that impose different demands on vision, motor control and language skills. In conventional reading, people navigate through the text with a series of brief eye movements called saccades, separated by pauses called fixations. People with mild to moderate visual impairment may use optical magnifiers, requiring coordination of hand movements, head movements, and eye movements. People with more severe visual impairment may use electronic magnifiers such as closed circuit TV.

There is a trade-off between the amount of magnification and the proportion of a printed page that is visible in the magnifier's field of view. Two problems result from the restricted field. First, there is the question of the number of letters in the field (window size) necessary to support the fastest reading. The critical number is at least four and can be greater, depending on the motor demands for magnifier scanning (cf. Beckmann & Legge, 1996; Legge, Pelli, et al., 1985). Second, the diminished field seen through the magnifier hides the global layout information on the page (Den Brinker & Beek, 1996).

Knowledge of the global layout of text is not very important for the sequential line-by-line reading of continuous prose. But nonsequential reading occurs in skimming text for gist or searching text for critical terms or hyperlinks. While the impacts of magnification and field size are fairly well understood for sequential text reading, relatively little is known about their impact on nonsequential reading.

Nonsequential reading is taking on greater importance with the growing use of computers at work and in the home. Screen magnification on computers has been implemented in commercially available software applications. Although these forms of adaptive technology have proven remarkably useful, they have generated new problems in dealing with the nonsequential display of information on computers.[1] It is expected that the growing use of hypertext in computer reading and increased reliance on graphical displays (typically nonsequential in their use) will impose extra burdens on reading by people with disabilities. This is an area in need of research.

It should also be noted that researchers have experimented with nontraditional methods for displaying text in hopes of finding a method particularly advantageous for people with low vision. For instance, the RSVP method (rapid serial visual presentation), involves displaying words of a text sequentially at the same place on a display screen, minimizing the need for eye movements. People with normal vision can read RSVP text much faster than conventional text (Rubin & Turano, 1992). Despite high hopes for a similar improvement in speed for people with low vision, RSVP provides only a modest benefit for readers with low vision (Fine & Peli, 1995; Harland et al., 1998; Rubin & Turano, 1994). A variant of RSVP, called ESP (elicited sequential presentation) provides a modest benefit in reading speed (Arditi, 1999). One disadvantage of RSVP and ESP is that they do away with global layout information altogether. Reading in the real world is not restricted to books, sheets of paper, and computer screens. Signage is important for mobility, both walking and driving. Spectacle-mounted or hand-held telescopes can be useful for finding signs, but the targeting process is time-consuming and is difficult to accomplish while the viewer is in motion. Stabilization of features in the magnified retinal image requires recalibration of the relationship

---

[1]Here are two examples. Imagine that the lower right quadrant of a computer screen is magnified so that it fills a low vision user's computer display. Activity outside this quadrant, such as menus, prompts or error messages, will simply not appear on the screen. Next, imagine using a screen magnifier to move through text with scroll bars. Either the text of interest or the scroll bars will be visible in the magnified view, but not both at the same time.

between head movements and compensatory eye movements, known as the visual vestibulo-ocular reflex (Demer et al., 1988). In short, while telescopes can be used for reading and other high-acuity distance tasks, there are serious practical limitations.

Other common reading tasks in the workplace include monitoring of dials and instrument panels, retail labels, and financial documents, including currency notes (National Materials Advisory Board & National Research Council, 1995).

It is important to keep in mind that many visually disabled people use nonvisual methods for reading in addition to or instead of print. Text can be read aloud by live assistants or recorded on audio tape. Digital documents can be spoken by speech synthesizers. With the advent of optical scanning, improved speech-recognition software, and the widespread creation of electronic documents, computer-based speech has become a realistic option for both vocational and pleasure reading. This technology has reduced the dependence of visually disabled readers on sighted assistants. It should be noted, however, that the sequential nature of auditory displays makes nonsequential text reading difficult. Some screen reader programs (such as JAWS by Freedom Scientific) have included special functions to help with nonsequential reading (e.g., a function that groups all hyperlinks on a web page into a single column).

Between 15,000 and 85,000 Americans use Braille (Legge et al., 1999). Although Braille reading speeds average about a factor of two lower than print reading speeds, Braille is especially valuable in contexts in which magnifiers or auditory displays are inconvenient. Word processing documents can be converted to Braille codes by software and embossed on Braille printers. Braille note takers (for example, Braille 'n Speak by Freedom Scientific or BrailleNote by PulseData) permit users to type Braille on a compact keyboard for later reproduction by synthetic speech, print, or embossed Braille.

There is a debate over the mode of instruction for teaching visually impaired children to read—print, Braille, or tape. In one view, children with low vision should learn to read print because the majority of written material appears in print. In another view, children should learn to read Braille because it is often more convenient than reading with a magnifier, and because it is hard to learn later in life when vision may decrease further. Almost everyone agrees that strict reliance on audio recordings is undesirable because it results in poor spelling and even illiteracy.

Measuring Reading

Reading performance has been evaluated in many ways. A brief review follows. Clinical tests of reading are discussed in the next section.

Reading Acuity and Critical Print Size. *Reading acuity* refers to the measurement of visual acuity using a test chart containing paragraphs, sentences, or words in typeset print. The test material for reading acuity is more congested and complex than the letter chart, which has relatively widely separated letters. Not only is the reading material more crowded, but there is more spatial integration required to correctly recognize individual words and word strings. Reading acuity is highly correlated with letter acuity, although some people with low vision, particularly those with macular degeneration, have poorer reading acuity than letter chart acuity (Lovie-Kitchin & Bailey, 1981). Reading acuity is typically measured at a near viewing distance such as 40 cm.

Newsprint, held at a distance of 40 cm (16 inches), would typically be at the limit of resolution of someone with reading acuity of 20/50. Accordingly, someone with a reading acuity poorer than 20/60 (a common definition of low vision) would be unable to read newsprint without bringing the page closer to the eye or using some other form of magnification.

A newer concept is *critical print size.* While reading acuity documents the angular size of the smallest print size for which reading is possible, a somewhat larger print size is required for fluent, effective reading. For a given viewing distance, the critical print size, two or more times larger than acuity letters, is the print size beyond which the size of characters no longer inhibits reading performance. Although optical and closed circuit television magnifiers are often prescribed to magnify selected specimens of printed material to achieve the observer's critical print size, it is only recently that critical print size has received attention from researchers.

For example, consider a person with 20/200 reading acuity whose critical print size is 3 times larger than their acuity limit. If 4-fold magnification brings typical newsprint to this person's acuity limit, then 12-fold magnification would be necessary to reach the critical print size for effective reading. Although 4-fold magnification might be easily accomplished with a hand-held optical magnifier, 12-fold magnification could require a more specialized magnifying device and a smaller field of view. The important point is that the nature of the prescribed magnifier, as well as the functional outcome, may depend on whether text letters are enlarged to the acuity limit, to the critical print size, or to an intermediate size.

DeMarco & Massof (1997) have surveyed the distribution of print sizes in 10 different sections of 100 U.S. newspapers. Median print sizes range from $M = 0.78$ (stock listings) to $M = 1.21$ (comic strips), corresponding to Snellen sizes (at 40 cm) of 20/40 to 20/60. (*M*-units indicate the distance in meters at which the letter height subtends 5 minutes of arc. For example, 1.0 *M* print subtends 5 minutes at a distance of 1 meter and is 1.45 mm high.) Anyone with a critical print size larger than 20/60 would be at a disadvantage in reading text similar to newspapers at a distance of 40 cm. At that distance, they would either read slowly (if at all) or would require some magnification.

Reading acuity and critical print size are familiar measures to eye care professionals because of their similarity to letter acuity. The following measures are less familiar and have been used more in rehabilitation or research contexts.

Reading Speed. Reading speed, in words per minute (wpm), has been widely used in psychophysical studies because it can be measured objectively, is reproducible, and is sensitive to variations in visual parameters (Carver, 1990; Legge, Pelli, et al., 1985; Tinker, 1963). Reading speed is a measure that reflects the dynamic nature of reading. One problem with this measure is that reading speed depends on the difficulty level of the reading material. Factors such as the component words, the sentence structure, and the simplicity or complexity of the content necessarily cause variations in difficulty from one passage to the next or from one observer to another. Mean word length varies from passage to passage, increasing with text difficulty. Carver (1990) has shown that differences in speed due to text difficulty can be reduced by measuring reading speed in "standard-length words" per minute, wherein each six characters count as one standard-length word. Carver has shown that, on average, a subject's reading speed is about constant in standard-length wpm across text difficulty, provided the grade level of the text does not exceed the reading level of the subject.

Average prose reading speed in English for normally sighted adults is about 250 wpm (cf. Legge et al., 1999). Whittaker & Lovie-Kitchin (1993) have identified three slower rates, based on clinical experience, associated with different levels of function in people with low vision: (1) spot reading (44 wpm), adequate for many tasks of daily life, such as reading mail, recipes, and labels; (2) fluent reading (88 wpm), and (3) high fluent reading (176 wpm). Note that their high fluent rate is well below the typically cited mean value for normally sighted reading speed. A sustainable reading speed of 176 wpm, while still slow for a normally sighted reader, would probably be adequate for meeting the needs of all but the most reading-intensive jobs. However, a person whose maximum reading speed is 90 wpm or less is functionally disadvantaged in reading, lying more than two standard deviations below the normal mean (Legge et al., 1992).

Accuracy. The percentage of words read aloud correctly is sometimes used, especially in cases in which it is expected that faulty control of eye movement may lead to missed portions of text or if the person is inclined to guess.

Endurance. Sometimes people with low vision can read rapidly for a short period, but the motor demands of a magnifier or the nature of the eye condition precludes lengthy sustained reading. There has been little study of reading endurance, but it is surely an important issue for some types of work.

Comprehension. Comprehension is tested in many cognitive and educational studies of reading. Standardized tests, such as the SAT or GRE, evaluate comprehension. It appears that comprehension is not much affected by eye condition or a person's maximum reading speed

(Legge, Ross, Maxwell, & Luebker, 1989). But there is some evidence that a greater cognitive load is associated with low vision reading. Dickinson & Rabbitt (1991) tested reading comprehension in normally sighted subjects with simulated low vision (optical blur and distortion). Free recall performance was impaired, although performance on multiple-choice questions was not. Further research is required to show whether these subtle effects are found in low vision reading.

Eye Movements. Saccade lengths and fixation times have been widely measured in linguistic and cognitive studies of reading. It is technically difficult to measure eye movements in people with low vision, especially those with scotomas (blind spots) in central vision. This is because eye-tracking hardware usually relies on a subject's careful fixation for proper calibration. Nevertheless, there have been several studies of eye movements in people with central scotomas from macular disease (Bullimore & Bailey, 1995; Rumney & Leat, 1994; Trauzettel-Klosinski et al., 1994). These studies typically find that slower reading is primarily due to abnormally short saccades, while fixation times are more nearly normal. Legge et al. (1997) have provided a theoretical analysis and computer simulation of saccade behavior in the presence of central scotomas.

Questionnaires. Surveys of visual status usually include questions about reading behavior, and standardized measuring instruments, such as the National Eye Institute Visual Function Questionnaire (discussed below), also include questions about reading. An important issue is the correlation between people's responses to these questions and their actual reading performance. In one study, a discrepancy was found in the responses of some people with mild visual impairment between measured reading speed and self-reports of reading difficulty on the Activities of Daily Vision questionnaire (Friedman et al., 1999). A small proportion of subjects reported minimal difficulty in reading newsprint despite measured reading speeds less than 80 wpm. The authors suggested that the discrepancy occurred for people who were undergoing changes in visual status during an acute phase of eye disease; they were not yet fully aware of the decline in their reading ability.

Clinical Tests of Reading

There are numerous clinical tests of reading acuity. Some use continuous text (e.g., Sloan & Brown, 1963), and some use randomly ordered words (Bailey & Lovie, 1980). A few reading charts have been designed to standardize the length and difficulty of the reading task in order to facilitate the quantitative assessment of reading speed in either clinical or research environments. These include the charts described in Bailey & Lovie (1980); the MNREAD chart (Mansfield et al., 1996); and the Colenbrander Chart (Precision Vision Catalogue). Figure 3-1 shows sample MNREAD data for a normally sighted subject and a person with age-related macular degeneration.

The Pepper Visual Skills for Reading Test (Baldasare et al., 1986) was designed to measure the effects of word length, line spacing, and other attributes of text on reading by visually impaired people.

Clinical tests of reading performance have been found to correlate with real-world reading performance in the home (West, Rubin, et al., 1997) or with magnifier-aided reading (Ahn & Legge, 1995; Lovie-Kitchin et al., 2000). They are better predictors of real-world reading performance than such standard clinical tests as letter acuity.

Design Characteristics for a Clinical Reading Test

There is consensus that tests of reading vision should provide not only a measure of the smallest print (angular size) that can be read, but also an assessment of reading speed as a function of print size. Reading acuity, critical print size, and maximum reading speed are three important parameters for characterizing reading vision. Some reading acuity tests are composed of unrelated words, but, for testing functional reading ability, tests with continuous text are preferred because the task is more representative of real-world reading tasks. The results from tests composed of unrelated words and continuous text are often similar; reading speeds are faster for continuous text than unrelated words, but the speeds are highly correlated across subjects (Legge, Ross, Luebker, & LaMay, 1989).

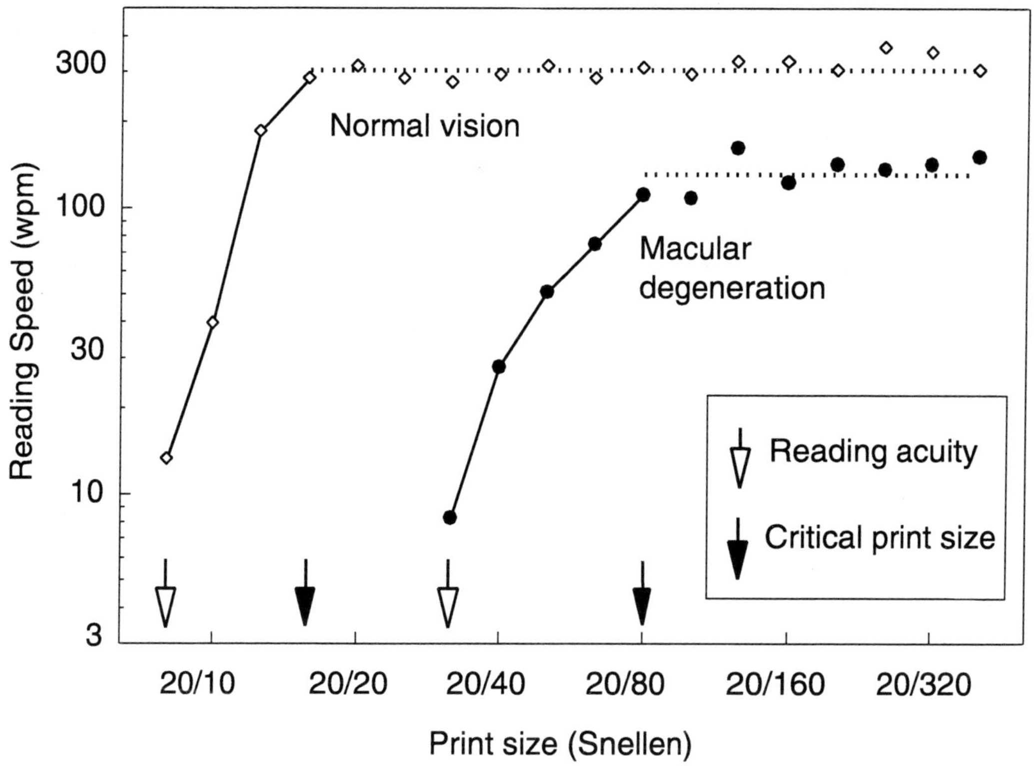

FIGURE 3-1. Illustrative data from the MNREAD Reading Acuity Chart for a subject with normal vision (upper curve) and a subject with age-related macular degeneration (lower curve). Reading speeds were obtained by measuring the time to read sentences composed of 60 characters (10 words) at each of several print sizes. Three parameters are shown for each curve: reading acuity (arrow at the left end), critical print size (arrow at the bend), and reading speed (dashed line). Source: Gordon E. Legge, unpublished.

For reading tests with continuous text, the charts should follow the same design principles that are recommended for letter charts for measuring distance visual acuity. The task should be essentially the same at each of the size levels. This requires a logarithmic progression of size, standardization of the typeface, and standardization of the layout and reading difficulty throughout the chart. The length of rows and the spacings between letters, between rows, and between adjacent size levels should be kept proportional to print size. The words and composition of the text should be such that the different passages have approximately equal difficulty. The number of characters per row should be approximately the same throughout the chart.

In order to ensure that reading acuity can be measured for all people, the range of print size should extend to print so small that it is beyond the resolution limit of people with normal vision when viewing the chart from a standard reading distance (e.g., 40 cm). The largest print size should be as great as practical, to accommodate the widest range of low vision subjects. High-quality printing is required to achieve good rendition of the print at the very small sizes.

The text used in reading tests should be simple enough to be read easily by most persons with the expected level of literacy. Simpler text may be necessary for testing young children. The choice of the length of the passages of text requires compromises between (a) sufficient text to estimate reading performance, (b) too much text to fit on the chart or screen at the large print end, and (c) time required by low vision subjects to read through the passages. The text may be single sentences or sequences of sentences forming paragraphs. From one print size to the next, there should not be a continuity of the story line. The average number of character spaces per row should be kept approximately the same at all size levels. If reading speeds are to be quantified, the length of the text samples at each size level should be specified in terms of number of words or characters. It is desirable that there be different versions of the chart available, should the test need to be repeated. The typeface should be representative of commonly used type. Most reading charts use Times Roman or a similar typeface.

Print size should be expressed in angular terms when measuring reading acuity and determining profiles of reading speed as a function of print size. Specifying both the height of the print and viewing distance provides a measure of angle. The height of letters in typeset print may be characterized by the height of the lowercase letters that have neither ascending nor descending limbs; the lowercase x is representative of such letters. The "x-height" may be expressed in millimeters or inches, but it is most common for M-units or points to be used to specify print size in reading tests. M-units indicate the distance in meters at which the letter height subtends 5 minutes of arc. For example, 1.0 M print at a distance of 1 meter subtends 5 minutes, is 1.45 mm high, and is equivalent to a 20/20 Snellen letter. At a standard reading distance of 40 cm, 1 M letters have the angular size of 20/50 Snellen letters. Points are units traditionally used in the printing industry: 1 point = 1/72 inch. For a sample of typeset print, the size in points measures from the top of the ascenders to the bottom of the descenders. For font styles such as those most commonly used in newspapers and books (e.g. Times, Century, Schoolbook), the x-height is approximately one-half of the total height of the print sample. Thus, in the Times font, 8 point print has an x-height of 4/72 inch = 1.41 mm. If there is a fixed reading distance, the print size may be labeled in terms of angular size as Snellen fractions or logMAR values.

Standardizing Testing Procedures

The conventional or traditional reading distance is 40 cm, although other viewing distances may be used. Persons with impaired vision may need or may prefer to hold the reading material much closer. Logarithmic print scaling can facilitate adjusting scores to allow for the change in distance. For any testing of reading vision, it is important to ensure that the person being tested has the accommodation and/or appropriate correction to ensure that the eye is in good focus for the viewing distance that is being used. In some occupational tasks, there may be constraints on the range of reading distances used in the workplace. For tests of reading vision to have functional relevance, it is appropriate to place the same constraints on viewing distances during the reading test.

When testing the ability to read, it is important that an appropriate optical correction be worn to ensure an in-focus image. People younger than the mid-forties should normally wear their usual distance vision glasses or contact lenses during testing. Their accommodation will normally be sufficient to focus clearly on the printed material at common reading distances.

Older persons with limited or no accommodation ability are likely to require reading glasses in order to achieve clear vision when performing reading tasks at close distances. The reading glasses may be in the form of single vision reading lenses, bifocal, trifocal, or progressive addition lenses. Some older persons with myopia may remove their distance vision glasses to achieve clear vision at a close distance. If a test of reading vision is being conducted at a set reading distance, care should be taken to ensure that any reading glasses provide the best focus for the test distance.

Real-world reading is typically binocular, so it is appropriate to test reading vision binocularly. (For specialized applications, it may be desirable to test reading performance in the left and right eyes separately.) Uniform instructions should apply across subjects and across print sizes for a given subject. If reading speed is measured, the instructions should promote the same reading strategy across all conditions, e.g., "Read the passage aloud, reading as quickly and accurately as possible." Most tests of reading vision use reading aloud because it is easier to score objectively. When reading aloud at faster speeds, the task of vocalization may limit performance. In principle, silent reading speeds can be measured by monitoring eye movements or by having the subject indicate when the text sample has been completed, although these techniques may be less reliable for purposes of disability determination.

Charts should be uniformly illuminated in a manner that avoids unwanted reflection glare. For compatibility with conditions for testing distance visual acuity, the luminance of the white background should be in the range 80 to 320 cd/m^2 .

Reading acuity is given by indicating the smallest print that can be read and specifying the test distance. Reading errors may be counted and recorded. There should be rules for what constitutes successful reading of a text sample. When reading speeds are to be quantified, there should be rules about extracting the reading speeds and for determining the smallest print.

All of the above criteria assume that the subject is literate in the language in which reading is being tested. Our discussion is based on testing in English, but reading tests are available or under development in other languages. We have not evaluated these here.

Evaluation

To evaluate reading as a potential measure of functional vision, the committee reviewed what is known about (1) the relationship to standard clinical measures of visual impairment and (2) common stimulus variables that may affect reading performance. Before discussing these topics in detail, we address some up-front questions.

What Is the Cause of the Reading Disability?

While most types of impaired vision result in reading problems, it is not the case that all reading problems result from impaired vision. In the United States, low literacy is a major societal problem. According to the National Institute for Literacy (http://novel.nifl.gov/nifl/faqs.html), the 1992 National Adult Literacy Survey revealed that between 21 and 23 percent of the adult population had level 1 literacy skills (i.e., they were unable to fill out most forms or read a simple story to a child). Other nonvisual causes of poor reading include testing in a nonnative language, dyslexia (or related higher-level disorders), or cognitive dysfunction. It is a policy decision whether it is important to ascertain the visual origins of a reading disability.

Assuming that reading disability needs to be ascribed to visual impairment, a diagnosed eye disorder or measurable visual impairment provides a prima facie case. If a nonvisual cause of reading disability is suspected, documentary evidence should be included in the assessment (e.g., a low score on the Mini-Mental Status Exam would be indicative of cognitive dysfunction). For many purposes of disability determination, rehabilitation specialists conduct an assessment including compulsory reports from eye care professionals to establish the visual origin of the disability. If a standardized measurement of reading performance was a part of disability determination, it is reasonable to expect that the origin of poor reading (visual or nonvisual) could be established with high confidence in most cases.

Age is a nonvisual factor requiring special consideration. There is evidence that age per se has greater impact on reading speed for people with low vision than for normal readers (Legge et al., 1992). It is also noteworthy that age has a greater impact on more challenging tests of visual function—such as low-contrast, low-luminance acuity—than it does on standard visual acuity (Haegerstrom-Portnoy et al., 1999).

Is There a Scale for Reading Disability?

The measures of reading performance that have received most attention from clinicians and vision researchers are reading acuity, critical print size, and reading speed. These measures are all reactive to eye problems and are to some degree decoupled from one another. How should they be combined in the determination of disability? This problem, like visual field testing, requires a method for collapsing multiple measures into a single score. In principle, there is no greater barrier in constructing a scale for reading disability than for constructing scales for functional acuity or functional field measurements.

Are Reading Measurements Too Variable?

Eye clinicians have had vastly more experience with acuity and field measurements than with reading measurements (although informal use of reading charts is common in refraction). Intuitively, it seems likely that acuity measurements are tighter and more reliable than reading measurements.

Surprisingly, well-controlled studies of the distribution of normal acuity and the reliability of repeat measurements are few and far between. In part, this is because suitably designed acuity charts and scoring methods have been developed only in recent years (Bailey &

Lovie, 1976; Ferris et al., 1982). Leat et al. (1999) summarized the small number of tightly controlled studies in which all subjects were screened to have no eye disorders, best refraction was used, and acuity charts were used with sufficient lines to avoid floor effects. Across studies (see Table 1 of Leat et al.), mean normal acuity was about –0.10 logMAR (Snellen 20/16) with a standard deviation of about 0.1 log unit (i.e., percentage error of about 26 percent). An identical standard deviation of 0.1 log units was obtained for a normal control group in a study of reading speeds for people with low vision by Legge et al. (1992). In a large sample study of older subjects in Marin County, California described by Haegerstrom-Portnoy et al. (1999), data from 748 subjects were analyzed[2] to compare the standard deviations of acuity measurement (near acuity measured with the SKILL test) and reading speed measurement (from the Pepper test). For subjects less than 65 years of age, the standard deviations were 0.09 and 0.10 log units for acuity and reading speed, respectively. The standard deviations of both tests grew with increasing age. For subjects over 90 years of age, the values were 0.18 and 0.24 log units for acuity and reading, respectively.

Although more studies are needed of both acuity and parameters of reading, preferably stratified by age, existing evidence indicates that variability of normal reading performance is not much greater than variability in acuity values.

Should Magnifiers Be Allowed During Testing?

Rehabilitation includes the prescription of reading magnifiers. Magnifiers increase the range of accessible print sizes and reduce the impact of vision impairment on reading. In other words, magnifiers reduce reading disability, although they do not affect visual impairment. It is reasonable to argue, therefore, that a person's reading disability should be assessed while using a magnifier. This would be analogous to evaluating the mobility of a paraplegic person in a wheelchair.

---

[2]John Brabyn, committee member, personal communication.

In opposition, it may be argued that the magnifier introduces too many uncertainties into the assessment of reading disability. For instance: Is it practical to use a suitable magnifier for reading tasks in the person's line of work? Has an appropriate magnifier been prescribed? Will the trade-off of field and print size, inherent in magnifiers, adversely affect work performance?

A hybrid approach might be to measure reading performance with and without a prescribed magnifier and compute reading disability as a weighted combination.

What About Manipulation?

When financial benefits are on the line, it is desirable to use tests that are immune to the subject's manipulation. Any behavioral tests of best sensory, motor, or cognitive function are vulnerable in this sense. Certainly, poor reading could be faked by a subject. As in the case of acuity testing, however, an experienced examiner could use subtleties of the test to ferret out manipulation. For instance, do the critical print size and reading acuity change appropriately when the viewing distance is halved or doubled? Is the person's reading acuity close to their distance Snellen acuity? How easily did they read the printed instructions given to them before the test? In short, assessment of reading disability may be no more vulnerable to manipulation than tests of visual impairment, such as acuity.

Relationship of Reading Performance to Impairments of Visual Functions

Reduced acuity, reduced contrast sensitivity, and loss of macular function are the primary visual impairments affecting reading for people with low vision.

Acuity

Reading the newspaper at a normal reading distance (40 cm or 16 in) is frequently taken as an example of a visually demanding task. According to DeMarco & Massof (1997), 75 percent of material in all newspapers exceeds 0.8 M print size. Letters of this size would be at the acuity limit of a person with 20/40 acuity (the print on medicine bottle labels can often be as small as 0.4 M).

Typically, people need letters larger than their acuity limit to read quickly and without fatigue. The increased print size for fluent reading—the acuity reserve or critical print size—is a factor of 2 or more larger than acuity letters (Mansfield et al., 1996; Whittaker & Lovie-Kitchin, 1993). Accordingly, even a person with 20/40 acuity would be at a visual disadvantage in a job with demands equivalent to newspaper reading.

Clinical tests of letter or reading acuity determine the tiniest letters that can be read. They are reasonably good predictors of the range of legible print sizes under optimal conditions. Conventional letter acuity measurements are not, however, good predictors of reading speed when adequate magnification compensates for acuity limitations (Legge et al., 1992; Whittaker & Lovie-Kitchin, 1993). A recent report indicates that near acuity measurement, based on text or unrelated words, is predictive of reading speeds in people with macular degeneration (Lovie-Kitchin et al., 2000).

Fields

Broadly speaking, field loss can be divided into macular loss, peripheral loss, or hemianopsia. Blind spots (scotomas) in the macular region at the center of the visual field are common in macular degeneration, the leading cause of low vision in the United States. When macular scotomas are present, reading is almost always severely affected (cf. Faye, 1984). The tight link between macular loss and reading difficulty is a strong argument for considering the status of the central fields in disability determination.

Why is macular field loss so detrimental to reading? People with central scotomas typically adopt a region of peripheral vision for fixation termed the *preferred retinal locus.* If peripheral vision were simply a low-resolution version of central vision, reading difficulty could be remedied by magnifying text presented to the preferred retinal locus. Magnification does help, but it does not restore people with macular degeneration to normal reading speed. Nor is it a question of eye movement control. Even when a text presentation method is used that minimizes the need for eye movements, people with central scotomas still read slowly (Rubin & Turano, 1994). Recently, Legge et al. (2001) reported evidence that the number of characters recognized in parallel, termed the *visual span,* shrinks in peripheral vision and imposes an inescapable bottleneck on reading speed.

Peripheral loss can affect reading if the region of remaining central vision gets so small that only a few letters can be seen at a time. This form of "tunnel vision" can occur in advanced cases of glaucoma or retinitis pigmentosa. In such cases, text composed of very large letters can be more difficult to read than text containing smaller letters. A similar situation occurs in some cases of macular scotoma in which the patient retains a small region of foveal function (Fletcher et al., 1999).

Hemianopsia refers to complete loss of either the left or right side of the visual field, usually due to stroke. Although both types of hemianopsias reduce reading speed, loss of the right visual field tends to produce greater deficits than loss in the left visual field (Trauzettel-Klosinski & Brendler, 1998).

Contrast Sensitivity

Contrast sensitivity deficits can be present when acuity and field are relatively intact (Elliott & Whitaker, 1992b), a finding that has motivated the development of special charts for measuring contrast sensitivity discussed in Chapter 2 (cf. Pelli et al., 1988).

Deficits in contrast sensitivity are related to reduced reading performance (Leat & Woo, 1997; Rubin & Legge, 1989; Whittaker & Lovie-Kitchin, 1993). The latter authors found that Pelli-Robson contrast sensitivity less than 1.05 was invariably associated with reduced reading speed. Rubin & Legge (1989) proposed that a subset of people with low vision (those with cataract and other forms of cloudy ocular media) shows normal reading performance after loss of contrast sensitivity is accounted for. For these people, contrast sensitivity can be used to predict reading performance.

The contrast polarity of text (white on black or black on white letters) has little effect on normal reading, but it can affect low vision reading. People with cloudy ocular media suffer from glare due to light scatter within the eye. They usually read white on black text faster and with better acuity than conventional black on white text (Legge, Rubin, & Schleske, 1987). Electronic magnifiers usually include a contrast polarity switch.

Visual Functions That Have Little Effect on Reading

For people with normal binocular vision, in which the two eyes are nearly matched, there are only slight effects on acuity or reading performance of binocular versus monocular viewing (Jones & Lee, 1981; Legge, Pelli, et al., 1985; Sheedy et al., 1986). For instance, Sheedy et al. found only a 3.7 percent reading speed advantage for binocular viewing. Stereo depth is not considered to be relevant to reading.

People with impaired vision usually see better with one eye than the other. When the interocular difference in vision is large, the better eye undoubtedly governs reading performance. There are clinical reports that the poorer eye sometimes interferes with reading. There is need for research to better understand binocular interactions in low vision.

Eye disease frequently results in color deficits, sometimes combining with inherited colored defects. The acquired color defects vary widely in type and severity. Although bright colors can provide helpful cues for people with low vision, there is no evidence that color coding facilitates reading. Based on current knowledge, maximizing luminance contrast is the best way to enhance text legibility, with color contrast secondary.

Search capacity is probably relevant to nonsequential reading (e.g., searching for hyperlinks on a web page.) The relevance of findings on preattentive and serial search to skimming and searching in reading is not well established.

Stimulus Properties and the "Reading Envelope"

It is important to understand how reading performance depends on the stimulus properties of the text for two reasons. First, reading as a real-world task is subject to wide variations in viewing conditions and text characteristics (undoubtedly true for on-the-job applications). We need to understand how these stimulus factors affect performance. Second, in designing tests of reading vision, it is important to know how viewing conditions affect performance.

Beginning with the seminal studies of Tinker and colleagues (summarized in Tinker, 1963), there have been many studies of the effects of text characteristics on reading performance in normal vision. Many of these studies help to define the reserve or "envelope" for reading—that is, the range of conditions over which fluent reading remains possible. Important examples include the effects of print size, text contrast and text luminance.

Reading performance is limited by angular print size, which is jointly determined by physical print size on the page (or screen) and viewing distance. Normal reading speed is at maximum for angular print sizes over a 10-fold range from about 0.2 to 2.0 deg (Legge, Pelli, et al., 1985). For people with reduced acuity, this range is contracted.

Normal reading speed is roughly independent of text contrast from 100 percent contrast down to 10 percent or a little lower, there being some interaction with character size (Legge, Rubin, & Luebker, 1987). It is this tolerance to contrast reduction that enables normally sighted people to read low-contrast xerox copies or poor-quality computer displays. It is not known if reduced contrast affects reading endurance. People with reduced contrast sensitivity have less tolerance to loss of text contrast.

Legge & Rubin (1986) showed that normally sighted reading speeds decrease only slightly over a wide range of moderate to low photopic text luminance, but they decrease more rapidly in scotopic vision.

Sloan (1969) measured acuity versus luminance for a diverse group of subjects with low vision. While some reached maximum acuity at lower luminance levels than required by normally sighted subjects, some subjects with macular degeneration required higher luminance to achieve maximum acuity. Sloan subsequently recommended bright task lighting as a reading aid for people with macular degeneration (Sloan et al., 1973). Bullimore and Bailey (1995) studied reading eye movements in persons with macular degeneration and found substantial changes in reading speeds with changes in illumination. In a recent study, Aquilante et al. (2000) measured reading speeds for normal subjects and subjects with central field loss from macular degeneration. They varied both luminance and print size. They found no qualitative difference between the normal and central loss subjects; both showed decreased reading speed when the luminance was low, with the effect of luminance increasing for print sizes near an individual's acuity limit. More research is needed to clarify the effects of luminance on reading in people with low vision.

The reading envelope of normal vision encompasses a wide range of print sizes, contrasts, and luminance levels. As a result, people can read fluently over a wide range of environmental conditions—variation in viewing distance, daylight or twilight, etc. One important effect of visual impairment is to shrink the envelope. Some people with mild visual impairment may read normally under optimal environmental conditions (e.g., the conditions in effect for a clinical test of reading), but they show a sharp decline with modest changes in text contrast or light level.

Recommendations

Reading is a necessary component of many jobs in the modern economy. Anyone with a reading disability due to vision impairment is restricted in the range of jobs available to them, and faces impediments in many other jobs. Almost everyone with low vision encounters reading difficulty. We can be confident that most people meeting the SSA's medical listing criteria for visual impairment (recommended by the committee to include tests of acuity, field, and contrast sensitivity) will encounter problems with visual reading. For this reason, an additional test of reading performance is unnecessary for those who meet the medical listing criteria.

But some people with visual impairments who fail to meet the listing criteria may experience reading problems that hamper their employability. For example, people with macular problems, notoriously difficult to measure with contemporary field tests, frequently have severe reading disabilities. Others may experience reading difficulty due to combined effects of acuity, contrast, or field deficits that, by themselves, do not meet the criteria.

The committee recommends that a test of reading vision should be included as a key component in the assessment of individuals with vision impairment who receive vocational assessment when their impairments do not meet the medical listing criteria. This should be implemented as soon as a well-normed reading test can be shown to meet test standards established by SSA. Any such assessment may take into consideration the impact on reading of viewing conditions or circumstances associated with an individual's vocational niche (e.g., a person whose reading performance deteriorates rapidly at moderate or low luminance may no longer be able to hold a job that requires reading at low light levels).

Three parameters of reading vision should be taken into account in evaluating disability. A person with *reading acuity* equivalent to 20/60 or worse will be unable to resolve text similar in size to newsprint if it is at a normal working distance of 40 cm (16 inches). A person whose *critical print size* is equivalent to 20/60 or less will be unable to read fluently most text in newspapers and other documents of equivalent print size if they are held at a normal reading distance. A person with a maximum *reading speed* of 90 words per minute or less will be functionally disadvantaged in reading.

Psychophysical and clinical studies of reading and vision have reached the point at which appropriate tests exist or can be designed to measure reading disability. This section has outlined the findings and design principles against which to judge candidate tests. We recommend the following criteria for tests of reading vision:

- Visual characteristics that are consistent with contemporary standards for acuity tests, including a logarithmic progression of print sizes;
- A range of print sizes containing large enough print to be useful with most visually impaired people and small enough to reliably measure reading acuity in normally sighted people;
- Text passages equated in layout across print sizes;
- Reproducible rules for estimating reading acuity, critical print size, and reading speed;
- Binocular testing, unless one eye interferes with the other in reading and the problem can be addressed by covering the interfering eye; and
- Text passages representative in font and letter spacing of commonly encountered real-world texts.

We recommend additional research to establish in more detail the distributions of reading acuity, critical print size, and reading speed in different age groups and the relationships between these measures and performance of work-related activities and the important tasks of daily life.

ORIENTATION AND MOBILITY

Ambulatory Mobility

Independent travel on foot and on public transit—an important prerequisite for employment and independent living—is severely affected by blindness and visual impairment. Indeed, an entire orientation and mobility (O&M) profession has evolved to address this problem (Blasch et al., 1997). The visual requirements for independent travel have received rather limited study compared with other tasks, such as flying a plane or driving an automobile, but enough is known for some conclusions to be drawn.

As the O&M acronym suggests, the independent travel problem for blind and visually impaired people is commonly broken down into two parts. Mobility is commonly thought of as the problem of maintaining a safe and straight path through the environment, avoiding obstacles, collisions, dropoffs, and excessive veering. Orientation is the more global navigation or wayfinding aspect of the problem, involving finding one's way from A to B and maintaining a knowledge of where one is, what direction one is facing, etc. (Blasch et al., 1997).

Theories of Orientation and Mobility

The use of visual information for maintaining a path through the environment and steering around obstacles has long been studied in terms of optical flow (Gibson, 1958, 1979). Navigation, a higher-order task, involves more elaborate spatial representations (Strelow, 1985). For example, "cognitive maps" (Tolman, 1948) loosely refer to a viewpoint-independent representation of spatial layout in environmental (allocentric) coordinates.

Evidence for the salience of landmarks in spatial representations has been used to argue for navigation based on "route memory" rather than cognitive maps. Route memory consists of chains of associations between perceived landmarks and motor movements (Schoelkopf & Mallot, 1995). Route memory relies on egocentric coordinates, and is ineffective for judging the relations between locations not on the same route. Route memory has often been ascribed to people with blindness or low vision to explain deficiencies in spatial tasks (cf. Thinus-Blanc & Gaunet, 1997). Path integration (Loomis et al., 1999) is yet another model for the cognitive aspect of navigation, probably most useful in exploring unknown environments.

It is likely that travelers invoke cognitive maps, route memory, or path integration depending on their task demands or training. The studies suggest the importance of visual landmarks in forming all of these cognitive representations, and impaired vision may make them harder to learn because of reduced access to landmarks.

Travel Needs of Blind and Partially Sighted Individuals

As mentioned earlier, the profession of orientation and mobility instruction has evolved to address the rehabilitation needs of blind and visually impaired persons relating to travel. A wide variety of training techniques and assistive devices have been developed specifically for this problem. To address mobility, people with little or no functional vision have to rely on canes or guide dogs in combination with training in the use of auditory and tactile cues, such as traffic sounds, echolocation, and surface texture, and various other techniques for safe travel. The cane allows direct detection of obstacles, surfaces, dropoffs and shorelines (walls, edges of pathways, etc., which have to be paralleled during travel) within the zone covered by its scanning pattern. It also allows indirect detection of large objects (walls, building entrances, etc.) via echoes derived from the tapping of its tip on the ground (Wiener & Lawson, 1997). Traffic sounds are used to orient one's path relative to the street and determine when crossings can be safely made. In the last resort, drivers may be able to see the white cane and avoid the blind pedestrian.

Travelers with significant residual vision can supplement these methods with visual detection of large obstacles, shorelines, and oncoming traffic. However, detection of other hazards such curbs, dropoffs, small objects on the ground that could be tripped over, and intersection crossing information, depend on the nature and amount of an individual's residual vision. Important factors include the effectiveness of the individual's vision function in the real world of varying light levels and viewing conditions, as well as the optical aids and training he receives to optimize its use (Geruschat & Smith, 1997).

The orientation aspect of travel is considerably complicated when vision is impaired or absent. This applies particularly to travel in unfamiliar surroundings—which many blind and visually impaired people consequently avoid. Access to landmarks and printed navigational signs, which are the sighted traveler's main cues, is effectively eliminated or severely reduced (Arditi & Brabyn, 2000). Blind travelers are taught a number of orientation techniques that rely heavily on memory, as well as cues involving sounds, smell, and touch. Examples include feeling the direction of the sun shining on the face, remembering the sounds and smells of different types of shops, memorizing the number of blocks along a route, and remembering as many cues as possible along a route that has been travelled before (Long & Hill, 1997). Persons with some residual vision can add visual information about large objects that can serve as landmarks in the environment. Signs, once located, may be read with a hand-held telescope if visual function is sufficient.

Direct Measures of Orientation and Mobility Performance

Beginning in the 1970s, researchers have used various methods of quantifying ambulatory travel performance for studies on electronic travel aids for blind persons and on the visual factors contributing to travel performance deficits. Such measurements are difficult partly because of the number of variables encountered (traffic, weather, presence of obstacles, etc.) in outdoor travel routes. Early efforts (e.g., Armstrong, 1972, 1975) used an outdoor test route to measure various aspects of safety, efficiency, and stress in an effort to evaluate new devices. Brabyn and Strelow (1977) designed a position sensing system using a computer for objectively measuring locomotion of blind subjects indoors. Dodds et al. (1983) extended the Armstrong technique with video recordings and the use of numerous parameters, such as time taken, productive walking index (percentage of time spent walking), cane and body contacts with obstacles and shorelines, steps taken, and curb incidents and lateral position on the pavement. Later researchers followed this general approach, using a wide variety of indoor and outdoor courses of varying realism and complexity (e.g., Haymes et al., 1996; Kuyk et al., 1998; Long et al., 1990; Lovie-Kitchin et al., 1990; Marron & Bailey, 1982). Some researchers lumped many of the items together as "mobility incidents" (Geruschat et al., 1998). Variations included the use of a secondary task (reaction time to randomly emitted tones) to gauge the mental effort imposed by the mobility task (Turano et al., 1998). Most of these approaches dealt only with the mobility aspect of the travel problem; fewer efforts have been made to measure the orientation aspect of travel skills. Crandall et al. (1999) used a variety of indoor and outdoor travel routes to test blind subjects' ability to find particular destinations with and without an infrared navigation device (Talking Signs), with the percentage of successful route completions as the main measure.

Due to difficulties such as specifying and implementing standard travel routes in different localities, defining measures that would be common to all routes, and incorporating orientation as well as mobility measurement, no standardized measure of orientation and mobility performance has been widely adopted. The use of simulators has received little attention in this field and could be a possible avenue for standardization. At the present time, however, it would be difficult to recommend any particular test as a benchmark for determining disability in terms of travel performance.

Aspects of Vision Function Affecting Orientation and Mobility

In *controlled environments,* in the absence of such hazards as dropoffs, small low-lying objects to trip over, or fast approaching traffic, the mobility aspects of travel can be performed with relatively poor vision. Pelli (1987), working with normally sighted subjects with simulated low vision in a controlled environment (a shopping mall), showed that obstacle avoidance is possible with severely reduced vision (acuity reduction achieved by blur, contrast reduction, and field restriction.) Studies of obstacle avoidance with low vision subjects (again, mainly in well-controlled environments) have usually shown that acuity level is not important, contrast sensitivity is somewhat important, and the total extent of the visual field is of major importance (Haymes et al., 1996; Kuyk et al., 1998; Long et al., 1990; Lovie-Kitchin et al., 1990; Marron & Bailey, 1982).

In the complex, *uncontrolled environments* found in the real world beyond experimental studies, hazards abound that are not easy for the individual with impaired vision to detect. Also, visual function is greatly reduced under the less than ideal conditions found in the real world (Brabyn et al., 2000; Kuyk et al., 1996). A brief discussion follows of the way the various hazards and problems interact with different measures of visual function.

Acuity. Laboratory studies aside, acuity is clearly a factor in real-world orientation and mobility. It is necessary, for example, in detecting and avoiding small objects or surface irregularities on the ground in front of the traveler in order to avoid tripping. Even making visual determinations about surface texture (e.g., is the patch ahead water or ice) requires acuity. Inability to see fine detail may make it difficult to distinguish between a dropoff and a shadow (Guth & Rieser, 1997). Some degree of acuity is obviously important in recognition of environmental landmarks. However the major area in which acuity is vital is in finding and reading the signs on which one depends for orientation and navigation. Signs are designed in overall size and in print size to be located and read by individuals with normal or near-normal acuity from the distance at which their particular information is needed (20/40 is a common standard for road signs). A person with, say, 20/100 acuity has to be 2.5 to 5 times as close as the signmaker envisaged in order to find and read the information. This decreases the chance that the individual will be able to find and use the information as intended. (Even if 5-fold magnification via a telescope is used, the viewable area will necessarily be reduced by at least a factor of 25, making location of the sign more difficult.)

Contrast Sensitivity. Visually guided travel is dependent on the ability to see objects (whether large or small) of widely varying contrast against their backgrounds. It is therefore not surprising that a number of studies have found an association between contrast sensitivity and mobility (Geruschat et al., 1998; Kuyk & Elliott, 1999; Kuyk et al., 1998; Marron & Bailey, 1982; Rubin et al., 1994; Turano et al., 1999). In nearly all cases, contrast sensitivity was a far better predictor of mobility performance than acuity (and often the only predictor). Many tripping hazards are of very low contrast. Examples include curbs, step-ups and step-downs, stairways, and dropoffs. Rubin et al. (2001) found an association between contrast sensitivity and self-reported difficulty going down steps. There are also driveway indentations crossing the sidewalk, wheelchair ramp borders, and discontinuities in the sidewalk pavement, such as the uplifting of one slab slightly above another by an underlying tree root. Good contrast sensitivity is needed to detect these hazards and avoid tripping and is therefore critical in ensuring safety (Geruschat & Smith, 1997).

Color contrast is also important in mobility. For example, it is generally accepted that yellow markings on stairs, etc., can help make low-contrast edges more visible to those with reduced vision.

Visual Fields. Not surprisingly, a number of mobility studies have found a relation between mobility performance and visual fields (Brown et al., 1986; Geruschat et al., 1998; Kuyk et al., 1998; Lovie-Kitchin et al., 1990; Marron & Bailey, 1982). The hazards referred to above lie in the lower visual field, making this part of the field extremely important for safety while walking (Lovie-Kitchin et al., 1990). Visual field defects can also make detection of hazards in other parts of the visual field difficult or unreliable. For example, hemianopic fields make detection of shorelines, traffic, or other hazards on one side or the other very difficult, with potentially catastrophic results. Very narrow visual fields reduce the chances that hazards of any kind will be detected, reducing the value of optic flow, widely thought to be important in mobility (Gibson, 1958). Visual fields also affect orientation. Rieser et al. (1992) asked subjects with low vision to judge from memory the directions and distances between landmarks in their neighborhoods. They found no effect of acuity level, but people with early onset of narrow visual fields tended to perform more poorly than others. Reduced field size could affect other aspects of navigation by reducing the probability of finding or noticing landmarks and navigational signs.

Adaptation and Glare. Difficulty adapting to poor or changing light levels is widely acknowledged to impact the mobility of many visually impaired persons (Szlyk et al., 1990). This problem is closely related to the visual function of glare recovery (see section on Glare and Light/Dark Adaptation in Chapter 2). Geruschat and Smith (1997, p. 63) assert that "The most frequently reported mobility problem for persons with low vision is lighting, inclusive of glare; light adaptation from outdoors to indoors and vice versa; dim and night lighting; and frequent changes in lighting." Kuyk et al. (1996) demonstrated that the ability of visually impaired individuals to avoid obstacles is significantly impaired under low illumination. Turano et al. (Turano et al., 1998) found that four of the six most difficult mobility situations for people with retinitis pigmentosa were related to lighting conditions. Certainly, all the problems mentioned above under acuity and contrast are made much worse under poor or changing light conditions. Both acuity and contrast sensitivity fall off rapidly as light level is reduced, making visually impaired persons even more subject to these hazards in dusk or nighttime conditions.

Glare recovery is also an important factor in real-world orientation and mobility. An inability to adapt rapidly to changing light conditions can be disabling for mobility when going from bright sun to indoors or vice versa. Glare recovery declines more with age than many other aspects of vision function (Brabyn, 1999), so this problem is particularly prevalent in older persons. Although it is not commonly measured in younger individuals, it is definitely an aspect of vision that needs to be taken seriously for its negative effects on mobility and safety. However current lack of standardized testing methods makes its adoption as a stand-alone criterion for disability problematic.

Disability glare, or disruption of vision due to veiling glare, can impede the detection and reading of navigational signs against a bright sky, as well as possibly affecting detection of traffic in some circumstances. People with certain forms of low vision, such as retinitis pigmentosa, have particularly severe problems with glare (Turano et al., 1998).

Binocular Vision. There is some evidence that binocular vision or stereopsis is important in mobility, as poor stereopsis has been associated with hip fractures, which in most cases result from falls, in some studies of older populations (Ivers et al., 2000).

Visuocognitive Factors. As noted in the discussion of theories of orientation and mobility, cognitive factors and memory abilities are important in orientation and navigation. For the mobility aspect of the task, the traveler often has to concentrate on the path ahead but be alert to hazards in the lower and horizontal visual fields. Therefore, recently developed tests of divided attention such as the useful field of view and the attentional visual field may be relevant, as they are in similar situations in the driving task (Brabyn, 1990; Brabyn et al., 1994; Owsley, 1994; Owsley et al., 1991). However these tests go beyond the realm of pure vision function.

Summary and Recommendations

The most important aspects of visual function for safe and efficient ambulatory orientation and mobility are contrast sensitivity, visual fields, and acuity. The next most important variable is adaptation to low or changing light conditions. Disability glare, binocular vision, and visuocognitive functioning are significant but of lesser importance and do not currently lend themselves well to stand-alone tests of visual disability in relation to independent travel. Research is needed on better quantification of these aspects of vision. Pending such standardization, they can be dealt with only by subjectively evaluating any disabling impact on mobility and other activities for individuals not meeting the SSA medical listing criteria.

Driving Mobility

Driving is a specialized type of mobility. Many jobs involve driving, including those that require workers to operate vehicles that transport goods (e.g., interstate truck drivers, local package delivery drivers) and those that involve the transport of people (e.g., bus drivers, taxi drivers). U.S. employment data from 1999 indicate that over 9.5 million persons in the United States were engaged in transportation and material moving occupations, with about half these jobs consisting of operation of a car, bus, or truck (Bureau of Labor Statistics, U.S. Department of Labor, 2000). There is a great deal of emphasis placed on driver safety in U.S. society. The concern is not just whether one can transport the goods or people to their destination, but whether one can do so in a way that does not endanger oneself, coworkers, passengers, or the public.

Investigations into the driving task typically focus on either *performance* or *safety*. Performance is usually operationalized as accuracy or latency of a driving maneuver or control input (e.g., staying in lane, braking to avoid a collision), exhibiting certain behaviors (e.g., using mirrors), or other measures, according to some graded scale. Safety is usually defined in terms of adverse driving events, such as crash involvement (e.g., at-fault crashes, injurious crashes) or moving violations (e.g., speeding, failure to obey traffic control devices). Measures of safety are often expressed statistically, such as a risk ratio or odds ratio in which a subgroup of drivers of special interest is compared with a reference group (e.g., visually impaired drivers compared with drivers who have 20/20 visual acuity or better). Although driving performance should be theoretically linked to driving safety, there is little empirical evidence for this link. This is probably due to the fact that there are numerous operator, vehicle, and environmental factors that influence driving performance and the likelihood of being involved in an adverse event (e.g., crash).

The research literature that examines the impact of vision impairment on driving is huge, with a recent review (Owsley & McGwin, 1999) listing over 200 references from the peer-reviewed literature and government publications. Most of these studies are not based on commercial drivers (i.e., those who drive in performing their jobs) but rather on drivers of personal vehicles. One major difference between the driving demands for drivers of personal vehicles and those of commercial drivers is that commercial drivers have high levels of driving exposure (i.e., miles driven per week, time on the road). Exposure is a key for understanding crash risk, since one's risk increases with exposure to the road. Exposure is also relevant from a fatigue and task-vigilance standpoint. Another noteworthy feature of the vision impairment and driving literature is that it is primarily based on older drivers. This is because vision impairment is more prevalent in late adulthood, and thus questions about the relationship of vision impairment and driving are more easily addressed among older populations. Finally, it is worthwhile to note that although the focus here is on drivers of ground vehicles, the impact of vision impairment on other types of transportation operators is also worthy of consideration (e.g., airline pilots, maritime pilots, rail engineers).

Below we summarize the vision impairment and driving literature, by type of vision impairment. The reader is also referred to recent reviews of this literature for additional details and commentary (North, 1985; Owsley & McGwin, 1999; Owsley, Stalvey, et al., 2001; Shinar & Schieber, 1991).

Visual Acuity

Visual acuity impairment (worse than 20/40 in the better eye or as measured binocularly) can hamper road sign visibility and also the avoidance of some obstacles in the roadway (Higgins et al., 1998; Wood, 1999). With respect to safety, however, visual acuity impairment, in the range that has been studied in detail (20/60 or better), does not appear to threaten road safety, or does so only weakly (Ball et al., 1993; Davison, 1985; Decina & Staplin, 1993; Gresset & Meyer, 1994; Henderson & Burg, 1974; Hills & Burg, 1977; Hofstetter, 1976; Humphriss, 1987; Ivers et al., 1999; Johansson et al., 1996; Marottoli, Cooney, et al., 1994; Marottoli, Richardson, et al., 1998; McCloskey et al., 1994; Owsley, Ball, Sloane, et al., 1991; Owsley, Ball, McGwin, et al., 1998). Drivers with significant acuity impairment tend not to be on the road, either because of state laws removing their licenses when visual acuity drops below a certain statutory requirement or because of self-restriction of their own driving (i.e., they remove themselves from the road or drastically reduce their exposure). Thus, it is difficult to evaluate crash risk in the population of drivers with severe acuity impairment (worse than acuity in the range of 20/70 to 20/100) because these individuals have low or no exposure.

Visual Fields

Studies simulating serious visual field restriction (binocular) have shown that a 40° radius visual field and smaller can compromise some aspects of driving performance (e.g., road sign identification, obstacle avoidance, reaction time) (Wood & Troutbeck, 1992, 1995; Wood et al., 1993). Simulation studies, while useful, must be cautiously generalized to actual driving performance by those with real visual field restrictions, since it is likely that the impact of a sudden, simulated field restriction is not identical to that of a naturally occurring restriction from an eye disease or neurological disorder. Those with the naturally occurring disorders may develop compensatory mechanisms (e.g., eye and head movements) over time. In several studies where real-world driving performance was assessed, drivers with actual (not simulated) field loss did not exhibit increased driving problems (Cashell, 1970; Council & Allen, 1974; Marottoli et al., 1998). The impact of binocular field restriction on driving performance appears to be an area in need of clarification. In studies addressing crash risk, drivers with severe binocular visual field loss (i.e., significant loss of peripheral vision in both eyes) appear to have twice the crash risk of those without this deficit (Ball et al., 1993; Johnson & Keltner, 1983).

Contrast Sensitivity

There are fewer studies on contrast sensitivity and driving than on acuity and visual field sensitivity, so conclusions about it must be more tentative. Simulated contrast sensitivity impairment appears to be associated with impaired driving performance (Wood & Troutbeck, 1992; Wood et al., 1993). Actual contrast sensitivity impairment in older drivers is associated with crash involvement in analyses not adjusted for confounding factors (Ball et al., 1993; Marottoli et al., 1998; Owsley, 1994). Severe contrast sensitivity impairment (Pelli-Robson score of 1.25 or less) due to cataract is significantly associated with a history of crash involvement, even if present in only one eye (Owsley, Stalvey, et al., 2001).

Visual Search/Attention

Impairment in visual search skills, including deficits in divided attention and slowed processing speed, are associated with crash involvement (Ball et al., 1993; Barrett et al., 1977; Kahneman et al.,

1973; Mihal & Barrett, 1976; Owsley, McGwin, & Ball, 1998). Even when drivers have good visual sensory function (acuity, peripheral vision), they can exhibit deficits in visual search skills (Ball & Owsley, 1991; Ball et al., 1993). This is a relatively common problem among older adults (Rubin et al., 1999). It appears that these sorts of higher-order, visual-processing skills are better predictors of high-risk drivers than visual sensory measures (Ball et al., 1993; Owsley, McGwin, et al., 1998; Rubin et al., 1999). This may be due to the fact that tests of visual attention rely on a more comprehensive set of visual skills, not just good visual sensory input. Although the data are not plentiful, it also appears that poor visual search skills are associated with poor on-road driving performance and performance in a driving simulator (Cushman, 1996; Duchek et al., 1998; Rizzo et al., 1997).

Monocularity

In most drivers the visual function in the two eyes is highly similar. However for a few individuals the visual capabilities of the eyes are drastically different, because of either an ocular or a neurological condition or trauma. There have been a few studies over the years that have examined the role of monocularity in driver safety and performance. In these studies, monocularity has been defined in a variety of ways, and sometimes no definition is given at all. A typical scenario in these studies is that one eye has good vision (usually meaning good acuity and/or visual field sensitivity), whereas the other eye can vary from no vision at all, to acuity worse than 20/200, to significant scotomas in the visual field. With respect to actual driving performance, simulated monocular vision, by occluding one eye, does not appear to impact driving maneuvers on a closed-road course (Wood & Troutbeck, 1992; Wood et al., 1993). Monocular truck drivers also reportedly carried out most maneuvers in a satisfactory fashion (McKnight et al., 1991). With respect to safety, drivers of personal vehicles with monocular field loss did not have an elevated crash rate compared with a control group of drivers with normal visual fields in both eyes (Johnson & Keltner, 1983). However, studies on commercial drivers who have high levels of driving exposure suggest that monocularity, defined as worse than 20/200 in one eye, elevates crash risk (Laberge-Nadeau et al., 1996; Maag et al., 1997; Rogers, Ratz, & Janke, 1987).

Other Aspects of Vision and Driving

A recent comprehensive review of the color vision and driving literature (Vingrys & Cole, 1988) indicates that color deficiency does not threaten road safety or performance. Color deficiency may pose difficulty in reading traffic control devices in some situations, but the critical cues on the road usually can be obtained through multiple sources of information, allowing drivers to compensate.

Dynamic visual acuity has a stronger unadjusted association to driver safety than does the conventional static acuity test, but the relationship is still weak (Hills & Burg, 1977; Shinar, 1977). Three decades ago, a study showed that performance in a motion perception task was one of the best correlates of self-reported crash involvement among a large battery of vision tests (Shinar, 1977), but motion processing abilities have not received serious examination in the literature in the ensuing years.

Disability glare problems are often discussed as a serious threat to driver safety (Wolbarsht, 1977) but one is hard-pressed to identify actual studies that scientifically confirm this notion. This failure to find an association may be due to methodological difficulties in defining glare and in measuring a multifaceted phenomenon, as well as to a poor understanding of what people mean when they say they have problems with glare.

Direct Measures of Driving Ability

There are no tests of actual driving ability that are widely available, have been standardized, and have proven validity and reliability for use with a wide range of individuals. Licensing agencies have protocols to assess driving performance for their own purposes in order to evaluate applicants for licensure, but these protocols are highly varied across states and agencies and tailored for the specific needs of each agency and the laws that govern them. On-road driving performance can be evaluated on the open road (i.e., public streets or highways) or on closed courses where other road users and obstacles are nonexistent or minimal. There are several challenges in developing a test of actual driving performance. Driving is a highly complex stream of behaviors, and the practical issue is to decide which ones are the most critical to measure. Second, actual driving involves processing a myriad of events, many of which are rather unexpected; closed courses seriously underestimate the complexity of the driving task because they are sheltered from this reality of the open road. Third, strict standardization of the driving performance evaluation is impossible on the open road because of its uncontrolled nature. Researchers interested in the impact of functional impairments on driving have had some success in developing on-road evaluations that are reliable and valid for cognitively impaired older drivers (Hunt et al., 1993; Odenheimer et al., 1994). However, there is no on-road driving evaluation with demonstrated validity and reliability for drivers of wide-ranging ages who are visually impaired.

An alternative to measuring actual on-road driving performance is to use driving simulators. Performance in simulated driving tasks allows for the evaluation of driving skills in a safe environment, which has heightened relevance when evaluating a driver who has a functional problem, such as visual loss. Simulators enable a controlled testing situation (both stimulus and response) that is easily standardized across testing sessions and drivers. One challenge in the design of simulated driving scenarios is determining the critical aspects of the roadway environment for inclusion in the simulator's scenes (Ball & Owsley, 1991). Other challenges are sufficient visual fidelity and spatial resolution (e.g., Padmos & Milders, 1992), establishing validity against the gold standard of actual driving performance (e.g., Reinach et al., 1997), and implementing interactive capabilities that sufficiently resemble actual driving. Driving simulators are becoming more popular both for driver training and in research, and these simulators can vary from a highly sophisticated use of computer technology with motion bases (e.g., Iowa Driving Simulator, see Reinach et al., 1997) to part-task simulators that focus on a few critical component skills (Doron simulator). The field of driving simulation is a rapidly growing field, but at present there is no driving simulator or protocol that has been deemed a standard.

Summary and Recommendations

There are no standard tests of actual driving ability currently available for determining driving fitness in those who are visually impaired. However, over the past few decades, research has identified aspects of vision impairment that elevate crash risk and hamper on-road driving performance. Severe visual field loss in both eyes doubles crash risk, and field constrictions resulting in a less than 40° radius field hamper obstacle avoidance on the road. Severe contrast sensitivity impairment due to age-related cataract (Pelli-Robson scores less than 1.25) elevates crash risk. Slow visual processing speed and divided attention problems also increase crash risk at least twofold; these problems are not detected by visual sensory tests (visual acuity, visual fields, contrast sensitivity). Thus in determining driving fitness, there is a need for a test that screens for these types of visual processing impairments. SSA should support research to develop such tests. Color deficiency does not by itself increase crash risk.

SOCIAL PARTICIPATION

The role of social interaction in a modern, service-oriented economy is very important. In a sample of 2,523 job categories, proportional to the distribution of employed adults in the United States as of 1993 (see Occupational Analysis section for a description of the findings from this database), 47 percent of jobs require a significant degree of advising and instructing, with more than 90 percent indicating the need for routine oral exchange of information. Moreover, in studies of persons with vision loss who describe problems encountered with their impairment, social interactions and activities comprised about 10 percent of the problems encountered (Mangione, Berry, et al., 1998). Social-type problems were the fourth most common type of problem mentioned in this largely older population. Clearly, the impact of any vision loss on social participation will vary enormously with the individual, the workplace, and the environment in which the individual must function. The manner in which the individual and his or her relatives, friends, coworkers, and the public adapt to the visually based constraints depends on a myriad of complex psychological, social, and workplace-related factors.

There is relatively scant literature on the role of vision in participation in social activities. Social interaction, receiving and acting on cues perceived from others, of course, has been examined in the literature of sociology and psychology, but not in the vision literature. The committee considered the tests of visual function that may be related to social participation (see Chapter 2). In addition, we reviewed the literature on vision-related tests that form specific analogues to social participation. This literature includes two distinct types of studies: those investigating performance-based tests, strongly based in vision, which are presumed to measure some function of social interaction, and those based on self-report of social functioning related to vision.

Performance Tests

The only performance-based tests that have been used to approximate the dimension of social interaction are tests of face recognition. Face recognition is important to personal interactions, but the task is also important for watching TV and movies and being in other audience situations (e.g., congregation, classroom). The task is complex, as multiple cues are used for recognition. Some of these are highly visible features, such as hair color, skin color, and facial hair; others require discerning more subtle detail, such as changes in the shape of the mouth, which may involve shading.

There are multiple versions of face recognition tests; some require the determination of the mood of the face presented, some require identification of well-known persons, and others require identifying a different person embedded in a series of different poses of the same person. The latter version of the test has been shown to have responses that are sensitive to race, education, and cognitive status apart from visual function (Rubin et al., 1997).

Most studies of visual impairment and the ability to see faces have used images of faces presented at a fixed or limited angular size—often at equivalent viewing distances that simulate a face within arm's length. The test is also performed typically at ideal light levels with maximum contrast in the photographs displayed, which may not be characteristic of the need to identify faces or read transient facial expressions in a working environment.

Being able to read faces depends in part on viewing distance, which in turn determines the angular size of the face at the viewer's eye, and there will inevitably be some association with visual acuity. In fact, persons with low vision, primarily represented as central acuity loss or severe visual field loss, report difficulties recognizing familiar faces and discerning facial expression changes (Bullimore et al., 1991). Alexander et al. (1988) studied a large group of subjects, conducting a battery of functional tests that included reading, reading clocks, and distinguishing colors, products, facial expressions. The faces were presented as fixed-size photographs, and it was found that the third of the sample that had the best visual acuity did best at recognizing expressions and the third with the poorest acuity had the worst performance at reading expressions. Bullimore et al. (1991) studied a small group of subjects ($n = 13$) with macular degeneration. They used photographs of faces and determined the equivalent viewing distances (EVD) required for recognition of identity and expression. These measures of performance were found to be very highly correlated to reading acuity scores and quite strongly correlated to letter chart visual acuity scores. Associations with peak contrast sensitivity and grating acuity were weaker. For some subjects, visual performance was measured under different luminance levels and the within-subject analyses showed parallel changes in the tests of face recognition and the test of reading and grating acuity. They found that the EVDs required for recognition of identity and of expression were very similar except in subjects with very poor visual acuity, for whom recognizing expressions became easier than recognizing identity.

Tests of central acuity and contrast sensitivity have been studied in relation to face recognition and are summarized by Higgins and Bailey (2000). In general, Bailey and colleagues have found a relationship between poor visual acuity, particularly reading acuity, and performance on recognizing facial expressions; modest correlations were also observed with contrast thresholds for sharp edges (Bullimore et al., 1991). However, others found poorer prediction of face recognition from acuity (Rubin & Schuchard, 1989).

There is disagreement on whether low spatial frequency information is all that is required for adequate face recognition, or whether high spatial frequency is also important. There are data to suggest that middle and low spatial frequencies are associated with face recognition (Owsley & Sloane, 1987; Owsley et al., 1981). Work by Peli suggests that the spatial frequency content centered at 8 cycles/face was important for face recognition in those with normal vision, but those with acuity loss preferred images with a center frequency of 16 cycles/face (Peli, Goldstein, et al., 1991; Peli, Lee, et al., 1994). As Bullimore et al. (1991) point out, the viewing distance for face recognition has an important impact on the influence of acuity versus contrast sensitivity.

In a comprehensive evaluation of vision in a population-based study, the SEE project, the contribution of loss of visual acuity, contrast sensitivity, visual field loss, and stereoacuity has been characterized relative to the decline in the ability to match faces in an older population of 2,520 adults. The test comprised a series of 20 presentations of four faces; in each set of four, three are the same person in different poses, and one is a different person. A full regression model, including adjustments for age, gender, race, education, and cognition, accounted for 37 percent of variance, with the vision variables accounting for 10 percent. Decrements in acuity, contrast sensitivity, visual field, and stereoacuity, independent of each other, were significantly associated with worsening scores in face recognition. While statistically significant, a very small decrement in face recognition was associated with visual field loss and stereoacuity loss, suggesting that these aspects of vision were less important predictors of the score on this test. The parameters suggest that a loss of recognition of one face (unit change) is associated with a three-line loss in visual acuity and a five-letter loss in contrast sensitivity. There was also an interaction in the data, which suggested that with 20/60 or better visual acuity in the better eye, contrast sensitivity was a major predictor of decreased ability to recognize faces. For visual acuity worse than 20/60, contrast sensitivity decrements contributed little to the decrease in face recognition (West, unpublished).

Self-Report of Social Interaction

Several quality of life scales include the dimensions of role function and social interaction. Unlike the performance-based tests, however, self-report of difficulties includes not only perceived limitations imposed by vision loss, but also such dimensions as expectations of performance and the use of compensatory strategies for visual loss. Thus, there are differences between the actual performance and the self-report of performance for many activities, including reading (Friedman et al., 1999).

Visual acuity loss has been associated with declines in the social function scales of the NEI VFQ-25 (Broman et al., 2001; Mangione, Berry, et al., 1998) and with limitations in communication and recreations and pastimes in the Sickness Impact Profile (SIP) (Scott et al., 1994). Parrish et al., in a study of people with glaucoma, found that binocular visual field impairment was not highly correlated with decrements in social function as measured by the SF-36 or NEI VFQ, once visual acuity impairment was considered (Parrish et al., 1997). Gutierrez et al. found an association with the VF-14 social function item and visual field status of the better eye, but the effect of concomitant acuity was not considered (Gutierrez et al., 1997). Research has studied groups of people with specific eye diseases, such as optic neuritis or age-related maculopathy, and evaluated the correlations of severity of disease with changes in the NEI VFQ; concomitant analyses using tests of vision in these patients were not done (Cole et al., 2000; Mangione et al., 1999).

In preliminary data from the SEE project, participants were asked if they attended social activities such as church, movies, and restaurants as often as they wished, and if not, whether the decline was due to vision. For attending movies or going to restaurants, contrast sensitivity decrement was the only vision variable significantly associated with a decline in social function ($p = .03$). Neither visual acuity impairment nor visual field loss was significantly associated, after also adjusting for gender, race, and education.

Summary and Recommendations

The importance of social interaction as a visually intensive task in the workplace environment is generally acknowledged. The use of an instrument for disability determination that would collect data on self-report of decrements in social interaction, or decrements in a performance-based test such as a test of face recognition, as the measure for this skill is not recommended at this time. First, the test of face recognition has an unknown relationship to the visual tasks involved in social interaction. Moreover, there is no standard test of face recognition, nor general agreement on the testing environment that should be used. The correlation with visual acuity and contrast sensitivity for both self-reported measures and face recognition tests suggests that incorporation of these tests as measures of visual function may capture some of the relevant disability in social interaction. Finally, a myriad of other sources of information (e.g., verbal and aural inputs) are also likely to be as critical (if not more so) for social interaction as is visual function. Therefore, tests of social participation should not have high priority at this time, although they merit reconsideration in the future.

TOOL USE AND MANIPULATION

The successful use and manipulation of hand-held tools is a complex task that varies with such components as the complexity of the tool, the reason for the use of the tool, the manual dexterity of the individual, the extent to which hand-eye coordination is needed to use the tool, and the visual demands of the tasks for which the tool is used. The myriad types of tools, coupled with the variety of tasks for which the tool is being used, do not allow for easy summarization of this topic. Thus, the impact of vision loss on tool use and manipulation will vary enormously with the tool, the tasks, and the individual.

The use of hand-held tools is widespread in the workplace, as suggested by the frequency of tool use (exclusive of controls or keyboard devices) mentioned as important to the job in a sample of 2,523 jobs proportional to the distribution of employed adults in the United States as of 1993 (see below for a description of the findings from this database). Fully 67 percent of jobs reportedly required more than a little use of hand-held machines or equipment, and 37 to 39 percent reported some use of nonprecision tools or instruments and measuring devices. In recent years, the use of tools such as a computer mouse or other hand-held pointing or input device that provides primarily visual feedback has become common for office workers and others whose work involves computer use.[3]

The visual demands required for jobs with these tools, as reported in the job sample, were varied. It should be noted that the database used to estimate visual demand was based on reports by job incumbents, supervisors, or job analysts of the need for near and far acuity, depth perception, and color vision for each task. Near acuity capability was reported as the most common demand, with a high proportion reporting that near acuity was of moderate to essential importance for tool use. Depth perception and color vision were less likely to be reported as important across all tool use tasks.

Research on the impact of vision loss, measured using standard tests, on performance involving use of tools in industry could not be located. In the past 10 years, the vision research community has borrowed from work done in the gerontology field to identify tasks of everyday living for which vision may have a significant input. Some

---

[3]While alternative input devices and software are available for visually impaired workers, these would be considered workplace accommodations in most cases. The committee did not investigate the frequency with which such accommodations are provided.

of these tasks involve the use of tools, such as sewing, writing a check, etc. There are many sets of these instrumental activities of daily living (IADL) tasks (Lawton & Brody, 1969; Nagi, 1976; Rosow & Breslau, 1966). There are both self-reports of function on these tasks and some standardized analogues for the tasks that can be performed. The literature contains references to the role of vision loss in self-reported difficulties with daily activities requiring tool use, such as garden tools, repair tools, sewing, and the like (see below); fewer data are available on actual performance of the tasks.

Vision and Performance Tests of Tool Use

Immediately following World War II, there was a great deal of physical ability testing being conducted in industry. This was due, in large part, to the ubiquity of machine manufacturing and assembly line subassembly work. As a result, a number of test batteries were developed to assess manual dexterity for near vision tasks. Representative batteries were the MacQuarrie Test for Mechanical Ability, the O'Connor Finger and Tweezer Dexterity Test, the Purdue Pegboard test, the Crawford Small Parts Dexterity Test, and the Minnesota Rate of Manipulation Test. Each of these test batteries is described in some detail by Guion (1965). These tests require the manipulation of some objects with small tools (e.g., tweezers or screwdrivers) or with one's fingers. These tests were introduced for the purpose of selecting applicants for industrial positions and have not been used as standard batteries for assessing visual impairment. Nevertheless, there are substantial normative data on these tests demonstrating their relationships (i.e., validity) to typical industrial activities. It would seem logical to adapt tests like these for assessing the consequences of various forms of visual impairment on tool use and manipulation in work settings. In conjunction with selected IADL tasks, such a battery might prove extremely useful in determining the extent to which an individual's visual impairment may influence safe and effective job performance.

Because there is no standard set of performance-based tests, few studies in this area have been done, and tasks were selected that have a visual component. One study may examine inserting a plug, using a key, and dialing a telephone (West, Munoz, et al., 1997) while others examine telling time and distinguishing products (Alexander et al., 1988), or threading a needle and using a screwdriver (Owsley, McGwin, et al., 2001). Typically, the time required to perform the task and the quality of the performance are graded for each subject. It should be noted again that performance among visually impaired (and nonimpaired) subjects varies greatly depending on such nonvisual factors as the use of compensatory strategies for using the tool, familiarity with the tool (e.g., a sewing needle), strength, dexterity, etc. The tools used for testing are simple and the tasks uncomplicated, which may or may not bear a resemblance to tool use tasks in industry.

Research from one population-based study of older persons indicates that visual acuity deficit and contrast sensitivity loss independently contribute to declines in performance on these tool-oriented tasks, adjusting for other confounders (West et al., in press). In another study, which combined visual acuity loss and/or visual field deficits into a category of "visual impairment," there was a correlation between visual impairment and performance on an index that included some tool use items (Haymes et al., 2001). It was not possible from this paper to separate out the tool use items specifically. Visual field deficits were less well correlated with performance than was loss of acuity. In a third study of people with retinitis pigmentosa, visual acuity and contrast sensitivity were the only measures of vision (which included visual fields and electroretinogram) associated with level of difficulty in performing such tasks as using a screwdriver, using a vending machine, and pouring water. Only contrast sensitivity was associated with dialing a phone or writing a check. None of the vision measures was associated with threading a needle. None of the vision measures was adjusted for correlations with the others (Szlyk et al., 2001).

In another study of 342 people enrolled in a longitudinal study of mobility, subjects were timed on completion of several tool use tasks, including using a screwdriver, threading a needle, dialing a number, and inserting a key in a lock (Owsley, McGwin, et al., 2001). Acuity, contrast sensitivity, and scores on a test of visual attention and visual processing (useful field of view) were measured for each person. The tool use tasks were all significantly related to acuity, while contrast sensitivity was independently associated with threading a needle and using a screwdriver. The useful field of view was associated with dialing a phone number. Age, education, comorbidities, and especially cognitive function were important predictors of performance in addition to vision. However, the contribution of vision to performance on these tasks was relatively low.

At present there are insufficient data that link performance on these tasks, or other measures, to actual tool use in an employment setting to be certain that a standard test battery of tool manipulation would be useful in assessing visual disability. The variation in visual demands, depending on the tool and task, also does not allow easy summarization of a single or multiple visual test that would capture deficits in this area.

Self-Report of Tasks Using Tools

Several scales in research instruments include the dimensions of reported difficulty with IADL tasks explicitly, although the tasks themselves may or may not involve the use of tools. Unlike the performance-based tests, however, self-report of difficulties includes not only perceived limitations imposed by vision loss, but also such dimensions as the impact from other comorbid conditions (such as arthritis) and expectations of performance (drill use by a carpenter versus an occasional user, for example). Thus, there are differences between the actual performance and the self-report of performance for many activities, including reading (Friedman et al., 1999).

Several studies have demonstrated that loss of vision, either as reported or measured using standard tests, is associated with self-reported loss of physical function, using instruments that include IADL tasks (Appollonio et al., 1995; Carabellese et al., 1993; Cassard et al., 1995; Dargent-Molina et al., 1996; Havlik, 1986; Jette & Branch, 1985; LaForge et al., 1992; Mangione, Lee, et al., 1998; Mangione et al., 1995; Rubin et al., 2001; Rudberg et al., 1993; Salive et al., 1994). In the vision-related quality of life scales, there is a domain of physical function in which tool use for daily activities is one component. Visual acuity loss has been associated with declines in the near acuity scales of the NEI VFQ-25, which contains tasks involving tool use, but it is not explicit (Broman et al., 2001).

Rubin et al. have investigated the association of multiple tests of vision with self-report of visual disability (the Activities of Daily Vision instrument). The instrument includes a near vision scale with questions on using such tools as a screwdriver and ruler and threading a needle (Rubin et al., 2001). Loss of visual acuity, contrast sensitivity, stereoacuity, and sensitivity to glare were independently associated with a score of 70 or below (on a scale of 0-100). In addition to vision, age, race, gender, education, cognition, and comorbid conditions also were associated with decrements in function. Peripheral visual field loss (outer 30°), using an 81-point single-intensity screening test, was not related to loss of self-reported function, but central visual field loss (central 30°) was independently related to loss of function. In a study of 62 people with retinitis pigmentosa, Szlyk et al. found a correlation of self-reported difficulties in several tool use tasks with loss of contrast sensitivity, loss of acuity, and loss of visual field (Szlyk et al., 2001). There was no adjustment for the correlation between the various measures of vision.

Summary and Recommendations

While the committee acknowledges that tool use is an important component of daily activities and in the workplace, there are insufficient data to recommend any battery of performance-based tests that include tools that would determine visual disability for this domain. Data suggest that visual acuity loss and contrast sensitivity loss in particular are related to both self-report of difficulty and slower performance using tools.

There are standard, performance-based tests of tool use that appear to be referable to industrial tool use, and we recommend that these should be studied for possible utility in helping to determine disability due to vision loss.

HEALTH-RELATED QUALITY OF LIFE

Health-related quality of life (HRQOL) is a reflection of how a person perceives and reacts to his or her health status as it relates to functioning and well-being. Vision may be an important component of HRQOL. It not only provides sensory input about the surroundings but also influences emotional well-being by enabling performance of activities essential for daily physical and social functioning. Indeed, self-reported difficulties with vision, such as trouble seeing or frequency of blurred vision, are associated with decrements in both physical and social functioning (Lee et al., 1997; Kington et al., 1997). In the social model of disability, visual impairment may thus be associated with undesirable social consequences.

In assessing the relationship between limitations in vision and the ability of individuals to participate in work, we use the general schema of the American Medical Association (AMA) guides for our conceptual framework. At one level, visual impairments are related directly to limitations in an individual's ability to do a job and to perform important tasks as well as to his or her mental health related to health and vision. At more basic levels, impaired vision functioning can be measured by performance on intermediate surrogates, such as reading speed or tool manipulation. Even more basic are measures that assess only visual and integrative vision function, such as visual field or visual acuity, which have traditionally been used as markers of more complex levels of visual performance. At still more basic levels, electrophysiological tests, such as electroretinograms or visual evoked potentials, assess the physiological function of the visual system.

People perceive and react differently to similar levels of diminished vision, and these perceptions and reactions may, in turn, affect functioning. The committee thus specifically sought to investigate issues surrounding HRQOL. As part of the inquiry into person-centered perspectives on assessment, we investigated the applicability of direct measures of vision-related functional status and health-related quality of life to the determination of vision-related disability, rather than or in addition to using intermediate surrogates.

There are two general strategies for characterizing a person's state of health or functional ability: objectively measuring it (with varying degrees of input from the individual) and relying on the person to report about it. For example, the traditional tests to assess visual function, even visual fields, are mostly objective physical measures. In contrast, self-ratings of functioning and well-being may be assessed by use of HRQOL questionnaires that are completed by the individual. Information derived from these questionnaires often differs from and may augment information derived from more objective measures.

These questionnaires typically consist of items, scales, and domains. An item is a single question. A scale contains the available categories for expressing a response to the question. A domain identifies a particular focus of attention, such as social functioning, physical functioning, mental health, etc., often represented by several items. Graded responses are required of each item, and a value is assigned to each response. Summation of values and linear transformation results in a subscale score (e.g., 0 to 100) for each domain. In addition to the individual domain scores, many instruments also provide a composite score.

Generic HRQOL Instruments

Instruments that measure HRQOL can be broadly divided into two classes: generic and disease- (e.g., vision-) specific. Generic instruments assess general concepts of health and well-being that are applicable across a range of different types of diseases, medical interventions, and population groups. In the context of visually impaired people, these instruments provide information beyond the immediate impact of a particular visual disorder or symptom; they identify and quantify the impact on wider aspects of daily living, such as self-care, mobility, and dependence. A desirable feature of generic instruments is that they permit comparison of quality of life among different diseases. For example, the impact of having "trouble seeing" has been compared with the impact of diabetes mellitus through the use of a standardized scoring metric (Lee et al., 1997). A weakness of generic instruments is that they often fail to detect subtle changes in specific aspects of quality of life related to a specific organ or functional system, such as those related to vision and vision impairment (Fryback et al., 1993). Serious medical problems are correlated with lower scores for the generic instruments. Thus, the presence of comorbid conditions must be ascertained and appropriate adjustments made.

Although a number of generic measures of HRQOL have been used for people with visual disorders, the Medical Outcomes Study Form-36 (SF-36) and the Sickness Impact Profile have been most popular. The SF-36 has been used to determine the impact on functional status and well-being of diminished vision (Mangione et al., 1994; Scott et al., 1999), age-related maculopathy (Mangione et al., 1999), glaucoma (Gutierrez et al., 1997; Parrish et al., 1997; Wilson et al., 1998), corneal transplantation (Musch et al., 1997), and treatment for choroidal melanoma (Cruickshanks et al., 1999). The SF-36 was used as the measure of general health-related quality of life in the National Institutes of Health-funded Ocular Hypertension Treatment Study and the Collaborative Longitudinal Evaluation of Kerataconus study (CLEK). The Sickness Impact Profile has been used to study quality of life for people with retinal vascular disease (Scott et al., 1994) and cataracts (Steinberg et al., 1994). Modified for the effects of glaucoma and glaucoma treatment, it was included as one of several questionnaires that were used to assess the quality of life in the Collaborative Initial Glaucoma Treatment Study, another clinical trial sponsored by the National Institutes of Health (Janz et al., 2001).

Studies of the various ophthalmic diseases and their association with scores of these generic health-related quality of life measures have not yielded consistent, unequivocal results. In the few studies in which a statistically significant association was found, the strength of the association was weak.

Vision-Specific HRQOL Instruments

Disease-specific instruments target specific symptoms and problems that are of greatest relevance to a given disease. By assessing health status issues that are more immediately affected, instruments of this type are typically more sensitive than generic instruments in evaluating clinically relevant aspects of specific diseases and in detecting changes over time.

The early vision-specific questionnaires focused predominantly or exclusively on issues related to diminished vision as a result of cataracts. The most widely used of these have been the Activities of Daily Vision Scale (ADVS) (Mangione et al., 1992) and the VF-14 (Steinberg et al., 1994). The ADVS is a reliable and valid measure of people's perceptions of functional visual impairment. The VF-14 is similar to the ADVS in content and differs mainly in that there are 14 visual activities of interest rather than 20. (Although these tests may not meet the strictest definition of health-related quality of life instruments because of their exclusive focus on visual functioning, they are popularly used and described as vision-related quality of life instruments.)

Studies using the ADVS and the VF-14 have demonstrated improvement in vision-targeted quality of life after cataract surgery in more than 80 percent of patients (Mangione et al., 1994; Steinberg et al., 1994). It has also been shown that postoperative changes in global satisfaction with vision correlate better with postoperative VF-14 scores than with visual acuity (Steinberg et al., 1994). Data from several studies suggest that vision-targeted quality of life questionnaires predict real-world visual capabilities better than objective measurement of visual acuity (Mangione et al., 1994; Steinberg et al., 1994). For example, a truck driver with problems performing his or her work may be measured as having 20/25 or even 20/20 vision. Whatever visual difficulties are being experienced by the truck driver will not be adequately assessed by a measurement of acuity but will be characterized by a vision-targeted quality of life questionnaire. These results suggest that these questionnaires may in some instances measure visual disability better than routine testing of distance visual acuity with Snellen charts.

The Visual Activities Questionnaire (VAQ) (Sloane et al., 1992) assesses some other dimensions of vision not captured by the ADVS or the VF-14—color discrimination and peripheral vision. This questionnaire was part of a panel of questions that was used to study HRQOL in the

Collaborative Initial Glaucoma Treatment Study. In the VAQ, higher scores (indicating more problems) on the peripheral vision subscale were associated with more visual field loss, but the strength of the correlation was relatively weak (Janz et al., 2001).

The National Eye Institute Visual Function Questionnaire (NEI-VFQ) (Mangione, Lee, et al., 1998) is a recently developed questionnaire that was designed to be relevant to the majority of visually impaired adults, regardless of the cause of the visual disability. Thus it may be more properly called function-specific than disease-specific. Items for the questionnaire were selected after analyses of transcripts from focus groups made up of people with many different ocular diseases. Because it systematically incorporates issues from multiple ocular conditions, the NEI-VFQ may be more appropriate than previous vision-specific instruments for use across a wide range of ophthalmic diseases and impairments. This questionnaire has been used in the assessment of HRQOL in a wide range of diseases, with published results available for people with low vision (Scott et al., 1999), glaucoma (Gutierrez et al., 1997; Parrish et al., 1997), diabetic retinopathy (Klein et al., 2001), and optic neuritis (Cole et al., 2000).

One of the interesting findings thus far reported with the NEI-VFQ is the decline in scores for many of the domains with increased glaucomatous field loss (Gutierrez et al., 1997; Parrish et al., 1997). Furthermore, field loss appears to be independent of visual acuity as a predictor of vision-targeted functioning.

Should Current Measures of HRQOL Be Used in the Disability Determination Process?

The recommendations of previous groups on assessment of visual functioning for disability determination have not addressed the use of health-related quality of life instruments. Although the 1994 Committee on Vision report mentioned the importance of patient perceptions (National Research Council, 1994), the technology and techniques were not sufficiently advanced to allow consideration of such methods. Since that report, substantial new knowledge and techniques have been developed, allowing us to at least consider the use of HRQOL assessments in disability determination.

The use of HRQOL assessments and instruments has only recently been recognized as an important adjunct to traditional clinical measures. Although these instruments are valid and reliable, it is important to note that they measure self-perceptions. Self-perception of function has many facets that are the product of several factors other than vision. Because of this, the usefulness of these instruments depends in part on the truthfulness of the responses and the lack of influence of other, confounding factors. For example, clinical depression has a very large effect on the reporting of ability to function, apart from any visual problems. Unlike many objective tests in which the responses can be verified, checks on the responses to HRQOL instruments are limited. The validity of a low score could thus be questioned in a situation in which there is incentive to be classified as functionally disabled.

The generic QOL instruments are not likely to be useful for SSA's purposes. Although it can be argued that data indicating decrement in general health and well-being with some level of diminished vision (acuity and/or visual field) would be helpful, such data currently do not exist. There is some potential in the use of vision-targeted quality of life instruments, particularly the NEI-VFQ. The major advantage of the NEI-VFQ is that its questions are relevant not only to people with cataract but also to those with a wide range of vision-related disorders. However, although studies have documented a decrement in scores (domain-specific and composite) with diminished vision functioning as measured by visual acuity and/or visual field, data relating a specific score to a specific level of functional performance or disability are not available. Thus, at present, a NEI-VFQ score is not translatable to a specific level of visual acuity or visual field impairment.

Summary and Recommendations

There is an emerging consensus that the consideration of HRQOL may provide important information in the assessment of functional disability. The committee affirms this view. In fact, our research on HRQOL informed and supported our final selection of functional vision domains. However, the value of self-reported data regarding issues of functional impairment due to vision is limited, and the potential for other factors being important and for "gaming" the assessments is great. These considerations led the committee to recommend that health-related quality of life measurements should not be used in the assessment of visual functioning for disability determination.

WORK SKILLS AND VISUAL FUNCTIONING

In approaching the question of how to determine if a worker is "disabled" for visual reasons from performing his or her job, various systems use a variety of surrogate markers. At the most basic level, these surrogates are measures such as visual acuity, visual field, or other psychophysical measures that test the performance of the visual system, although with a required level of participation by the individual. Even more basic levels of assessment, such as electrophysiological testing, that do not require such participation, have not been used to determine disability in adults. As understanding of the often minimal relationship between the traditional surrogates of visual skills and abilities and an individual's actual abilities to perform important tasks (for example, tool use and reading) has grown, greater attention has been paid to higher levels of surrogates that are more directly and closely related to job skills.

In an effort to better understand the relationships between visual skills and abilities and workplace requirements, the committee pursued several avenues of empirical data collection. First, an analysis of the most common standard vision measures—visual acuity, visual fields, and contrast sensitivity—in relation to actual performance on various tasks such as tool use and reading was conducted using the Salisbury Eye Evaluation study data. Some of these findings were discussed in the sections on social interaction and tool use. Second, a literature review and analysis of the relationship of vision measures—visual acuity and visual field loss—to subjects' self-reported functioning and health-related quality of life was conducted and is reported in the preceding section on health-related quality of life instruments.

Third, available labor databases were assessed and analyzed to determine how important facets of vision were related to the performance of job tasks for Department of Labor (DOL) job categories. This third effort was designed to provide a model for determining which visual measures should be weighted more heavily in specific job categories (those in which that visual measure is rated to be more important) and is the subject of this section. It seeks to create a template for more specific and tailored job disability assessments by determining how visual measures should be weighed in determining vision-related disability for each job category and the underlying job tasks that exist within each category. Together, these three efforts will, in the future, allow policy makers to better understand and refine the thresholds for determining vision-related disability for specific job categories.

Job Analysis Using Labor Databases

Job analysis is a process used to examine both the essential functions (i.e., important and frequent tasks) that constitute a job and the knowledge, skills, abilities, and other characteristics that a worker should possess in order to successfully carry out those essential functions. In one form or another, job analysis has been integral to the process of personnel selection since the 1920s. There are two basic types of job analysis, job-oriented and worker-oriented. The job-oriented approach emphasizes the conditions of work, or the results of work. It concentrates more on the accomplishments of work than on the behavior of the worker. The worker-oriented approach "focuses more on the human behaviors that compose the job in question" (Landy, 1989). Currently, more data exists for the use of worker-oriented analyses.

The Position Analysis Questionnaire

Although thousands of worker-oriented job analyses of thousands of job titles have been completed in the past 50 years, most analyses have been completed using idiosyncratic and often poorly defined and inconsistently applied job analysis methods. This makes it very difficult to aggregate the results of those analyses in any meaningful way. Ernest McCormick of Purdue University sought to address these concerns by launching an empirically based project to develop a generic worker-oriented job analysis device that would permit the accumulation of data and the construction of a database for comparing and contrasting job requirements (including such sensory/perceptual requirements as visual requirements). The result of that effort is the Position Analysis Questionnaire (PAQ), a worker-oriented job analysis system that analyzes jobs based on 187 job elements that describe work activities and work situation variables. The PAQ has been accumulating job analyses since the 1970s.

The development and the validation of the PAQ have been documented by its creators (McCormick et al., 1972). The system itself is well described in technical manuals and technical reports (e.g., McCormick & PAQ Services, Inc., 1977; McCormick et al., 1977). As a result of the process by which the PAQ was developed, validated, and standardized, it is the job analytic device most widely used by employers in the United States. Consequently, the PAQ database includes information on "2000 [now 2,523] jobs that characterize the structure of the U.S. labor force" (McCormick & Jeanneret, 1988). These job titles represent several hundred thousand actual analyses (i.e., multiple analyses of each job title, with the cumulative number of discrete observations varying for each job title from a few to several thousand) done for several thousand different employing organizations. To date, the PAQ has not been used in scholarly analyses, nor has it been used to understand the sensory relationships to job performance in general as opposed to a specified job title.

Department of Labor Occupational Information Network

A second database examined by the committee is the Occupational Information Network (O*NET) system, which provides an online, comprehensive, interactive database system of job descriptions developed by the Employment and Training Administration (ETA) of the U.S. Department of Labor (DOL). The original database used in O*NET 98 (subsequently refined and updated) is based largely on data supplied and refined by occupational analysts from sources such as the *Dictionary of Occupational Titles* (DOT) (U.S. Employment Service, 1991). Groups of five or six occupational analysts and graduate students in industrial and organizational psychology, working independently, rated each of the occupations using the appropriate survey. O*NET is intended to replace the existing *Dictionary of Occupational Titles.*

The operational model of O*NET is the Content Model, which includes a questionnaire divided into six sections that represent the major elements for categorizing and classifying job information. The six areas of the Content Model, the characteristics on which each job is rated, are: (1) worker characteristics, (2) worker requirements, (3) occupation requirements, (4) experience requirements, (5) occupation-specific requirements, and (6) occupation characteristics. Under worker characteristics is the category sensory abilities. Under sensory abilities are located seven visual abilities: near vision, far vision, visual color discrimination, night vision, peripheral vision, depth perception, and glare sensitivity (Hubbard et al., 2000). While the structure is promising, O*NET analysis is not yet able to provide meaningful analysis of jobs by worker characteristics. Furthermore, the current O*NET database is not yet a representative sample of the U.S. working population and has not yet been widely used.

Usability of the PAQ Database

The PAQ database includes 2,523 job titles with specific ratings. Each job was assigned to one of the nine DOL aggregate job categories, such as clerical or agriculture and fisheries. On the basis of these nine larger groupings, the PAQ database was adjusted to be proportional to the distribution of the employed adults in the United States as of 1993. This was accomplished through a weighting of responses to reflect data from the DOL, using the first digit of the DOT code (McCormick et al., 1998b). Therefore, if 3 percent of the jobs were in agriculture and fisheries, then 3 percent of the jobs in the database are in agriculture and fisheries. The PAQ assesses jobs and not the people holding jobs.

In assessing how codes were developed and assigned, our analysis revealed that there are 1,817 unique DOT job codes and the rest are overlapping codes, with data created using a bootstrap technique to take all the persons who responded within that job code and create another entry for that job code, to arrive at the number of 2,523. For each job title, there may have been anywhere from one to several hundred measurement sessions. For each measurement session, there may be one or more observations by different persons (job incumbent, supervisors, consultants, analysts). Because of the proprietary nature of this database, the committee could not determine how many job title assessments are based on only one or very few respondents. It was reported by the developers of the PAQ (Richard Jeanneret, personal communication) that the number is very small. The response in the database for each job title is the average response for all persons who analyzed that job title (thus, the average reponses may include decimals, although the input responses are integers).

There are additional significant limitations in the potential generalizability of the PAQ analysis results. First, the data collected do not arise from a random sample of jobs within each of the 1,817 unique job titles or the nine aggregate categories. Second, and even more importantly, among individuals with specific jobs, the selection of the sample may not be representative of all persons holding that specific job. Furthermore, the responses for each specific job are aggregated over time, starting from the 1970s. As a result, there may be potential biases from changes in jobs that occur over time for which the ratings have not sufficiently reflected the new methods and concerns. This is of particular concern given the averaging of all responses over the past 30 years. For example, 30 years ago, the use of "hand-held control devices" encompassed very different tasks than it does today, when the use of a computer mouse and other such input devices is included in this category. Similarly, 30 years ago, before computers were common on office desks, most managers would not have reported much use of keyboards.

Other limitations to the PAQ database are inherent in the method of data collection by multiple observers. Individuals who perform the job, their supervisors, and experts in the field may each rate the job. Ratings may therefore vary with individual interpretations of the standards used for the ratings, with raters' understanding of the visual functions they are rating, and with the raters' depth of knowledge of the job's requirements.

Despite these limitations, we did not identify a comparable or better data structure for job analyses in the United States. The validity of the PAQ system has been tested over 30 years by the employer and business communities, which use its results for employment and planning purposes. Reliability ratings suggest that the PAQ has reasonable interrater and test-retest performance (McCormick et al., 1998a). The unique benefits of the PAQ system suggest that it may be used carefully to augment our understanding of vision and vision decrements in the workplace, despite its proprietary nature and the lack of previous use for these purposes.

The PAQ instrument gathers information on the following visual and perceptual characteristics of jobs: near visual acuity, far visual acuity, depth perception, and color discrimination. It does not include assessments of visual field or contrast sensitivity. Furthermore, it measures near vision differently than the other three variables (see below).

Nevertheless, it is possible to enter the database and examine the visual demands in one or all of these categories for specific jobs, job families or categories, or broad occupational groupings. And it is possible to concentrate on the specific visual demands of particular tasks within or across jobs (e.g., the use of hand-held tools, the manipulation of fixed or variable controls, assembly or disassembly tasks). However, because of the data source limitations noted above, the committee chose to use analyses limited only to the nine

TABLE 3-1 Ratings of the Importance to the Job of Aspects of Vision (percentage)

Level of Importance	Near Acuity	Far Acuity	Depth Perception	Color Perception
Does not apply	0.5	38.1	46.6	47.3
Very minor	3.0	23.0	24.2	24.6
Low	17.6	19.6	14.6	13.9
Moderate	69.2	13.2	9.8	9.1
High	8.8	5.2	4.1	3.8
Extreme	0.9	1.0	0.8	1.3

Source: Position Analysis Questionnaire database of 2,523 job title ratings.

aggregate DOL levels and not to use results from variation at the individual job title level.

The PAQ was thus used to determine how important vision is to job category performance in the aggregate and across the nine standard DOL job categories. The first analysis is the distribution of responses to the four main vision items. Respondents were asked to rate the importance to their job of far acuity (defined as differences in seeing characteristics beyond arm's reach), near acuity (defined as the amount of detail that must be seen within arm's reach), depth perception (defined as judging the distances between objects), and color perception (defined as differentiating objects or details on the basis of color). As the definitions were worded, only the response for near acuity captures "blind or working in darkness" at the zero end of the scale; the rest of the vision categories score "0" as "does not apply." Therefore, the distribution for near acuity is much less skewed than for the other vision variables.

As seen in Table 3-1, for the distribution of job titles in the database, far acuity, depth perception, and color perception are of low or minor importance—or do not apply—to 80 percent or more of respondents. However, 69 percent of the respondents rated near acuity as of moderate importance, with 10 percent rating it as of high or extreme importance. While it is clear that the distributions are sensitive to the structure of the response choices, it is also apparent that the respondents placed considerable importance on near acuity for job performance.

The second analysis is the distribution of responses indicating the importance of four main vision items according to the nine major job categories (Table 3-2). The levels are numerically coded as <3 = low or minor importance; 3 = moderate importance; 4 = high importance;

TABLE 3-2 Rating of the Importance of Vision to Job Performance by Broad Category of Job (percentage)

Vision Importance	Prof/Tech	Clerical	Service	Ag/Fish
Near Acuity				
Not Applicable to Low	11	14	45	51
Moderate	77	82	46	49
High	11	4	8	0
Extreme	1	0	1	0
Far Acuity				
Not Applicable to Low	84	93	69	52
Moderate	11	4	23	24
High	4	3	5	19
Extreme	1	0	2	5
Depth Perception				
Not Applicable to Low	88	98	82	61
Moderate	8	2	13	25
High	4	1	3	11
Extreme	0	0	1	3
Color Perception				
Not Applicable to Low	87	94	80	89
Moderate	9	4	12	11
High	3	2	7	0
Extreme	1	1	1	0
(N)	737	707	352	75

Source: Position Analysis Questionnaire database of 2,523 job title ratings.

5 = extreme importance. Differences by category are apparent. Service jobs and agricultural/fisheries jobs do not rate near acuity as important as do the professional/technical and clerical and sales jobs. However, depth perception is rated more important for jobs in agriculture/fisheries and benchwork, compared with professional and clerical jobs. There is uniformity in the low rating given to the importance of color vision across jobs.

Process	Machine/Trades	Bench-work	Structural	Misc.
36	19	12	17	42
57	67	63	69	46
5	13	22	12	11
2	1	3	2	1
68	78	90	67	56
26	16	9	20	26
5	6	1	13	16
1	0	0	1	2
77	74	72	69	73
17	19	14	22	15
5	6	10	8	9
1	1	4	1	3
82	83	72	75	77
12	11	16	17	16
6	5	7	6	6
1	2	5	2	2
139	191	105	87	110

Conclusions

The committee sought to determine if empirical data existed to help understand the relationship between visual skills and abilities and workplace performance and job requirements. Two datasets were identified as being potentially useful. The first, O*NET, was determined to not yet be a representative nor usable data source at this time, although it may become so in the future. The second, the PAQ, was judged to provide information that would otherwise be unavailable.

With the appropriate understanding of the limitation of the PAQ database design, its limitations in execution, and the weighted nature of the data, the PAQ provides information of an otherwise inaccessible nature and was thus used as presented by the committee in a limited fashion. The key limitations of the database reflect in part its proprietary nature and include the following:

- Representativeness of the U.S. job market (not people) exists only at the aggregate nine-category level, not for any of the 2,523 specific job titles nor across the aggregate of job titles;
- Each of the 2,523 job titles has an unknown number of measurement sessions and an unknown number of observations per measurement session;
- The cumulative measurements for each job title are averaged over a 30-year time period and thus may not fully capture changes in workplace requirements as job functions change over time;
- The PAQ was intended to be used for other purposes than the one the committee is undertaking;
- The vision variables are limited (no contrast sensitivity and no visual field items) and the near vision variable is measured differently from far vision, color, or depth perception.

The results of our analyses demonstrate that facets of vision remain important to many jobs across the range of job titles or the nine aggregate DOL categories. They also demonstrate, however, that the importance of vision and of the four measures of visual function being rated—near acuity, far acuity, color, and depth perception—vary across the job categories and specific work or job skills. Because of concerns about the data, we have chosen to limit the analyses to no more detail than the nine categories. We make the following specific points:

- Analyses of the PAQ database demonstrate that near visual acuity is rated to be of high or extreme importance in 9.7 percent of 2,523 job titles, while far acuity is of similar import in 6.2 percent, depth perception in 4.9 percent, and color perception in 4.1 percent. An additional 69.2 percent of job ratings place near acuity as of moderate importance, while only 13.2 percent so rate far acuity, 9.8 percent depth perception, and 9.1 percent color perception. Thus, the importance of focusing more attention on near acuity assessment for disability determination is suggested.

- At the same time, the weight to be given to near acuity or to the other vision variables should vary depending on the sector of the economy (i.e., job classification) in question. While 89 percent of professional and technical job ratings indicate that near vision is of at least moderate importance, only 55 percent of service job ratings and 49 percent of agricultural or fisheries job ratings do so. In contrast, 48 percent of agricultural or fisheries job ratings indicate that distance acuity is of at least moderate importance, while only 7 percent of clerical jobs rate it that highly. Depth perception is commonly rated of at least moderate importance only in agricultural and fishing jobs (39 percent) and least important in the clerical sector job ratings (2 percent). Finally, color is most important to the benchwork (28 percent of ratings) and structural (25 percent of ratings) job ratings and least important in the clerical (6 percent).

- When analyzed by specific job skills relative to each of the nine DOL categories and each of the vision variables, each of these two earlier patterns is seen again. Thus, vision remains relatively important for most job skills, although there is some variation across labor categories and the specific visual task varies by job skill even within the same labor category.

RECOMMENDATIONS FOR TESTS OF VISUAL TASK PERFORMANCE

The committee's review of the potential for using tests of performance of vision-related tasks determined that for most of the task domains we examined, SSA should not attempt to test performance as a part of its disability determination process, using the tests now available. The one important exception is for reading. The committee also determined that health-related quality of life measures, although useful as indicators of important tasks and activities of daily life that are affected by vision loss, are not appropriate as tests for use in disability determination. The specific recommendations are presented below.

Reading

The committee recommends that a test of reading should be included in the vocational factors steps (Steps 4 and 5) of the disability determination process as soon as a well-normed reading test can be shown to meet test standards to be established by SSA. Reading tests are available that should be able to meet such criteria after modest additional research and development efforts, and we recommend that SSA support such research. We recommend the following criteria for reading tests:

- Visual characteristics that are consistent with contemporary standards for acuity tests, including a logarithmic progression of print sizes;
- A range of print sizes containing large enough print to be useful with most visually impaired people and small enough print to reliably measure reading acuity in normally sighted people;
- Text passages equated in layout across print sizes;
- Reproducible rules for estimating reading acuity, critical print size, and reading speed;

- Binocular testing, unless one eye interferes with the other in reading and the problem can be addressed by covering the interfering eye; and
- Text passages representative in font and letter spacing of commonly encountered real-world texts.

We recommend additional research to establish in more detail the distributions of reading acuity, critical print size, and reading speed in different age groups, and the relationships between these measures and performance of work-related activities and the instrumental activities of daily life.

Mobility

The committee recommends no testing of ambulatory or driving mobility at this time. The evidence suggests that most ambulatory mobility problems will be captured by tests of visual functions: contrast sensitivity, visual fields, and acuity. The committee recommends that mobility problems related to other functions not tested (glare, light adaptation, binocularity, or visuocognitive problems) should be subjectively evaluated for their disabling impact, pending development of acceptable tests of such functions.

For driving mobility, although we recommend no task-based testing at this time, the committee recommends that SSA support development of tests of more complex visual functions that have been shown to affect driving safety, such as divided attention and visual processing speed.

Tool Use and Manipulation

The committee recommends no testing of tool use tasks directly at this time, but we do recommend that SSA support research into adapting commonly used industrial tests that involve tool use for future application to detection of vision-related disability.

Social Participation

The committee recommends no use of any instrument currently available to test the impact of vision loss on social participation. Current research measures, such as tests of face recognition, are not appropriate for such use. Tests of visual acuity and contrast sensitivity should capture some of the relevant disability in social participation. Tests of social participation should not have high priority at this time, although they may merit reconsideration in the future.

Health-Related Quality of Life

The committee's examination of HRQOL instruments indicates that these instruments can provide valuable information for the assessment of the general relationships of visual impairments to functional disability, but they are not likely to be useful as tests for determining disability in individual claimants. A major weakness is that the instruments rely on self-report of functional status and are thus subject to gaming by claimants motivated to demonstrate loss of function in order to qualify for benefits.

4

ASSESSMENT OF VISION IN INFANTS AND CHILDREN

The testing of vision in infants and children has been treated separately from the testing of adults because infants and children often cannot be tested with the same materials and techniques as adults. In addition, the course of visual and cognitive development must be taken into account in evaluating infants' and children's visual abilities, and special techniques often must be used, especially to test infants and preschoolers, that cannot be held to the same standards that apply to tests for adults. The testing of children's vision is important to SSA because Title XVI of the Social Security Act provides for SSI benefits for children with disabilities, and acceptable methods must be specified for determining disability in this population. This chapter reviews the major issues in testing infants' and children's visual acuity, fields, and contrast sensitivity and offers some recommendations for testing to ensure fair evaluation of their visual abilities.

ASSESSMENT ISSUES

Infants

A major difficulty in assessment of vision in infants is that they cannot be tested with the standard tools that are used with adults. A second difficulty is that studies have shown that even normal infant vision is greatly inferior to that of normal adults. Thus, adult standards are not appropriate for use with infants. A third difficulty in determining the visual status of infants is that their vision is not static; it generally improves rapidly during the first postnatal year. In both normal and visually at-risk infants, the time course of the measured improvement in vision depends on both the assessment technique used and the aspect of vision that is being assessed. Finally, assessment of vision in infants is complicated by the fact that evidence of normal or abnormal visual status at one age is not necessarily predictive of what the visual status will be at a later age. That is, visual development during infancy is highly plastic and can be interrupted or modified by either external or internal environmental factors.

Because of the immaturity of the infant's visual system and the dynamic nature of visual development during the first postnatal months, any program for the assessment of visual status in infants must recognize two important points. First, the results of visual assessment must be compared with normative data from infants of the *same age*, tested with the *same assessment tool*. Comparing results to norms based on data from adults or older children or to infants tested with a different procedure can lead to a misdiagnosis of visual impairment. Second, results of visual assessments conducted during infancy are not necessarily predictive of visual status later in life. An infant whose vision appears normal early in life may later show visual impairment if the visual system fails to undergo the considerable amount of development that normally occurs between infancy and adulthood. Similarly, some infants who appear visually impaired early in life show normal visual responses several weeks or months later.

Existing Social Security Administration (SSA) regulations appear to recognize these two points. In defining "marked" and "extreme" limitations, the regulations indicate the importance of evaluating the young child relative to test norms and to age. In section §416.926a Functional equivalence for children of 20 CFR Ch. III (4-1-99 Edition), "marked" and "extreme" limitations are defined relative to test norms, with a marked limitation being a score that is ≥2 but <3 standard deviations below the norm for the test, and an extreme limitation being a score that is ≥3 standard deviations below the norm. What is implied but not specifically stated in these criteria is that the norm is specific to the age of the child.

In the same section of the SSA regulations, a second definition takes into account the age of the infants in a different way. This definition states that a "marked" limitation is present when a child between birth and age 3 years is functioning at more than one-half but not more than two-thirds of chronological age, and an "extreme" limitation is present when the child is functioning at one-half chronological age or less. This definition is problematic, because visual development does not progress linearly during infancy and early childhood; therefore, an infant of one age who is functioning at one-half chronological age may be substantially more impaired than an infant of another age who is functioning at one-half chronological age. For example, the visual acuity deficit experienced by a 6-month-old infant whose acuity is equivalent to that of a 3-month-old is substantially larger than the visual acuity deficit experienced by a one-year-old child whose acuity is equivalent to that of a 6-month-old. This is because visual acuity improves rapidly between birth and age 6 months, but it improves only slightly between ages 6 and 12 months (Mayer & Dobson, 1982; Norcia & Tyler, 1985). Existing SSA regulations also recognize the dynamic nature of visual development. SSA Publication No. 05-10026, dated October 2000, indicates that the law requires that a continuing disability review be conducted at least every three years for recipients under age 18 whose conditions are likely to improve, and not later than 12 months after birth for infants whose disability is based on low birthweight.

Preschool-Age Children

Between infancy, which is generally considered to end at age 1 year, and a child's entry into the school system at age 5 to 6 years, there is a period during which the child shows considerable development, in both vision and cognitive skills. As a result, the tools that can be used to assess vision in children in the preschool-age range vary, depending on age and cognitive abilities. With toddlers, it is usually necessary to use tools similar to those developed for use with infants, but adapted to the toddler's very short attention span. In contrast, the oldest preschool children can often be tested with assessment tools similar or identical to those used with adults.

As with infants, the changing visual and cognitive status of the young child makes it especially important that visual assessment results of preschool children be compared with results from normal children of the *same age* tested with the *same technique*. This is recognized by the Social Security Administration regulations, as described above. The need to compare a child's visual status with age-based and instrument-based norms is important for older preschool children as well as for toddlers, since even these children, who can often complete visual assessment procedures designed for adults, typically show normal results that are below those of typical adults.

As in infancy, the changing visual and cognitive status of the preschool child means that periodic review of the child's visual abilities, as measured with the most sophisticated procedure that the child is capable of performing, is advisable. SSA recognizes the need for repeated assessment of visual status in the developing child by requiring continuing disability reviews as noted above.

School-Age Children

In general, children of normal intelligence who have reached 5 to 6 years of age can be tested with the same procedures that are used to assess visual function in adults. However, their results are typically lower than those of adults, and therefore it is important to compare the results of school-age children with data from normal children of the same age. In addition, it is often useful when testing the youngest school-age children to use modified procedures that permit the child to respond in a nonverbal manner.

Adults and School-Age Children Who Cannot Perform Standard Tests of Visual Function

Some adults and school-age children cannot be tested using standard adult tests of visual function, due to limitations related to language, physical, or cognitive abilities. For these individuals, useful information about their visual capabilities may be obtained by assessing them with tests designed for younger children or infants. However, it is important to recognize that (1) the results of tests designed for younger children and infants are typically less accurate than results based on tests designed for adults and (2) tests designed for younger children and infants often use stimuli (e.g., large grating targets) that may fail to reveal visual deficits that would be evident if standard stimuli (e.g., letter targets) could be used.

VISUAL ACUITY

Visual acuity is a measure of the finest detail that can be resolved or recognized by the visual system. Visual acuity can be reduced by the optical blur produced by imperfect optics of the eye (refractive error), which can be corrected by spectacle or contact lens correction, or it can be reduced by neural deficits, which cannot be corrected optically. Because visual acuity deficits due to refractive error are correctable and therefore do not result in a disability, visual acuity assessment should be conducted with the individual wearing best optical correction. For adults, best correction is typically evaluated by manifest refraction, in which the adult judges which lenses produce optimal ability to read an eye chart. For infants, very young children, and multiply handicapped individuals with whom manifest refraction cannot be performed, the estimate of best correction must be made using objective techniques, such as autorefraction or retinoscopy.

The visual acuity of school-age children can usually be tested using standard letter acuity tests that are designed for use with adults. Testing of preschool-age children often requires modified visual acuity tests, composed of a limited subset of letters or symbols that can be identified or matched to a card that is held by the child. Infants and children younger than 3 years usually cannot identify letters or symbols verbally or by matching. The most successful way to assess their visual acuity is through observation of their visual system's electrophysiological responses or eye movement responses to repetitive grating (striped) or checkerboard patterns. This strategy of assessing an infant's *resolution acuity* rather than his or her *recognition acuity* may underestimate the depth of some visual acuity deficits (e.g., amblyopia or lazy eye), but it currently provides the best method for assessing a young child's visual capability.

Impairments of visual acuity can hinder children's social and academic development (Hyvärinen, 1994, 1998a, 1998b). Early identification of visual impairment can assist parents, teachers, and eye care practitioners in providing suitable modifications in a child's social and educational environment (Hyvärinen, 1994, 1998a, 1998b; Jose & Rosenbloom, 1990; Kalloniatis & Johnston, 1990; McAlpine & Moore, 1995).

Visual acuity is the one aspect of visual function for which there are well-established, validated tools for assessment of infants and young children. Furthermore, age-normative data are available for most of these assessment tools. Therefore, assessment of visual acuity is the primary method that is currently available for quantification of visual impairment in infants and preschool-age children. Although no standardized tools have yet been developed to measure the effect of visual impairment on quality of life in infants and children, results of visual acuity testing have been shown to be related to a young child's daily activities and the way the child interacts with the environment (Katsumi et al., 1995).

Assessment in Infants

Fixation and Following

In most clinical settings, the eye care practitioner makes a qualitative assessment of an infant's vision, based on his or her ability to show steady fixation of a target and to follow the target using smooth pursuit movements. However, the ability to fix and follow does not necessarily indicate normal visual acuity, since many older children with 20/200 or worse visual acuity fix and follow well (Day, 1990). Similarly, failure to show normal fixation and following shortly after birth is not necessarily predictive of a later visual deficit but may simply be an indicator of delayed visual maturation (Fielder et al., 1985; Illingworth, 1961).

Visual Evoked Potential

The visual evoked potential (VEP, also called the visual evoked response or VER) is an electrical signal generated by the occipital cortex of the brain in response to visual stimulation. It is recorded through one or more electrodes placed on the scalp over the visual cortex. Visual acuity can be estimated by recording VEP responses to patterned stimuli, such as phase-alternating, black and white gratings, in which the overall luminance of the target remains constant but the spatial configuration of the pattern changes. Typically, as the size of the pattern elements decreases, the amplitude of the VEP decreases, with the result that the visual acuity threshold can be estimated as the finest grating or the smallest check size that results in a measurable VEP (for details of recording and scoring techniques, see Norcia, 1994). Normative data are available for VEP acuity for infants between birth and age 1 year (McCulloch et al., 1999; Norcia & Tyler, 1985). However, use of the VEP for measurement of visual acuity in individual infants has been limited to a relatively small number of clinical sites, undoubtedly due to the expense of the equipment and the technical expertise required to conduct the test.

The advantages of using the pattern VEP for measurement of visual acuity in infants are several: (1) measurements can be made quickly, within a time span over which most infants will remain cooperative and will fixate on the stimulus; (2) the procedure requires minimal response from the infant; (3) the VEP can be a good indicator of macular function, since it is generated primarily by the area of visual cortex that receives input from the macular region; and (4) data on the distribution of acuity results in normal infants of different ages are available, making it possible to interpret an infant's visual acuity score in terms of number of standard deviations below normal, as suggested in the current SSA regulations.

There are limitations on the pattern VEP for assessment of visual acuity in infants: (1) the testing equipment is expensive and not widely available; (2) technical expertise is required for conducting the procedure and interpreting the responses; (3) it can be difficult to obtain a measurable response from infants with such oculomotor abnormalities as nystagmus and such neuromotor abnormalities as cerebral palsy, which may cause muscle artifacts that obscure the visual signal; and (4) infants older than 9 months may resist having electrodes attached.

Forced-Choice Preferential Looking (FPL)

The basis of the forced-choice preferential looking procedure is that infants show preferential fixation of a patterned stimulus in comparison to a homogeneous field. Thus, visual acuity can be measured by observing an infant's eye movement responses to black and white gratings paired with a gray stimulus matched to the space-averaged luminance of the gratings.

The version of the procedure that is commercially available and is most widely used to measure visual acuity in infants is the acuity card procedure (Teller et al., 1986). In this procedure, the tester shows the infant a series of gray cards, each containing a black and white grating on the left or the right of a central, small peephole. Prior to testing, the cards are arranged in a stack, face-down, proceeding from coarser to f … tester presents each card to the infant several tim … 180° to change the left-right po … to presentation. The tester, w … rating on each card, watches th … ble and decides, based on the i … avior in response to repeated … nfant can resolve the grating … on) of the grating. After this … tester is permitted to look at … grating.

… e finest grating that the tester … rmative data have been … ure for both binocular and … n birth and 1 year, as well for … age (Courage & Adams, 1990; … ura, 1995).

… used successfully in a wide range … g acuity in visually at-risk infants. In … y for retinopathy of prematurity … cedure was used to measure acuity in … ts with birthweights less than 1,251 g, … etinopathy of prematurity in the … 1994). In the multicenter Ross … card procedure was used to test vision … and 12 months in 197 infants, in order … on visual function and growth (Auestad … ous single-center reports of the … rd procedure to evaluate visual status in infants with … developmental abnormalities, including, for example, cerebral visual impairment (Eken et al., 1996; van Hof-van Duin et al., 1998), severe ocular disorders (Fielder et al., 1991), Down syndrome (Courage et al., 1994), and cerebral hypoxia (van Hof-van Duin & Mohn, 1984).

The advantages of using the acuity card procedure for measurement of visual acuity in infants are that: (1) measurements can be made quickly, within a time span over which most infants will remain cooperative and will fixate the stimulus; (2) the procedure allows the tester to interact with the infant visually between card presentations, which helps to maintain the infant's interest in the testing procedure; (3) the procedure relies on the infant's natural eye movement responses to a patterned stimulus; (4) the procedure is easy to learn; (5) the cost of the equipment is relatively low; (6) the procedure can be used with infants of all ages, as well as with children whose developmental age is that of an infant; (7) with modifications in the positioning of the cards, the procedure can be used to test infants with oculomotor abnormalities, such as nystagmus; and (8) data are available on the distribution of acuity results in normal infants of different ages, making it possible to interpret an infant's visual acuity score in terms of number of standard deviations below normal, as suggested in the current SSA regulations.

There are limitations on the acuity card procedure for assessment of visual acuity in infants: (1) results depend on the integrity of the tester in remaining masked to the location of the gratings on the cards during their presentation (the purpose of remaining masked is to ensure that an unbiased assessment of visual acuity status is obtained); (2) cards must be kept free of dirt and smudges that could attract the infant's attention away from the grating target; (3) grating acuity may underestimate recognition (letter) acuity loss in infants with strabismic amblyopia or macular disease; and (4) variability of acuity scores in normal infants is greater than that reported in VEP studies of normal infants—approximately 0.2 log unit for acuity cards (Courage & Adams, 1990; Mayer et al., 1995) versus approximately 0.13 log unit for VEP (Norcia & Tyler, 1985).

Predictive Value of Results

Data are not available on the extent to which VEP measures of acuity obtained during infancy predict visual acuity during childhood, perhaps because of the limited sites at which VEP testing of infants is conducted. However, several studies have examined the extent to which acuity card results in infancy correlate with recognition acuity results during childhood.

The largest study involved a comparison of grating acuity obtained with the acuity card procedure at age 1 year and recognition (letter) acuity obtained with the Early Treatment for Diabetic Retinopathy Study (ETDRS) charts (Ferris et al., 1982) at age 5.5 years in 616 children who were participants in the multicenter CRYO-ROP study (Dobson et al., 1999). Of the 93 eyes in which vision was too poor to quantify at 1 year with the acuity cards, 90 remained without quantifiable vision at 5.5 years, and three showed measurable letter acuity of 20/400, 20/500, and 20/1600, respectively. Of the 347 eyes that had acuity at 1 year that was in the normal range, which was defined as the mean for the age ±2 standard deviations (Mayer et al., 1995; Salomão & Ventura, 1995), 84.7 percent showed acuity of 20/40 or better at 5.5 years, and none showed acuity of 20/200 or worse. Of the 193 eyes that had acuity in the below-normal range at one year (down to approximately 3 standard deviations below the mean for age), most (74.1 percent) showed acuity of 20/40 or better at 5.5 years, and only four (2.1 percent) showed acuity of 20/200 or worse at 5.5 years. Correlation analysis indicated, however, that grating acuity score at age 1 year accounted for only 2.9 percent of the variance in recognition acuity scores at 5.5 years. Thus, infants with grating acuity in the normal or near normal range at 1 year are likely to have normal recognition acuity at 5.5 years, and those with acuity too poor to be measured with acuity cards will continue to have impaired vision at age 5.5 years. However, the grating acuity score obtained with the acuity cards at age 1 year cannot be used to predict a child's recognition acuity score upon reaching kindergarten age.

Two other single-center studies have reported similar results. Mash and Dobson (1998) compared grating acuity results during infancy (at 4, 8, and 11 months from the infant's due date) with letter acuity results (using the letters HOTV) at age 4 years in 129 children treated in the neonatal intensive care unit for preterm birth or perinatal complications. Their data showed that 89 to 92 percent of children who had normal grating acuity during infancy showed normal letter acuity at age 4 years. However, grating acuity scores during infancy accounted for only 5 to 11 percent of the variance in letter acuity at 4 years. Similarly, Hall et al. (2000) found that normal grating acuity during infancy was highly predictive of normal recognition acuity scores at ages 3 to 10 years in infants at risk for visual disorders.

However, when individual pairs of scores were considered, there was no significant correlation between early grating acuity and later recognition acuity.

Assessment in Preschool-Age Children

While it is difficult to test children under 5 years of age with adult letter visual acuity charts, such as the ETDRS charts (Ferris et al., 1982), tests have been developed that are more "child friendly" yet meet many of the requirements set forth by the Committee on Vision (National Research Council, 1980) for assessment of visual acuity in adults. A recent report from the Maternal and Child Health Bureau/ National Eye Institute-sponsored task force on preschool vision screening (Hartmann et al., 2000) illustrates three of these tests: the HOTV letter chart, the Lea symbols chart (which uses four symbols: house, heart, square, and circle), and the tumbling E chart.

In the illustrations shown in the task force report, each of the charts contains lines of five letters or symbols each, with the distances between symbols and between lines spaced in logarithmic steps, similar to the ETDRS charts. An advantage of both the HOTV and Lea symbols charts is that they use left-right symmetric optotypes, which overcome the young child's difficulty with horizontal laterality (Graham et al., 1960; Rudel & Teuber, 1963; Wohlwill, 1960). In addition, a near visual acuity version of the Lea symbols chart is available, which permits assessment of visual acuity at 40 cm.

Two other tests that use left-right symmetric letters, with a logMAR progression in letter size, are the Glasgow acuity cards (McGraw & Winn, 1993) and the BVAT (Mentor, Inc.) crowded HOTV test. Each Glasgow acuity card contains four of six letters (X, V, O, H, U, and Y), with the four letters surrounded by a crowding bar. In the BVAT crowded HOTV test, single letters (H, O, T, and V) are presented surrounded by crowding bars, with logarithmic steps between letter size presentations. The crowding bars surrounding the single letters in the HOTV test help to prevent the overestimation of visual acuity that occurs in certain types of visual abnormality, such as amblyopia, when acuity is tested with single letters (Flom, 1991).

Another advantage of the HOTV and Lea symbols tests, as well as the Glasgow acuity cards, is that a lap card is available for each test, so that the child who is reluctant to identify the letters or symbols verbally can identify the symbols by pointing to them on the lap card. This same strategy can be used with neurodevelopmentally delayed older children and adults whose cognitive or literacy skills prevent them from being tested with standard adult letter acuity charts.

Success rates for 3- and 4-year-old children have been reported to be poor for the tumbling E test (Friendly, 1978), higher for the HOTV chart (Friendly, 1978; Hered et al., 1997), and highest for the Lea symbols charts (Hered et al., 1997). Unfortunately, however, large-scale normative data are not available for preschool-age children tested with any of these logMAR tests, although published screening recommendations state that children in this age range should be able to identify optotypes on the 20/40 line (American Academy of Pediatrics Committee on Practice and Ambulatory Medicine, Section on Ophthalmology, 1996; Hartmann et al., 2000).

Success rates for assessment of recognition acuity in children less than 3 years of age are very low (McDonald, 1986), due to the inability of young children to identify or match letters or symbols. In addition, it is difficult to get children in this age range to sit still and cooperate for electrophysiological (VEP) measurement of resolution (grating) acuity.

The only quantitative methods that have been used successfully for assessing visual acuity in substantial numbers of children between 1 and 2 years of age are rapidly conducted forced-choice preferential looking measures of resolution (grating) acuity, such as the Teller acuity card procedure (McDonald et al., 1986). Normative data for children between 1 and 4 years of age have been published by several groups (Heersema & van Hof-van Duin, 1990; Courage & Adams, 1990; Mayer et al., 1995; Salomão & Ventura, 1995), making it possible to interpret a child's visual acuity score in terms of number of standard deviations below normal, as suggested in the current SSA regulations.

Assessment in School-Age Children

As discussed in Chapter 2, the standard method of visual acuity assessment in adults is a logMAR chart, such as the Bailey-Lovie chart (Bailey & Lovie, 1976) and the Early Treatment for Diabetic Retinopathy Study (ETDRS) charts (Ferris et al., 1982). These tests have also been used successfully in studies of school-age children.

In a study of 106 10-year-old children with no ocular abnormalities who were tested with ETDRS charts, Myers et al. (1999) reported a mean monocular distance visual acuity of –0.009 logMAR (20/19.6) in the right eye and –0.004 (20/19.8) in the left eye, with a standard deviation of approximately one logMAR line (0.082 and 0.090 log unit for the right and left eyes, respectively). In a study of younger children (n = 31, 5.5 to 7 years of age) with no ocular or cerebral pathology who were tested with the Bailey-Lovie chart, Dowdeswell et al. (1995) reported a mean monocular acuity of 0.10 logMAR (20/25.2), with a standard deviation of 0.08 log unit.

The multicenter CRYO-ROP study reported successful use of ETDRS charts in a group of over 200 5.5- to 6-year-old very low birthweight children (mean birthweight, 800 g, SD 165; mean gestational age 26.3 weeks, SD 1.8), who were at risk for visual deficits due to severe retinopathy of prematurity (Cryotherapy for Retinopathy of Prematurity Cooperative Group, 1996). After excluding 56 cryotherapy-treated eyes and 85 control eyes judged to have no quantifiable pattern vision, an ETDRS acuity score was obtained for 116/177 (65.5 percent) of treated eyes and 90/145 (62.1 percent) of control eyes in this group of very premature children, many of whom had significant developmental delay (Msall et al., 2000). At age 10 years, ETDRS monocular distance acuity scores were obtained for 144 (91.7 percent) of 157 treated eyes and 106 (90.6 percent) of 117 control eyes that were sighted (Cryotherapy for Retinopathy of Prematurity Cooperative Group, 2001c).

Dowdeswell et al. (1995) also used a logMAR (Bailey-Lovie) chart to measure distance visual acuity in young, school-age children (5.5 to 7 years) who were born prior to term (<32 weeks gestation).

Monocular acuity results were successfully obtained in 65 (95.6 percent) of the sample of 68 children.

For near acuity, versions of both the Bailey-Lovie and ETDRS charts are available for assessment. Myers et al. (1999), who tested 106 healthy, full-term 10-year-old children with the near ETDRS charts, reported a mean monocular near visual acuity of –0.011 logMAR (20/19.5) in the right eye and –0.018 (20/19.2) in the left eye, with a standard deviation of approximately one logMAR line (0.10 and 0.11 log unit for the right and left eyes, respectively). In their study of 5.5- to 7-year-old healthy children tested with the near Bailey-Lovie chart, Dowdeswell et al. (1995) reported a mean monocular near acuity of 0.045 logMAR (20/18), with a standard deviation of 0.12 log unit.

Dowdeswell et al. (1995) reported that out of their group of 68 children 5.5 to 7 years of age who were born more than 8 weeks prior to term, 59 (86.8 percent) were able to complete near acuity testing of each eye. Among very low birthweight children with severe retinopathy of prematurity who were tested at age 10 years in the CRYO-ROP study, ETDRS monocular near acuity scores were obtained in 144 (91.7 percent) of 157 treated eyes and 105 (90.5 percent) of 116 control eyes that were sighted (Cryotherapy for Retinopathy of Prematurity Cooperative Group, 2001c).

In the CRYO-ROP study, children were provided with a lap card containing large (6-cm high) examples of the 10 letters that appear on the ETDRS charts (Cryotherapy for Retinopathy of Prematurity Cooperative Group, 1996, 2001c). This permitted children to match (point to), rather than verbally identify, the letters on the ETDRS charts.

Assessment in Those Who Cannot Perform Standard Tests

Registry data indicate that, in general, over half of children who have visual impairments also have other impairments, including mental retardation, cerebral palsy, hearing impairments, and epilepsy (Yeargin-Allsopp et al., 1992; Johnson-Kuhn, 1995; Ferrell et al., 1998; Viisola, 2000). In many cases, these children may be unable to perform visual acuity tests appropriate for their chronological age;

however, useful information about their visual functioning may be obtained through assessment tools designed for younger children or infants (Orel-Bixler et al., 1989; Scharre & Creedon, 1992; Haegerstrom-Portnoy, 1993; O'Dell et al., 1993; Mackie et al., 1996; Westall et al., 2000). Similarly, successful measurement of visual acuity has been reported in adults with severe cognitive impairment, through the use of the Teller acuity card procedure (Marx et al., 1990).

Recommendations

If possible, the visual acuity of children should be assessed with the methods that are recommended for adults, i.e., with refractive error corrected, using charts with a standard number of optotypes per line and a logarithmic progression of optotype size and spacing from line to line on the chart. Most school-age children can be tested using standard adult visual acuity charts and following the standard procedure, in which the patient identifies verbally each letter on the chart.

Many preschool-age children cannot verbally identify letters on an adult visual acuity test, and therefore modified procedures and/or charts may be required. The modifications may be as simple as providing a lap card to permit the 5-year-old to match, rather than verbally identify, the letters on an adult acuity chart. Alternatively, for the 3-year-old, it may be necessary to use familiar shapes rather than letters on the acuity chart, and to reduce the number of symbols that the child must identify during testing. Regardless of whether the preschool-age child is tested with a standard adult test, such as the ETDRS chart or Bailey-Lovie chart, or with a test designed for preschoolers, such as the Lea symbols test, it is important to compare the child's results with the results of other children of the same age tested with the same method, rather than with the results of adults, since visual acuity typically does not reach adult levels prior to a child's entering elementary school (Atkinson et al., 1988; Dowdeswell et al., 1995).

Measurement of visual acuity using letter or symbol optotypes is not possible in infants. However, infants' visual acuity can be tested with electrophysiological techniques (limited availability) and behavioral techniques (more widespread availability) that use resolution acuity targets, such as a black-and-white grating or checkerboard. These techniques have been used successfully with infants and young children in both research and clinical settings. Visual acuity results from normally sighted children between birth and age 1 to 2 years show a rapid improvement over the first six postnatal months, followed by a more gradual improvement over the next one to two years. This longitudinal change in visual acuity supports SSA's use of "number of standard deviations below age norm" in the disability determination process, as well as its requirement for periodic reassessment of the visual status of children who meet disability requirements. The fact that the longitudinal change in visual acuity is not linear, however, indicates that another SSA regulation—the one that recommends comparing the visual acuity results of a potentially visually disabled child with results of normal children of half that child's age—is inappropriate. This is because the degree of visual impairment represented by the vision of a child who is one-half the age of the child being evaluated will differ based on the child's age, being a smaller deficit when the child is in the 1- to 2-year age range than when the child is in the birth to 6-month age range.

Methods that have been developed for use with infants and young children have the potential to be useful for assessment of visual acuity in older children and adults who are too cognitively impaired to be tested with standard adult acuity charts. However, it is important to remember that tests that are based on eye movement responses to large grating stimuli may underestimate the visual acuity deficit of a patient with conditions that affect the macula, such as macular degeneration and amblyopia.

Issues Needing Further Study

Although there are methods available for assessment of visual acuity in children from birth through adolescence, additional research is needed to establish age-related norms for acuity scores obtained with these methods, as well as to provide data on the reliability and validity of each method.

More research is also needed to document the level of visual acuity that represents disability among older children and adults whose neurodevelopmental status prevents them from being tested with standard adult visual acuity tests, but who can be tested with methods designed for infants and young children.

Finally, it is important that studies be conducted with children to evaluate the effect of different levels of visual acuity deficit on everyday activities and quality of life, both for children without additional impairments and for children and adults whose other impairments make it necessary for their visual acuity to be assessed with tools developed for use with infants and younger children.

VISUAL FIELDS

The visual field is typically assessed using small spots of light that are illuminated briefly at various peripheral locations (static perimetry) or are moved inward from the periphery (kinetic perimetry) while the subject fixates on a central target. However, standard static perimetry techniques are difficult to use with children younger than about 8 years of age, and adult kinetic perimetry procedures typically cannot be used with children younger than 5 or 6 years of age.

In children, as in adults, severely restricted visual fields can have a detrimental effect on an individual's mobility, ability to read or benefit from visually presented information, and ability to interact socially. There is a long history of using perimetry and visual field testing to evaluate the status of peripheral vision in adults in both clinical and research settings. Automated static perimetry is available in the offices of most eye care practitioners, and the limitations of restricted visual field extent and of nonseeing areas within the visual field have been widely studied. For children who are old enough cognitively to be tested in a standard adult perimeter, the results of testing can provide an accurate indicator of visual field restrictions. Quantitative techniques for evaluating visual fields in younger children and infants, however, are available only in a small number of research and clinical settings. Thus, at the current time, quantitative evaluation of visual fields in infants and young children is not a practical means of evaluating disability in infants and preschool-age children.

Assessment in Infants

Confrontation Techniques

Quantitative perimetry is not widely available for assessment of visual fields in infants. Therefore, assessment of large visual field deficits in infants is usually made using confrontation techniques. The examiner faces the infant and attracts his or her attention centrally. Then an assistant introduces a toy or a light into the far periphery, and the examiner watches to see if the infant makes a rapid eye or head movement in the direction of the peripherally presented toy or light. A deficit that can be detected by this method is likely to be functionally significant in the future (Day, 1990).

White Sphere Kinetic Perimetry

Techniques for quantitative perimetry in infants are available, but their use has been primarily in research settings. The most widely used is the white sphere kinetic perimetry procedure (Mohn & van Hof-van Duin, 1986), in which an infant is induced to fixate on a centrally located white sphere while an assistant moves a second white sphere centrally from the far periphery along one of the arms of a single- or double-arc black perimeter. An observer hidden behind a black curtain watches to make sure that the infant is looking centrally at the beginning of each trial and indicates when the infant makes an eye movement away from center. The location of the peripheral white sphere when the infant makes an eye movement toward that target is used as an estimate of visual field extent along that perimeter arm. Normative data, available for infants between birth and 12 months of age, indicate that a gradual enlargement of the measured visual field from approximately 30° in each direction to nearly adult levels occurs during this time period (Mohn & van Hof-van Duin, 1986; van Hof-van Duin et al., 1992).

Overall, the advantages of white sphere kinetic perimetry include the availability of normative data against which to compare the results of visually at-risk infants, the use of relatively simple equipment, the ease with which the procedure can be used with any infant who has sufficient vision to fixate on a central target, and the quantitative nature of the test results. Disadvantages include the lack of availability of testing equipment in most clinical settings, the need for two adults (an observer plus an assistant to present the peripheral target), the imprecision of the test results due to the limited attention span of the infant for repeated presentations of the peripheral target, and the continued presence of a central target, which may interfere with some infants' ability to respond when the peripheral target is presented.

Static Perimetry

Several research labs have conducted studies of infants using static perimetry, in which the infant's eye movement responses are observed when a stationary stimulus is presented at different locations in the peripheral field (Lewis & Maurer, 1992; Harvey et al., 1997c). The advantages of static perimetry include the ability to extinguish the central fixation target during presentation of the peripheral stimulus, as well as the ability to identify precisely the location of the peripheral target when it was looked at by the infant. The major disadvantage of static perimetry is that strategies have not yet been devised for eliciting enough trials from an individual infant to quantify that infant's visual field status (Maurer & Lewis, 1991).

Perimetry in Visually At-Risk Infants

White sphere kinetic perimetry has been used in a number of studies of visually at-risk infants, including those with retinopathy of prematurity (Fetter et al., 1992), perinatal asphyxia (Luna et al., 1995), periventricular leukomalacia (Scher et al., 1989), and intraventricular hemorrhage (Harvey et al., 1997b). Data from a limited number of longitudinal studies of at-risk infants suggest that normal visual field extent in early infancy is not necessarily predictive of normal visual field extent in later infancy or early childhood, but that restricted visual fields in early infancy are usually, but not always, predictive of later visual field deficits (Harvey et al., 1997b; Luna et al., 1995).

As in assessment of other aspects of vision in infants and young children, it is important to compare visual field data from visually at-risk infants with data obtained from normal infants of the same age tested with the same procedure, since the age at which measured visual field extent reaches adult levels is highly dependent on characteristics of the stimuli used during testing (Mohan & Dobson, 2000).

Assessment in Preschool-Age Children

The only quantitative method that has been widely used to assess visual field extent in preschool children who cannot cooperate for perimetry using standard adult procedures is the white sphere kinetic perimetry technique that was developed for use with infants (Mohn & van Hof-van Duin, 1986). The technique has the advantage that normative data are available for preschool-age children (Quinn et al., 1991; Wilson et al., 1991; van Hof-van Duin et al., 1992). In addition, the technique has been used successfully to assess visual field extent in at-risk preschool children, including single-center studies of children who experienced intraventricular hemorrhage (Harvey et al., 1997b), perinatal asphyxia (Luna et al., 1995), bronchiopulmonary dysplasia (Harvey et al., 1997a), periventricular leukomalacia (Cioni et al., 2000), and cerebral visual impairment (van Hof-van Duin et al., 1998), and a multicenter study of visual field extent in 5.5-year-old children who had undergone cryotherapy for severe retinopathy of prematurity (Quinn, Dobson, et al., 1996).

The disadvantages of the white sphere kinetic perimetry technique are that it is personnel-intensive and not widely available in clinical settings. Therefore, clinical assessment of visual fields in preschool children who cannot be tested with Goldmann perimetry is generally limited to confrontation techniques.

By permitting the tester to use the child's eye movement responses, rather than buzzer-pressing, to indicate detection of a peripheral stimulus, successful measurement of visual field extent using Goldmann perimetry has been accomplished in both normal and visually at-risk children between 3 and 5 years of age (Cummings et al., 1988; Mayer et al., 1991; Quinn et al., 1991; de Souza et al., 2000). Although normative Goldmann perimetry data for preschool children have not been published, data from Quinn et al. (1991) show that visual field extent, as measured with Goldmann perimetry, increases between age 4 and 10 years. This means that data obtained from visually at-risk preschool-age children tested with the Goldmann perimeter should be compared with data from normal children of the same age, and not with normative data from adults.

Although automated static perimetry is used routinely to measure the sensitivity of the central 30° of the visual field of adults in both clinical and research settings, successful use of automated static perimetry in children younger than age 5 years has not been reported.

Assessment in School-Age Children

Goldmann Perimetry

Goldmann perimetry has been used successfully in a number of studies to measure visual field extent in normal, school-age children (Lakowski & Aspinall, 1969; Liao, 1973; Quinn et al., 1991; Matsuo et al., 1998; Myers et al., 1999). Several investigators have reported developmental increases in measured visual field extent in school-age children. Quinn et al. (1991) showed an increase in measured visual field extent in children between ages 4 and 10 years, as did Lakowski and Aspinall (1969) for a group of 6- to 11-year-old children and Liao (1973) for a group of 6- to 12-year-old children. It is unclear whether this developmental increase in measured visual field extent is the result of sensory maturation or is due to other factors, such as age-related improvements in response time, cognitive processing, or attentional abilities. Nevertheless, the finding of age-related differences in measured visual field extent highlights the importance of using age-based norms when deciding whether a child's visual field extent is within the normal range.

Goldmann perimetry has been useful in measurement of visual field extent in school-age children with a variety of visual disorders, including severe retinopathy of prematurity with or without peripheral retinal ablation (Takayama et al., 1991; Quinn, Miller, et al., 1996; Cryotherapy for Retinopathy of Prematurity Cooperative Group, 2001b), aphakia following removal of unilateral or bilateral dense, central cataracts (Bowering et al., 1997), congenital glaucoma (de Souza et al., 2000), and visual field loss from use of the drug Vigabatrin to treat epilepsy (e.g., Vanhatalo et al., 1999; Wohlrab et al., 1999; Russell-Eggitt et al., 2000).

In standard Goldmann perimetry, the person being tested is required to press a buzzer to indicate the appearance of a peripheral target. Because this response can be difficult for young children, several investigators have reported using young children's eye movements away from the fixation target to indicate detection of the peripheral target (Cummings et al., 1988; Mayer et al., 1991; Quinn et al., 1991; Quinn, Miller, et al., 1996). Data from children ages 4 to 10 years (Quinn et al., 1991) and adults (Mayer et al., 1991) indicate no significant differences in measured visual extent when a buzzer or eye movements were used to indicate detection of the peripheral target.

Automated Static Perimetry

The first reported use of automated static perimetry in normal school-age children was by Bowering et al. (1997, 1993). These researchers used an Octopus 500 perimeter to measure the sensitivity of 7-, 8-, and 9-year-old children and adults to a 0.43° light presented at approximately 20° in the nasal field or 30° in the temporal field. The results showed no significant change in sensitivity with age, but there was a tendency for greater variability in the sensitivities of the younger children than in those of older children and adults.

Recently, Safran, Tschopp and colleagues reported a series of carefully conducted studies of the feasibility, validity, and normative values for testing 5- to 8-year-old normal children with the Octopus 2000R automated perimeter (Safran et al., 1996; Tschopp, Safran, et al., 1998a, 1998b; Tschopp, Viviani, et al., 1999). The results indicated that, following a specially designed training phase, 80 percent of 5-year-olds and all children ages 6 through 8 years were able to complete a 100-trial screening procedure (Tschopp et al., 1998a). In addition, 40 percent of 5-year-olds, 70 percent of 6-year-olds, 90 percent of 7-year-olds, and all 8-year-olds were able to complete a full quantitative evaluation, based on 200 trials or more (Tschopp et al., 1998a). Normative data indicated lower sensitivity than that of a comparison group of 24- to 30-year-old adults at 17/24 locations tested in 5-year-olds, 6/40 locations tested in 6-year-olds, 2/76 locations (both at 27° eccentricity) in 7-year-olds, and 1/76 locations (at 27° eccentricity) in 8-year-olds (Tschopp et al., 1998b). Although Tschopp et al. (1999) found that age differences in sensitivity to peripheral stimuli were related more to differences in attentiveness than to sensory differences across ages, their studies highlight the importance of comparing automated static perimetry results from at-risk children with data from normal children of the same age tested with the same equipment and procedure.

An alternative strategy for testing 6- to 12-year-old children with static perimetry was reported recently by Morales and Brown (2001). Monocular perimetry was performed on the Octopus 1-2-3 perimeter using the TOP-32 short perimetry program, with a "video games" explanation of the task and a 1-minute training trial. Although variability was higher in younger children than in older children, all 50 children in the study were able to complete the TOP-32 program in less than 3.5 minutes per eye. Specificity (normal field result in a normal child) was 78 percent for the total sample and 89 percent when data from 6- and 7-year-olds was excluded.

Automated static perimetry (Octopus 500 perimeter) was used successfully by Bowering et al. (1993) to measure visual field constriction at one nasal and one temporal location in 7- to 9-year-old children who had been treated for a dense and central cataract in one or both eyes. Results were compared with those of normal 7- to 9-year-old children tested with the same procedure. Similarly, Kremer et al. (1995) used automated static perimetry (Humphrey perimeter) to document constriction of the visual field in the eyes of 10 children who had been treated with cryotherapy for retinopathy of prematurity between 10 and 14 years prior to testing. Recently, Donahue and Porter (2001) reported using the Swedish interactive thresholding algorithm (SITA), a new testing strategy for the Humphrey perimeter, to test visual fields in children between 6 and 17 years of age with visual field defects.

Two modifications have been used by investigators to increase the proportion of young school-age children who can be tested successfully with automated static perimetry. First, investigators have reduced the number of peripheral stimulus presentations that the child is required to complete. For example, Bowering et al. (1993) tested children with stimuli centered around one nasal and one temporal location. Tschopp et al. (1998b) tested 5-year-olds with only 32 percent of the test locations used with 7- and 8-year-olds and adults, and 6-year-olds with only 53 percent of the number of locations used with older age groups. Morales and Brown (2001) used a commercially available ultra-short program that employs a "lateral bracketing" strategy to estimate threshold sensitivities for 76 test points in the central 30° of the visual field in less than 3 minutes. A second modification used by Tschopp et al. to increase testability in young children was an extensive training protocol, in which a series of positive reinforcement procedures was used to teach the child to respond when "stars" appeared, but not to respond to sounds in the perimeter that were not accompanied by the appearance of a star. Morales and Brown found that a training session of approximately one minute was all that was needed for children to be able to complete the ultra-short Octopus TOP-32 program.

In summary, although it is possible to test many young school-age children with automated static perimetry, care must be taken to ensure that the child understands and can perform the task prior to beginning the actual measurement of sensitivity at different locations within the visual field. In addition, the short attention span of young children may limit the degree of detail with which the sensitivity visual field can be mapped. By the time children reach ages 8 to 10 years, however, most can provide reliable data for sensitivity across the same area of the visual field that can be tested in adults.

Assessment in Those Who Cannot Perform Standard Tests

In contrast to the variety of tools that have been developed to assess visual acuity in infants and children who cannot be tested with standard adult techniques, there are no well-developed, widely available tools for assessment of visual fields in individuals who lack the physical or cognitive ability to perform kinetic or static perimetry procedures developed for use with adults. Minor modifications, such as observation of an individual's eye movements in response to perimetry targets, can permit testing of individuals who are physically or cognitively unable to provide the standard button-press results, but estimation of deficits in the visual field of the individual with severe neurodevelopmental delay or physical disabilities that prevent use of a standard perimeter is generally limited to confrontation testing.

Recommendations

If possible, visual fields of children should be assessed with the method that is recommended for adults, i.e., automated static perimetry. For children who are too young to be tested with standard adult perimetry procedures, there are no widely available, quantitative perimetry techniques and therefore no standardized methods for evaluating disability related to restricted visual fields.

Issues Needing Further Study

More research is needed to develop, norm, and validate methods for assessing visual fields in children too young to be tested with standard adult perimetry procedures. In addition, there is a need for more age-based normative data for standard adult perimetry procedures, so that the results from individual children can be compared with results from normal children of the same age, rather than with normative data from adults.

Another area in which research is needed concerns the effect of visual field deficits on activities of daily living and quality of life in children. Such investigation should include children old enough to be tested with adult perimetry procedures, as well as children and adults whose cognitive development is not sufficient to allow them to be evaluated with adult perimetry procedures.

CONTRAST SENSITIVITY

In adults, contrast sensitivity is measured by determining the least amount of contrast an individual needs to detect a difference in luminance between adjacent parts of a pattern. Laboratory studies have used measurements of contrast sensitivity in infants to produce a simulated view of what various patterns and scenes look like to an infant (Banks & Salapatek, 1981; Teller, 1997). However, there are no widely available, normed and validated tools for assessment of contrast sensitivity in infants or preschool-age children.

While visual acuity provides a measure of the finest detail that an individual can resolve, results of contrast sensitivity testing provide information on the individual's ability to detect patterns of all sizes, and thus they provide a more complete description of an individual's visual environment than can be obtained from a visual acuity score. Because the world of the infant and young child is built around global perceptions, rather than attention to fine detail as is required in reading, it is likely that assessment of contrast sensitivity would provide a more accurate estimate of an infant's or young child's ability to function visually than would a measure of visual acuity. However, the development of techniques for assessing contrast sensitivity in infants and young children has lagged far behind the development of techniques for assessing visual acuity. Therefore, at this time, visual acuity is the only aspect of spatial vision that can be assessed in a child too young to be tested with adult measures of contrast sensitivity.

Currently, methods to assess contrast sensitivity in adults require the individual to identify low contrast letters or to indicate, for a series of black and white gratings, the lowest contrast at which each pattern is detectable. Use of letters in the first type of test and the need for a large number of trials in the second type of test prevent either from being useful in the assessment of preschool-age children and infants.

Assessment in Infants

Although both normal infants (Adams et al., 1992) and infants with Down syndrome (Courage et al., 1997) have been tested successfully with an acuity card type of contrast sensitivity test and normative data are available for infants (Adams & Courage, 1996), the test is not ready for widespread use, due to poor test-retest reliability, long test times, and lack of commercial availability (Adams et al., 2000).

Measurement of contrast sensitivity in infants is also possible using the pattern VEP, and initial normative data are available (Norcia et al., 1990). However, it is unlikely that this technique will achieve widespread use, due to the expense of the equipment and the technical expertise required to interpret the results.

Assessment in Preschool-Age Children

The primary tests used to evaluate contrast sensitivity in adults are the Vistech chart (Ginsburg, 1984) and the Pelli-Robson charts (Pelli et al., 1988). Although the Vistech and Pelli-Robson contrast sensitivity charts have been used successfully with children as young as 5 years of age, they are not practical for use with younger children, due to the difficulty the children have in identifying grating orientation of stimuli on the Vistech chart and their inability to identify the letters used as stimuli on the Pelli-Robson charts (Rogers, Bremer, & Leguire, 1987; Scharre et al., 1990).

A potentially useful contrast sensitivity test for this age group is the low contrast version of the Lea Symbols test (Precision Vision, La Salle, IL). In this test, as in the Pelli-Robson charts, the symbols are of a constant size but contrast varies by row. Rydberg and Han (1999) reported using the low contrast version of the Lea Symbols test successfully with children between 3 years 9 months and 6 years of age who had normal vision or visual impairment due to ocular disease or amblyopia. However, normative data are not yet available for this test and, because it requires identification or matching of symbols, it is unlikely that the test would be useful for measurement of contrast sensitivity in children younger than about 3 years of age.

Another potentially useful procedure for assessment of contrast sensitivity is an "alley-running" procedure developed by Atkinson and colleagues (1981) to measure contrast sensitivity of 3- to 5-year-old children in a research setting. However, this procedure has received no follow-up development for use in clinical settings.

For children younger than age 3 years, it may be possible to measure contrast sensitivity with an acuity card procedure, similar to that used to measure grating acuity in this age range. Initial data obtained from normal 2- and 3-year-olds (Adams & Courage, 1993) indicate that it is possible to measure contrast sensitivity in children at the younger end of the preschool age range with this type of contrast sensitivity test (Adams et al., 1992). However, test times are relatively long (average = 12 min) and the cards are not yet commercially available.

Assessment in School-Age Children

Scharre et al. (1990) provided normative data on the Vistech chart for 5-, 6-, and 7-year-olds, showing that sensitivity increases with age, and that even at age 7 years, contrast sensitivity at all five spatial frequencies tested is lower than that of adults. Rogers, Bremer, and Leguire (1987) also found that Vistech contrast sensitivity in children younger than 7 years of age is lower than that of adults. Both Scharre et al. and Rogers et al. attempted to test children younger than 5 years of age, but they reported low success rates for test completion in these younger children.

Powls et al. (1997) tested 163 11- to 13-year-old, normal birthweight children using the Vistech chart and reported that results for the two lowest spatial frequencies were similar to those of adults, but that the children were less sensitive to the three highest spatial frequencies than were adults. In contrast, Fitzgerald (1989) reported that children were relatively more sensitive to high spatial frequency gratings than the adults who were tested to produce the Vistech chart norms.

Unlike the Vistech chart, which measures contrast sensitivity for individual spatial frequencies, the Pelli-Robson charts provide a single contrast sensitivity value based on multi-spatial-frequency letter targets. Using the Pelli-Robson charts, Fitzgerald et al. (1993) reported a mean *binocular* contrast sensitivity for 49 children ages 8 to 12 years of 1.89 log units (SD 0.97), which is within the range of values (1.75 to 1.91 log units) reported for *monocular* testing of young adults (Elliott, Sanderson, & Conkey, 1990; Elliott & Whitaker, 1992a; Beck et al., 1993). In contrast, Myers et al. (1999), in a study of 106 healthy, full-term 10-year-olds, reported mean monocular contrast sensitivities of 1.69 log units (SD 0.12) for the right eye and 1.66 (SD 0.11) for the left eye, lower than that typically reported for adults but similar to the mean monocular Pelli-Robson contrast sensitivity value of 1.62 (SD 0.08) reported by Dowdeswell et al. (1995) for healthy 5.5- to 7-year-old children.

Dowdeswell et al. (1995) reported obtaining monocular Pelli-Robson contrast sensitivity results in 61 (89.7 percent) of 68 children 5.5 to 7 years of age with gestational ages of less than 32 weeks. Pelli-Robson charts were also used to measure contrast sensitivity at age 10 years in the CRYO-ROP study. A measure of contrast sensitivity was obtained in 143 (91.7 percent) of 156 treated eyes and 102 (90.3 percent) of 113 control eyes that were sighted (Cryotherapy for Retinopathy of Prematurity Cooperative Group, 2001a). Results showed that eyes of children in the CRYO-ROP study were more likely to show normal contrast sensitivity in the presence of reduced visual acuity than normal visual acuity in the presence of reduced contrast sensitivity, supporting data from studies of adults, which indicate that visual acuity and contrast sensitivity measure different aspects of visual function.

To assist children in identifying the orientation of the grating patterns on the Vistech chart, Scharre et al. (1990) provided children with a pointer that could be aligned in the same orientation as the grating pattern or with a hand-held grating pattern that could be used to match the orientation of the pattern on the chart. No studies have reported adaptations of the Pelli-Robson procedure for use with young children, but it should be possible to create a lap chart that would allow the child to match, rather than to identify the letters verbally, similar to the lap card that has been used for assessment of letter visual acuity in young children (Cryotherapy for Retinopathy of Prematurity Cooperative Group, 1996, 2001c).

Assessment in Those Who Cannot Perform Standard Tests

There are no well-developed, widely available tools for assessment of contrast sensitivity in individuals who lack the ability to identify or match the orientation of the grating stimuli on the Vistech chart or to identify or match the letters on the Pelli-Robson charts.

Recommendations

In children whose visual acuity is measurable but below the normal range, it would be beneficial to evaluate their overall spatial vision by assessment of their contrast sensitivity. This is possible in children who have the cognitive skills to be tested with measures of contrast sensitivity developed for use with adults. For children who are too young to be tested with standard adult contrast sensitivity measures, there are no widely available techniques for assessment of contrast sensitivity and therefore no standardized methods for evaluating disability related to deficits in contrast sensitivity.

Issues Needing Further Study

More research is needed to develop, norm, and validate methods for assessing contrast sensitivity in children too young to be tested with standard adult procedures. In addition, there is a need for more age-based normative data for standard adult contrast sensitivity procedures, so that the results from individual children can be compared with results from normal children of the same age, rather than with normative data from adults.

Another area in which research is needed concerns the effect of contrast sensitivity deficits on activities of daily living and quality of life in children. This investigation should include children old enough to be tested with adult contrast sensitivity procedures, as well as children and adults whose cognitive development is not sufficient to allow them to be evaluated with adult procedures.

REFERENCES

Adams, A.J., Verdon, W.A., and Spivey, B.E. (1998). Chapter 19: Color vision. In T.D. Duane, W.E. Tasman, and E.A. Jaeger (eds.), *Duane's foundations of clinical ophthalmology*. Philadelphia, PA: Lippincott, Williams and Wilkins.

Adams, A.J., Wong, L.S., Wong, L., and Gould, B. (1988). Visual acuity changes with age: Some new perspectives. *American Journal of Optometry and Physiological Optics, 65*(5), 403-406.

Adams, R.J., and Courage, M.L. (1993). Contrast sensitivity in 24- and 36-month-olds as assessed with the contrast sensitivity card procedure. *Optometry and Vision Science, 70*(2), 97-101.

Adams, R.J., and Courage, M.L. (1996). Monocular contrast sensitivity in 3- to 36-month-old human infants. *Optometry and Vision Science, 73*(8), 546-551.

Adams, R.J., Courage, M.L., and Drover, J.R. (2000). Retest variability of human infant contrast sensitivity: How many tests are sufficient? *Optometry and Vision Science, 77*(2), 90-95.

Adams, R.J., Mercer, M.E., and Courage, M.L. (1992). A new technique to measure contrast sensitivity in human infants. *Optometry and Vision Science, 69*(6), 440-446.

Ahn, S.J., and Legge, G.E. (1995). Psychophysics of reading. XIII. Predictors of magnifier-aided reading speed in low vision. *Vision Research, 35*(13), 1931-1938.

Alexander, M.F., Maguire, M.G., Lietman, T.M., Snyder, J.R., Elman, M.J., and Fine, S.L. (1988). Assessment of visual function in patients with age-related macular degeneration and low visual acuity. *Archives of Ophthalmology, 106*(11), 1543-1547.

American Academy of Pediatrics Committee on Practice and Ambulatory Medicine, Section on Ophthalmology. (1996). Eye examination and vision screening in infants, children, and young adults. *Pediatrics, 98*(1), 153-157.

American Medical Association. (1993). *Guides to the evaluation of permanent impairment* (4th ed.). Chicago, IL: American Medical Association.

American Medical Association. (2001). *Guides to the evaluation of permanent impairment* (5th ed.). Chicago, IL: American Medical Association.

American Medical Association and the Committee on Medical Rating of Physical Impairment. (1958). Guides to the evaluation of permanent impairment: The visual system. *The Journal of the American Medical Association, 168*, 475-485.

American National Standards Institute International Standards. (1986a). *ISO/DIS 8596. Optics and optical instruments - visual acuity testing - standard optotype and its presentation.*

American National Standards Institute International Standards. (1986b). *ISO/DIS 8597. Optics and optical instruments - visual acuity testing - correlation of optotypes.*

Anderson, D.R., and Patella, V.M. (1999). *Automated static perimetry* (2nd ed.). St. Louis, MO: Mosby.

Appollonio, I., Carabellese, C., Magni, E., Frattola, L., and Trabucchi, M. (1995). Sensory impairments and mortality in an elderly community population: A six-year follow-up study. *Age and Ageing, 24*(1), 30-36.

Aquilante, K., Yager, D., and Morris, R. (2000). Are low vision patients with central visual field loss more sensitive to changes in luminance when reading than are age-matched normals? In *Vision science and its applications 2000, OSA technical digest series.*

Arditi, A. (1999). Elicited sequential presentation for low-vision reading. *Vision Research, 39*(26), 4412-4418.

Arditi, A., and Brabyn, J.A. (2000). Signage and wayfinding. In B. Silverstone, M.A. Lang, B.P. Rosenthal, and E.E. Faye (eds.), *The Lighthouse handbook on vision impairment and vision rehabilitation* (Vol. 2). Oxford University Press.

Arditi, A., and Cagenello, R. (1993). On the statistical reliability of letter-chart visual acuity measurements. *Investigative Ophthalmology and Visual Science, 34*(1), 120-129.

Armstrong, J.D. (1972). *An independent evaluation of the Kay Binaural Sensor.* Nottingham, England: University of Nottingham.

Armstrong, J.D. (1975). Evaluation of man-made systems in the mobility of the visually handicapped. In R.M. Pickett, and T.J. Triggs (eds.), *Human factors in health care.* Lexington, MA: Lexington Books.

Atkinson, J., Anker, S., Evans, C., Hall, R., and Pimm-Smith E. (1988). Visual acuity testing of young children with the Cambridge Crowding Cards at 3 and 6 months. *Acta Ophthalmologica, 66*(5), 505-508.

Atkinson, J., French, J., and Braddick, O.J. (1981). Contrast sensitivity function of preschool children. *British Journal of Ophthalmology, 65*(8), 525-529.

Attebo, K., Mitchell, P., and Smith, W. (1996). Visual acuity and the causes of visual loss in Australia: The Blue Mountains Eye Study. *Ophthalmology, 103*(3), 357-364.

Auestad, N., Montalto, M.B., Hall, R.T., Fitzgerald, K.M., Wheeler, R.E., Connor, W.E., Neuringer, M., Connor, S.L., Taylor, J.A., and Hartmann, E.E. (1997). Visual acuity, erythrocyte fatty acid composition, and growth in term infants fed formulas with long chain polyunsaturated fatty acids for one year: Ross Pediatric Lipid Study. *Pediatric Research, 41*(1), 1-10.

Bailey, I.L., and Bullimore, M.A. (1991). A new test for the evaluation of disability glare. *Optometry and Vision Science, 68*(12), 911-917.

Bailey, I.L., and Lovie, J.E. (1976). New design principles for visual acuity letter charts. *American Journal of Optometry and Physiological Optics, 53*(11), 740-745.

Bailey, I.L., and Lovie, J.E. (1980). The design and use of a new near-vision chart. *American Journal of Optometry and Physiological Optics, 57*(6), 378-387.

Bailey, I.L., Bullimore, M.A., Raasch, T.W., and Taylor, H.R. (1991). Clinical grading and the effects of scaling. *Investigative Ophthalmology and Visual Science, 32*(2), 422-432.

Baldasare, J., Watson, G.R., Whittaker, S.G., and Miller-Shaffer, H. (1986). The development and evaluation of a reading test for low vision individuals with macular loss. *Journal of Visual Impairment and Blindness, 80*(6), 785-789.

Ball, K.K., and Owsley, C. (1991). Identifying correlates of accident involvement for the older driver. *Human Factors, 33*(5), 583-595.

Ball, K.K., Owsley, C., Sloane, M.E., Roenker, D.L., and Bruni, J.R. (1993). Visual attention problems as a predictor of vehicle crashes in older drivers. *Investigative Ophthalmology and Visual Science, 34*(11), 3110-3123.

Ball, K.K., Roenker, D.L., and Bruni, J.R. (1990). Developmental changes in attention and visual search throughout adulthood. In J.T. Enns (ed.), *The development of attention: Research and theory. Advances in psychology* (pp. 489-508). Amsterdam, Netherlands: North-Holland.

Banks, M.S., and Salapatek, P. (1981). Infant pattern vision: A new approach based on the contrast sensitivity function. *Journal of Experimental Child Psychology, 31*(1), 1-45.

Barlow, H.B. (1972). Dark and light adaptation: Psychophysics. In D. Jameson, and L.M. Hurvich (eds.), (Vol. 7, Chap. 4, pp. 1-55). New York, NY: Springer-Verlag.

Barrett, G.V., Mihal, W.L., Panek, P.E., Sterns, H.L., and Alexander, R.A. (1977). Information-processing skills predictive of accident involvement for younger and older commercial drivers. *Industrial Gerontology, 4*, 173-182.

Beck, R.W., Diehl, L., Cleary, P.A., and The Optic Neuritis Study Group. (1993). The Pelli-Robson letter chart: Normative data for young adults. *Clinical Vision Sciences, 8*, 207-210.

Beckman, C., Scott, R., and Garner, L.F. (1992). Comparison of three methods of evaluating glare. *Acta Ophthalmologica, 70*(1), 53-59.

Beckmann, P.J., and Legge, G.E. (1996). Psychophysics of reading. XIV. The page navigation problem in using magnifiers. *Vision Research, 36*(22), 3723-3733.

Bengtsson, B., and Heijl, A. (1998a). Evaluation of a new perimetric threshold strategy, SITA, in patients with manifest and suspect glaucoma. *Acta Ophthalmologica Scandinavica, 76*(3), 268-272.

Bengtsson, B., and Heijl, A. (1998b). SITA Fast, a new rapid perimetric threshold test. Description of methods and evaluation in patients with manifest and suspect glaucoma. *Acta Ophthalmologica Scandinavica, 76*(4), 431-437.

Bengtsson, B., and Heijl, A. (1999a). Comparing significance and magnitude of glaucomatous visual field defects using the SITA and Full Threshold strategies. *Acta Ophthalmologica Scandinavica, 77*(2), 143-146.

Bengtsson, B., and Heijl, A. (1999b). Inter-subject variability and normal limits of the SITA Standard, SITA Fast, and the Humphrey Full Threshold computerized perimetry strategies, SITA STATPAC. *Acta Ophthalmologica Scandinavica, 77*(2), 125-129.

Bengtsson, B., Heijl, A., and Olsson, J. (1998). Evaluation of a new threshold visual field strategy, SITA, in normal subjects. Swedish Interactive Thresholding Algorithm. *Acta Ophthalmologica Scandinavica, 76*(2), 165-169.

Bengtsson, B., Olsson, J., Heijl, A., and Rootzen, H. (1997). A new generation of algorithms for computerized threshold perimetry, SITA. *Acta Ophthalmologica Scandinavica, 75*(4), 368-375.

Blake, R., and Fox, R. (1973). The psychophysical inquiry into binocular summation. *Perception and Psychophysics, 14*(1), 161-185.

Blasch, B.B., Wiener, W.R., and Welsh, R.L. (1997). *Foundations of orientation and mobility* (2nd ed.). New York, NY: AFB Press.

Bowering, E.R., Maurer, D., Lewis, T.L., and Brent, H.P. (1993). Sensitivity in the nasal and temporal hemifields in children treated for cataract. *Investigative Ophthalmology and Visual Science, 34*(13), 3501-3509.

Bowering, E.R., Maurer, D., Lewis, T.L., and Brent, H.P. (1997). Constriction of the visual field of children after early visual deprivation. *Journal of Pediatric Ophthalmology and Strabismus, 34*(6), 347-356.

Brabyn, J.A. (1990). Summary of proceedings of the Conference on Driver Competency Assessment. (pp. 52-54).

Brabyn, J.A. (1999). Visual function in the oldest old. *Proceedings of the 15th Biennial Eye Research Seminar: Research to prevent blindness.*

Brabyn, J.A., and Strelow, E.R. (1977). Computer-analyzed measures of characteristics of human locomotion and mobility. *Behavior Research Methods, Instruments and Computers, 9*(5), 456-462.

Brabyn, J.A., Haegerstrom-Portnoy, G., Schneck, M.E., and Lott, L.A. (2000). Visual impairment in older people under everyday viewing conditions. *Journal of Visual Impairment and Blindness, 94*(12), 741-755.

Brabyn, J.A., Schneck, M.E., and Haegerstrom-Portnoy, G. (1995). Measured and self-reported visual function in the elderly. *Investigative Ophthalmology and Visual Science Supplement, 36*, 3075.

Brabyn, J.A., Schneck, M.E., Haegerstrom-Portnoy, G., and Steinman, B. (1994). Vision test performance and accident proneness in drivers over the age of 55. In *Proceedings, vision science and its applications topical meeting* (Vol. 2pp. 210-213). Optical Society of America.

British Standards Institution. (1968). *Specification for test charts for determining distance visual acuity*. London, England.

Broman, A.T., Munoz, B., West, S.K., Rodriguez, J., Sanchez, R., Snyder, R., and Klein, R. (2001). Psychometric properties of the 25-item NEI-VFQ in a Hispanic population: Proyecto VER. *Investigative Ophthalmology and Visual Science, 42*(3), 606-613.

Brown, B., Brabyn, L., Welch, L., Haegerstrom-Portnoy, G., and Colenbrander, A. (1986). Contribution of vision variables to mobility in age-related maculopathy patients. *American Journal of Optometry and Physiological Optics, 63*(9), 733-739.

Brown, B., Zadnik, K., Bailey, I.L., and Colenbrander, A. (1984). Effect of luminance, contrast, and eccentricity on visual acuity in senile macular degeneration. *American Journal of Optometry and Physiological Optics, 61*(4), 265-270.

Bullimore, M.A., and Bailey, I.L. (1995). Reading and eye movements in age-related maculopathy. *Optometry and Vision Science, 72*(2), 125-138.

Bullimore, M.A., Bailey, I.L., and Wacker, R.T. (1991). Face recognition in age-related maculopathy. *Investigative Ophthalmology and Visual Science, 32*(7), 2020-2029.

Bureau of Labor Statistics, U.S. Department of Labor. (2000). *Occupational outlook handbook, 2000-01 edition, bulletin 2520.* Washington, DC: Superintendent of Documents, U.S. Government Printing Office.

Burg, A. (1967). *The relationship between test scores and driving record: General findings.* (Report No. 67-24). Los Angeles: Department of Engineering, UCLA.

Burg, A. (1968). *Vision test scores and driving record: Additional findings.* (Report No. 68-27). Los Angeles: Department of Engineering, UCLA.

Burkhauser, R.V., Daly, M.C., and Houtenville, A.J. (2000). How working age people with disabilities fared over the 1990s business cycle. In P.P. Budetti, R.V. Burkhauser, J.M. Gregory, and H.A. Hunt (eds.), *Ensuring health and income security for an aging workforce.* Kalamazoo, MI: W.E. UpJohn Institute for Employment Research.

Cagenello, R., Arditi, A., and Halpern, D.L. (1993). Binocular enhancement of visual acuity. *Journal of the Optical Society of America A. Optics and Image Science, 10*(8), 1841-1848.

Campbell, F.W., and Green, D.G. (1965). Monocular versus binocular visual acuity. *Nature, 208*(6), 191-192.

Carabellese, C., Appollonio, I., Rozzini, R., Bianchetti, A., Frisoni, G.B., Frattola, L., and Trabucchi, M. (1993). Sensory impairment and quality of life in a community elderly population. *Journal of the American Geriatrics Society, 41*(4), 401-407.

Carrasco, M., and Chang, I. (1995). The interaction of objective and subjective organizations in a localization search task. *Perception and Psychophysics, 57*(8), 1134-1150.

Carrasco, M., and Frieder, K.S. (1997). Cortical magnification neutralizes the eccentricity effect in visual search. *Vision Research, 37*(1), 63-82.

Carver, R.P. (1990). *Reading rate: A review of research and theory.* San Diego, CA: Academic Press.

Cashell, G.T.W. (1970). Visual function in relation to road accidents. *Injury, 2*(1), 8-10.

Cassard, S.D., Patrick, D.L., Damiano, A.M., Legro, M.W., Tielsch, J.M., Diener-West, M., Schein, O.D., Javitt, J.C., Bass, E.B., and Steinberg, E.P. (1995). Reproducibility and responsiveness of the VF-14. An index of functional impairment in patients with cataracts. *Archives of Ophthalmology, 113*(12), 1508-1513.

Charman, W.N. (1985). Visual standards for driving. *Ophthalmic and Physiological Optics, 5*(2), 211-220.

Chung, S.T.L., Mansfield, J.S., and Legge, G.E. (1998). Psychophysics of reading. XVIII. The effect of print size on reading speed in normal peripheral vision. *Vision Research, 38*(19), 2949-2962.

Cioni, G., Bertuccelli, B., Boldrini, A., Canapicchi, R., Fazzi, B., Guzzetta, A., and Mercuri, E. (2000). Correlation between visual function, neurodevelopmental outcome, and magnetic resonance imaging findings in infants with periventricular leucomalacia. *Archives of Disease in Childhood: Fetal and Neonatal Edition, 82*(2), F134-F140.

Cole, S.R., Beck, R.W., Moke, P.S., Gal, R.L., and Long, D.T. (2000). The National Eye Institute Visual Function Questionnaire: Experience of the ONTT. Optic Neuritis Treatment Trial. *Investigative Ophthalmology and Visual Science, 41*(5), 1017-1021.

Consilium Ophthalmologicum Universale Visual Functions Committee. (1988). Visual acuity measurement standard. *Italian Journal of Opthalmology, II*, 15.

Council, F.M., and Allen, J.A. (1974). *A study of the visual fields of North Carolina drivers and their relationships to accidents*. Chapel Hill: Highway Safety Research Center, University of North Carolina.

Courage, M.L., and Adams, R.J. (1990). Visual acuity assessment from birth to three years using the acuity card procedure: Cross-sectional and longitudinal samples. *Optometry and Vision Science, 67*(9), 713-718.

Courage, M.L., Adams, R.J., and Hall, E.J. (1997). Contrast sensitivity in infants and children with Down syndrome. *Vision Research, 37*(11), 1545-1555.

Courage, M.L., Adams, R.J., Reyno, S., and Kwa, P.G. (1994). Visual acuity in infants and children with Down syndrome. *Developmental Medicine and Child Neurology, 36*(7), 586-593.

Crandall, W., Brabyn, J.A., Bentzen, B.L., and Myers, L. (1999). Remote infrared signage evaluation for transit stations and intersections. *Journal of Rehabilitation Research and Development, 36*(4), 341-355.

Cronly-Dillon, J.R. (1991). *Vision and visual dysfunction.* Boca Raton: CRC Press.

Cross, A.W. (1985). Health screening in schools: Part 1. *The Journal of Pediatrics, 107*(4), 487-494.

Cruickshanks, K.J., Fryback, D.G., Nondahl, D.M., Robinson, N., Keesey, U., Dalton, D.S., Robertson, D.M., Chandra, S.R., Mieler, W.F., Zakov, Z.N., Custer, P.L., Del Priore, L.V., and Albert, D.M. (1999). Treatment choice and quality of life in patients with choroidal melanoma. *Archives of Ophthalmology, 117*(4), 461-467.

Cryotherapy for Retinopathy of Prematurity Cooperative Group. (1996). Multicenter trial of cryotherapy for retinopathy of prematurity: Snellen visual acuity and structural outcome at 5 1/2 years after randomization. *Archives of Ophthalmology, 114*(4), 417-424.

Cryotherapy for Retinopathy of Prematurity Cooperative Group. (2001a). Contrast sensitivity at age ten years in children who had threshold retinopathy of prematurity. *Archives of Ophthalmology, 119*, 1129-1133.

Cryotherapy for Retinopathy of Prematurity Cooperative Group. (2001b). Effect of retinal ablative therapy for threshold retinopathy of prematurity: Results of Goldmann perimetry at age ten years. *Archives of Ophthalmology, 119*, 1120-1125.

Cryotherapy for Retinopathy of Prematurity Cooperative Group. (2001c). Multicenter trial of cryotherapy for retinopathy of prematurity: Ophthalmological outcomes at ten years. *Archives of Ophthalmology, 119*, 1110-1118.

Cummings, M.F., van Hof-van Duin, J., Mayer, D.L., Hansen, R.M., and Fulton, A.B. (1988). Visual fields of young children. *Behavioural Brain Research, 29*(1-2), 7-16.

Cushman, L.A. (1996). Cognitive capacity and concurent driving performance in older drivers. *International Association of Traffic and Safety Sciences Research, 20*(1), 38-45.

Dargent-Molina, P., Hays, M., and Breart, G. (1996). Sensory impairments and physical disability in aged women living at home. *International Journal of Epidemiology, 25*(3), 621-629.

Davison, P.A. (1985). Inter-relationships between British drivers' visual abilities, age and road accident histories. *Ophthalmic and Physiological Optics, 5*(2), 195-204.

Day, S. (1990). History, examination and further investigation. In D.S. Taylor (ed.), *Pediatric ophthalmology* (pp. 47-64). Boston, MA: Blackwell Scientific Publications.

de Souza, E.C., Berezovsky, A., Morales, P.H., de Arruda Mello, P.A., de Oliveira Bonomo, P.P., and Salomão, S.R. (2000). Visual field defects in children with congenital glaucoma. *Journal of Pediatric Ophthalmology and Strabismus, 37*(5), 266-272.

de Waard, P.W., IJspeert, J.K., van den Berg, T.J., and de Jong, P.T.V.M. (1992). Intraocular light scattering in age-related cataracts. *Investigative Ophthalmology and Visual Science, 33*(3), 618-625.

Decina, L.E., and Staplin, L. (1993). Retrospective evaluation of alternative vision screening criteria for older and younger drivers. *Accident Analysis and Prevention, 25*(3), 267-275.

DeLuca, M., Spinelli, D., and Zoccolotti, P. (1996). Eye movement patterns in reading as a function of visual field defects and contrast sensitivity loss. *Cortex, 32*(3), 491-502.

DeMarco, L.M., and Massof, R.W. (1997). Distributions of print sizes in U. S. newspapers. *Journal of Visual Impairment and Blindness, 91*(1), 9-13.

Demer, J.L., Porter, F.I., Goldberg, J., Jenkins, H.A., and Schmidt, K. (1988). Dynamic visual acuity with telescopic spectacles: Improvement with adaptation. *Investigative Ophthalmology and Visual Science, 29*(7), 1184-1189.

Den Brinker, B.P.L.M., and Beek, P.J. (1996). Reading with magnifiers. *Ergonomics, 39*(10), 1231-1248.

Dickinson, C., and Rabbitt, P.M.A. (1991). Simulated visual impairment: Effects on text comprehension and reading speed. *Clinical Vision Sciences, 6*, 301-308.

Dobson, V., Quinn, G.E., Siatkowski, R.M., Baker, J.D., Hardy, R.J., Reynolds, J.D., Trese, M.T., Tung, B., and Cryotherapy for Retinopathy of Prematurity Cooperative Group. (1999). Agreement between grating acuity at age 1 year and Snellen acuity at age 5.5 years in the preterm child. *Investigative Ophthalmology and Visual Science, 40*(2), 496-503.

Dobson, V., Quinn, G.E., Summers, C.G., Saunders, R.A., Phelps, D.L., Tung, B., Palmer, E.A., and Cryotherapy for Retinopathy of Prematurity Cooperative Group. (1994). Effect of acute-phase retinopathy of prematurity on grating acuity development in the very low birth weight infant. *Investigative Ophthalmology and Visual Science, 35*(13), 4236-4244.

Dodds, A.G., Carter, D.D., and Howarth, C.I. (1983). Improving objective measures of mobility. *Journal of Visual Impairment and Blindness, 77*(9), 438-442.

Donahue, S.P., and Porter, A. (2001). SITA visual field testing in children. *Journal of the American Association for Pediatric Ophthalmology and Strabismus, 5*(2), 114-114.

Dowdeswell, H.J., Slater, A.M., Broomhall, J., and Tripp, J. (1995). Visual deficits in children born at less than 32 weeks' gestation with and without major ocular pathology and cerebral damage. *British Journal of Ophthalmology, 79*(5), 447-452.

Duchek, J.M., Hunt, L., Ball, K.K., Buckles, V., and Morris, J.C. (1998). Attention and driving performance in Alzheimer's disease. *Journals of Gerontology. Series B, Psychological Sciences and Social Sciences, 53*(2), P130-P141.

Ehrlich, M.I., Reinecke, R.D., and Simons, K. (1983). Preschool vision screening for amblyopia and strabismus. Programs, methods, guidelines. *Survey of Ophthalmology, 28*(3), 145-163.

Eken, P., de Vries, L.S., van Nieuwenhuizen, O., Schalij-Delfos, N.E., Reits, D., and Spekreijse, H. (1996). Early predictors of cerebral visual impairment in infants with cystic leukomalacia. *Neuropediatrics, 27*(1), 16-25.

Elliott, D.B. (1998). Contrast sensitivity and glare testing. In J. Benjamin, and I. Borish (eds.), *Clinical refraction* (pp. 203-241). Butterworths.

Elliott, D.B., and Bullimore, M.A. (1993). Assessing the reliability, discriminative ability, and validity of disability glare tests. *Investigative Ophthalmology and Visual Science, 34*(1), 108-119.

Elliott, D.B., and Whitaker, D. (1992a). Clinical contrast sensitivity chart evaluation. *Ophthalmic and Physiological Optics, 12*(3), 275-280.

Elliott, D.B., and Whitaker, D. (1992b). How useful are contrast sensitivity charts in optometric practice? Case reports. *Optometry and Vision Science, 69*(5), 378-385.

Elliott, D.B., Gilchrist, J., and Whitaker, D. (1989). Contrast sensitivity and glare sensitivity changes with three types of cataract morphology: Are these techniques necessary in a clinical evaluation of cataract? *Ophthalmic and Physiological Optics, 9*(1), 25-30.

Elliott, D.B., Hurst, M.A., and Weatherill, J. (1990). Comparing clinical tests of visual function in cataract with the patient's perceived visual disability. *Eye, 4*(Pt 5), 712-717.

Elliott, D.B., Sanderson, K., and Conkey, A. (1990). The reliability of the Pelli-Robson contrast sensitivity chart. *Ophthalmic and Physiological Optics, 10*(1), 21-24.

Elliott, D.B., Trukolo-Ilic, M., Strong, J.G., Pace, R., Plotkin, A., and Bevers, P. (1997). Demographic characteristics of the vision-disabled elderly. *Investigative Ophthalmology and Visual Science, 38*(12), 2566-2575.

Elliott, D.B., Yang, K.C., and Whitaker, D. (1995). Visual acuity changes throughout adulthood in normal, healthy eyes: Seeing beyond 6/6. *Optometry and Vision Science, 72*(3), 186-191.

Fawcett, G.M. (1996). *Living with disability in Canada: An economic portrait.* Hull, Quebec: Human Resources Development Canada, Office for Disability Issues.

Faye, E.E. (1984). *Clinical low vision* (2nd ed.). Boston, MA: Little, Brown.

Ferrell, K.A., Shaw, A.R., and Deitz, S.J. (1998). *Project PRISM: A longitudinal study of developmental patterns of children who are visually impaired.* (Report No. CFDA 84.0203c; H02310188). Greeley, CO: University of Northern Colorado, Division of Special Education.

Ferris, F.L., and Bailey, I.L. (1996). Standardizing the measurement of visual acuity for clinical research studies: Guidelines from the Eye Care Technology Forum. *Ophthalmology, 103*(1), 181-182.

Ferris, F.L., Kassoff, A., Bresnick, G.H., and Bailey, I.L. (1982). New visual acuity charts for clinical research. *American Journal of Ophthalmology, 94*(1), 91-96.

Fetter, W.P., van Hof-van Duin, J., Baerts, W., Heersema, D.J., and Wildervanck de Blecourt-Devilee, M. (1992). Visual acuity and visual field development after cryocoagulation in infants with retinopathy of prematurity. *Acta Paediatrica, 81*(1), 25-28.

Fielder, A.R., Fulton, A.B., and Mayer, D.L. (1991). Visual development of infants with severe ocular disorders. *Ophthalmology, 98*(8), 1306-1309.

Fielder, A.R., Russell-Eggitt, I.R., Dodd, K.L., and Mellor, D.H. (1985). Delayed visual maturation. *Transactions of the Ophthalmological Societies of the United Kingdom, 104*(Pt 6), 653-661.

Fine, E.M., and Peli, E. (1995). Scrolled and rapid serial visual presentation texts are read at similar rates by the visually impaired. *Journal of the Optical Society of America A. Optics and Image Science, 12*(10), 2286-2292.

Fischer, F.P., and Wagenaar, J.W. (1954). Binocular vision and fusion movements. *Documenta Ophthalmologica, 7*(8), 359-391.

Fitzgerald, A. (1989). Normal contrast sensitivity in 200 children aged seven to 13 years. *Australian Orthoptic Journal, 25*, 10-16.

Fitzgerald, A., Mitchell, J., and Munns, J. (1993). Pelli-Robson contrast sensitivity on 122 children aged six to twelve years. *Australian Orthoptic Journal, 29*, 40-45.

Fletcher, D.C., Schuchard, R.A., and Watson, G.R. (1999). Relative locations of macular scotomas near the PRL: Effects on low vision. *Journal of Rehabilitation Research and Development, 36*(4), 356-364.

Flom, M.C. (1991). Contour interaction and the crowding effect. *Problems in Optometry, 3*, 237-257.

Flom, M.C., and Neumaier, R.W. (1966). Prevalence of amblyopia. *Public Health Reports, 81*(4), 329-341.

Friedman, S.M., Munoz, B., Rubin, G.S., West, S.K., Bandeen-Roche, K., and Fried, L.P. (1999). Characteristics of discrepancies between self-reported visual function and measured reading speed. Salisbury Eye Evaluation Project Team. *Investigative Ophthalmology and Visual Science, 40*(5), 858-864.

Friendly, D.S. (1978). Preschool visual acuity screening tests. *Transactions of the American Ophthalmological Society, 76*, 383-480.

Fryback, D.G., Dasbach, E.J., Klein, R., Klein, B.E.K., Dorn, N., Peterson, K., and Martin, P.A. (1993). The Beaver Dam Health Outcomes Study: Initial catalog of health-state quality factors. *Medical Decision Making, 13*(2), 89-102.

Funkhouser, A., and Funkhouser, F. (1991). The effects of weighting the "mean defect" visual field index according to threshold variability in the central and midperipheral visual field. *Graefes Archive for Clinical and Experimental Ophthalmology, 229*(3), 228-231.

Geisler, W.S., and Chou, K.L. (1995). Separation of low-level and high-level factors in complex tasks: Visual search. *Psychological Review, 102*(2), 356-378.

Geruschat, D.R., and Smith, A. (1997). Low vision and mobility. In B.B. Blasch, W.R. Wiener, and R.L. Welsh (eds.), *Foundations of orientation and mobility* (2nd ed., pp. 60-103). New York, NY: AFB Press.

Geruschat, D.R., Turano, K.A., and Stahl, J.W. (1998). Traditional measures of mobility performance and retinitis pigmentosa. *Optometry and Vision Science, 75*(7), 525-537.

Gibson, J.J. (1958). Visually controlled locomotion and visual orientation in animals. *British Journal of Psychology, 49*, 182-194.

Gibson, J.J. (1979). *The ecological approach to visual perception*. Boston, MA: Houghton Mifflin.

Ginsburg, A.P. (1984). A new contrast sensitivity vision test chart. *American Journal of Optometry and Physiological Optics, 61*(6), 403-407.

Glaser, J.S., Savino, P.J., Sumers, K.D., McDonald, S.A., and Knighton, R.W. (1977). The photostress recovery test in the clinical assessment of visual function. *American Journal of Ophthalmology, 83*(2), 255-260.

Glovinsky, Y., Quigley, H.A., Drum, B., Bissett, R.A., and Jampel, H.D. (1992). A whole-field scotopic retinal sensitivity test for the detection of early glaucoma damage. *Archives of Ophthalmology, 110*(4), 486-490.

Goode, K.T., Sloane, M.E., Ball, K.K., Roenker, D.L., Roth, D.L., Myers, R.S., and Owsley, C. (1998). Useful field of view and other neurocognitive indicators of crash risk in older adults. *Journal of Clinical Psychology in Medical Settings, 5*, 425-440.

Graham, F.K., Berman, P.W., and Ernhart, C.B. (1960). Development in preschool children of the ability to copy forms. *Child Development, 31*, 339-359.

Gresset, J.A., and Meyer, F.M. (1994). Risk of accidents among elderly car drivers with visual acuity equal to 6/12 or 6/15 and lack of binocular vision. *Ophthalmic and Physiological Optics, 14*(1), 33-37.

Guion, R.M. (1965). Personnel testing. (pp. 288-295). New York, NY: McGraw-Hill.

Guth, D., and Rieser, J.J. (1997). Perception by blind and visually impaired pedestrians. In B.B. Blasch, W.R. Wiener, and R.L. Welsh (eds.), *Foundations of orientation and mobility* (2nd ed., pp. 9-38). New York, NY: AFB Press.

Gutierrez, P.R., Wilson, M.R., Johnson, C.A., Gordon, M.O., Cioffi, G.A., Ritch, R., Sherwood, M.B., Meng, K., and Mangione, C.M. (1997). Influence of glaucomatous visual field loss on health-related quality of life. *Archives of Ophthalmology, 115*(6), 777-784.

Haegerstrom-Portnoy, G. (1993). New procedures for evaluating vision functions of special populations. *Optometry and Vision Science, 70*(4), 306-314.

Haegerstrom-Portnoy, G., Brabyn, J.A., Schneck, M.E., and Jampolsky, A. (1997). The SKILL Card. An acuity test of reduced luminance and contrast. Smith-Kettlewell Institute Low Luminance. *Investigative Ophthalmology and Visual Science, 38*(1), 207-218.

Haegerstrom-Portnoy, G., Schneck, M.E., and Brabyn, J.A. (1999). Seeing into old age: Vision function beyond acuity. *Optometry and Vision Science, 76*(3), 141-158.

Haegerstrom-Portnoy, G., Schneck, M.E., Lott, L.A., and Brabyn, J.A. (2000). The relation between visual acuity and other spatial vision measures. *Optometry and Vision Science, 77*(12), 653-662.

Hall, H.L., Courage, M.L., and Adams, R.J. (2000). The predictive utility of the Teller acuity cards for assessing visual outcome in children with preterm birth and associated perinatal risks. *Vision Research, 40*(15), 2067-2076.

Hamadache, A. (1990). *Literacy, human rights and peace.* Geneva: International Bureau of Education.

Harland, S., Legge, G.E., and Luebker, A. (1998). Psychophysics of reading. XVII. Low-vision performance with four types of electronically magnified text. *Optometry and Vision Science, 75*(3), 183-190.

Hartmann, E.E., Dobson, V., Hainline L., Marsh-Tootle, W., Quinn, G.E., Ruttum, M.S., Schmidt, P.P., and Simons, K. (2000). Preschool vision screening: Summary of a Task Force report on behalf of the Maternal and Child Health Bureau and the National Eye Institute Task Force on Vision Screening in the Preschool Child. *Pediatrics, 106*(5), 1105-1116.

Harvey, E.M., Dobson, V., and Luna, B. (1997a). Long-term grating acuity and visual-field development in preterm children who experienced bronchopulmonary dysplasia. *Developmental Medicine and Child Neurology, 39*(3), 167-173.

Harvey, E.M., Dobson, V., and Narter, D.B. (1997c). The influence of a central stimulus on visual field measurements in children from 3.5 to 30 months of age. *Optometry and Vision Science, 74*(9), 768-774.

Harvey, E.M., Dobson, V., Luna, B., and Scher, M.S. (1997b). Grating acuity and visual-field development in children with intraventricular hemorrhage. *Developmental Medicine and Child Neurology, 39*(5), 305-312.

Havlik, R.J. (1986). Aging in the eighties, impaired senses for sound and light in persons age 65 years and older: Preliminary data from the Supplement on Aging to the National Health Interview Survey: United States, January-June 1984. In National Center for Health Statistics *Advance data from vital and health statistics* (Vol. 125, pp. 1-7).

Haymes, S.A., Guest, D., Heyes, A.D., and Johnston, A.W. (1996). Mobility of people with retinitis pigmentosa as a function of vision and psychological variables. *Optometry and Vision Science, 73*(10), 621-637.

Haymes, S.A., Johnston, A.W., and Heyes, A.D. (2001). The development of the Melbourne low-vision ADL index: A measure of vision disability. *Investigative Ophthalmology and Visual Science, 42*(6), 1215-1225.

Hedin, A., and Lovsund, P. (1986). Effects of visual field defects on driving performance. *Documenta Ophthalmologica Proceedings Series, 49*, 541-547.

Heersema, D.J., and van Hof-van Duin, J. (1990). Age norms for visual acuity in toddlers using the acuity card procedure. *Clinical Vision Sciences, 5*, 167-175.

Helveston, E.M., and Ellis, F.D. (1984). *Pediatric ophthalmology practice* (2nd ed.). St. Louis, MO: Mosby.

Henderson, R.L., and Burg, A. (1974). *Vision and audition in driving.* (Report No. DOT HS-801 265). Washington, DC: Department of Transportation.

Hered, R.W., Murphy, S., and Clancy, M. (1997). Comparison of the HOTV and Lea Symbols charts for preschool vision screening. *Journal of Pediatric Ophthalmology and Strabismus, 34*(1), 24-28.

Higgins, K.E., and Bailey, I.L. (2000). Visual disorders and performance in specific tasks requiring vision. In B. Silverstone, M.A. Lang, B.P. Rosenthal, and E.E. Faye (eds.), *The Lighthouse handbook on vision impairment and vision rehabilitation.* Oxford University Press.

Higgins, K.E., Wood, J.M., and Tait, A. (1998). Vision and driving: Selective effect of optical blur on different driving tasks. *Human Factors, 40*(2), 224-232.

Hills, B.L., and Burg, A. (1977). *A reanalysis of California driver vision data: General findings.* Crowthorn, England: Transport and Road Research Laboratory.

Hofstetter, H.W. (1973). From 20-20 to 6-6 or 4-4? *American Journal of Optometry and Archives of American Academy of Optometry, 50*(3), 212-221.

Hofstetter, H.W. (1976). Visual acuity and highway accidents. *Journal of the American Optometric Association, 47*(7), 887-893.

Holladay, J.T., Prager, T.C., Trujillo, J., and Ruiz, R.S. (1987). Brightness acuity test and outdoor visual acuity in cataract patients. *Journal of Cataract and Refractive Surgery, 13*(1), 67-69.

Home, R. (1978). Binocular summation: A study of contrast sensitivity, visual acuity and recognition. *Vision Research, 18*(5), 579-585.

Houtenville, A.J. (2001). *The economic experience of persons with chronic vision-related conditions*. Unpublished paper prepared for NRC Committee on Disability Determination for Individuals with Visual Impairments.

Howard, I.P., and Rogers, B.J. (1995). *Binocular vision and stereopsis*. New York, NY: Oxford University Press.

Hsia, Y., and Graham, C.H. (1965). Color Blindness. C.H. Graham (Editor), *Vision and visual perception* (pp. 395-413). New York: John Wiley and Sons.

Hubbard, M., McCloy, R., Campbell, J., Nottingham, J., Lewis, P., Rivkin, D., and Levine, J. (2000). Raleigh, NC: National O*Net Consortium.

Humphriss, D. (1987). Three South African studies on the relation between road accidents and drivers' vision. *Ophthalmic and Physiological Optics, 7*(1), 73-79.

Hunt, L., Morris, J.C., Edwards, D., and Wilson, B.S. (1993). Driving performance in persons with mild senile dementia of the Alzheimer type. *Journal of the American Geriatrics Society, 41*(7), 747-752.

Hyvärinen, L. (1994). Assessment of visually impaired infants. *Low Vision and Visual Rehabilitation, 7*, 219-225.

Hyvärinen, L. (1998a). *Assessment of low vision for educational purposes: Part 1.* Espoo, Finland: LEA-Test Ltd.

Hyvärinen, L. (1998b). *Assessment of low vision for educational purposes: Part 2.* Espoo, Finland: LEA-Test Ltd.

Illingworth, R.S. (1961). Delayed visual maturation. *Archives of Disease in Childhood, 36*, 407-409.

International Society for Low Vision Research and Rehabilitation. (1999). *Guide for the evaluation of visual impairment*. San Francisco, CA: Pacific Vision Foundation.

Ivers, R.Q., Mitchell, P., and Cumming, R.G. (1999). Sensory impairment and driving: The Blue Mountains Eye Study. *American Journal of Public Health, 89*(1), 85-87.

Ivers, R.Q., Norton, R., Cumming, R.G., Butler, M., and Campbell, A.J. (2000). Visual impairment and risk of hip fracture. *American Journal of Epidemiology, 152*(7), 633-639.

Jackson, G.R., Owsley, C., Cordle, E.P., and Finley, C.D. (1998). Aging and scotopic sensitivity. *Vision Research, 38*(22), 3655-3662.

Jacobson, S.G., Voigt, W.J., Parel, J.M., Apathy, P.P., Nghiem-Phu, L., Myers, S.W., and Patella, V.M. (1986). Automated light- and dark-adapted perimetry for evaluating retinitis pigmentosa. *Ophthalmology, 93*(12), 1604-1611.

Janz, N.K., Wren, P.A., Lichter, P.R., Musch, D.C., Gillespie, B.W., and Guire, K.E. (2001). Quality of life in newly diagnosed glaucoma patients: The Collaborative Initial Glaucoma Treatment Study. *Ophthalmology, 108*(5), 887-897.

Jette, A.M., and Branch, L.G. (1985). Impairment and disability in the aged. *Journal of Chronic Diseases, 38*(1), 59-65.

Johansson, K., Bronge, L., Lundberg, C., Persson, A., Seideman, M., and Viitanen, M. (1996). Can a physician recognize an older driver with increased crash risk potential? *Journal of the American Geriatrics Society, 44*(10), 1198-1204.

Johnson, C.A. (1993). *Final report on entry level vision standards for licensing and registration examiners in the California Department of Motor Vehicles.*

Johnson, C.A., and Brintz, N. (1994). California youth authority vision validation project: Final report. Entry level vision standards for group supervisors and youth counselors. *California Department of the Youth Authority technical report* (pp. 1-280).

Johnson, C.A., and Brintz, N. (1996). California Department of the Youth Authority vision study: Final report. Entry-level vision standards for parole agents. *California Department of the Youth Authority technical report* (pp. 1-256).

Johnson, C.A., and Brintz, N. (1997). California Department of the Youth Authority vision study: Final report. Entry-level vision standards for academic teachers in the California Department of the Youth Authority. *California Department of the Youth Authority technical report* (pp. 1-103).

Johnson, C.A., and Day, T. (1994a). California Department of Fish and Game vision study: Final report. Entry level vision standards for fish and game wardens. *California Department of Fish and Game technical report* (pp. 1-224).

Johnson, C.A., and Day, T. (1994b). California Department of Parks and Recreation vision study: Final report. Entry level vision standards for park rangers. *California Department of Parks and Recreation technical report* (pp. 1-234).

Johnson, C.A., and Keltner, J.L. (1983). Incidence of visual field loss in 20,000 eyes and its relationship to driving performance. *Archives of Ophthalmology, 101*(3), 371-375.

Johnson, C.A., Casson, E.J., and Zadnik, K. (1992). *Final report on entry level correctional officer vision standards for the California Department of Corrections.*

Johnson, C.A., Keltner, J.L., and Lewis, R.A. (1987a). Automated kinetic perimetry: An efficient method of evaluating peripheral visual field loss. *Applied Optics, 26,* 1409-1414.

Johnson, C.A., Keltner, J.L., and Lewis, R.A. (1987b). JAWS (Joint Automated Weighting Statistic): A method of converting results between automated perimeters. Documenta ophthalmologica proceedings series 49 *Seventh annual visual field symposium* (pp. 563-568). Dordrecht: Dr. W. Junk Publishers.

Johnson-Kuhn, J. (1995). The Blind Babies Foundation: Registry of early childhood visual impairment in central and northern California. In J. Bernas-Pierce (ed.), *The Hoyt-Akeson selected readings in pediatric ophthalmology*. San Francisco: Blind Babies Foundation.

Jones, R.K., and Lee, D.N. (1981). Why two eyes are better than one: The two views of binocular vision. *Journal of Experimental Psychology: Human Performance and Perception, 7*(1), 30-40.

Jose, R.T., and Rosenbloom, A.A. (1990). The visually impaired child. In A.A. Rosenbloom, and M.W. Morgan (eds.), *Principles and practice of pediatric optometry* (pp. 361-387). Philadelphia, PA: Lippincott.

Kahneman, D., Ben-Ishai, R., and Lotan, M. (1973). Relation of a test of attention to road accidents. *Journal of Applied Psychology, 58*(1), 113-115.

Kalloniatis, M., and Johnston, A.W. (1990). Visual characteristics of low vision children. *Optometry and Vision Science, 67*(1), 38-48.

Katsumi, O., Chedid, S.G., Kronheim, J.K., Henry, R.K., Denno, S., and Hirose, T. (1995). Correlating preferential looking visual acuity and visual behavior in severely visually handicapped children. *Acta Ophthalmologica Scandinavica, 73*(5), 407-413.

Keltner, J.L., and Johnson, C.A. (1987). Visual function, driving safety, and the elderly. *Ophthalmology, 94*(9), 1180-1188.

Keltner, J.L., Johnson, C.A., Spurr J.O., and Beck, R.W. (1999). Comparison of central and peripheral visual field properties in the optic neuritis treatment trial. *American Journal of Ophthalmology, 128*(5), 543-553.

Kington, R., Rogowski, J., Lillard, L., and Lee, P.P. (1997). Functional associations of "trouble seeing". *Journal of General Internal Medicine, 12*(2), 125-128.

Kirchner, C., Schmeidler, E., and Todorov, A. (1999). *Looking at employment through a lifespan telescope: Age, health, and employment status of people with serious visual impairment.* New York, NY: American Foundation for the Blind (subcontractor to Rehabilitation Research and Training Center on Bindness and Low Vision, Mississippi State University).

Klaver, C.C.W., Wolfs, R.C.W., Vingerling, J.R., Hofman, A., and de Jong, P.T.V.M. (1998). Age-specific prevalence and causes of blindness and visual impairment in an older population: The Rotterdam Study. *Archives of Ophthalmology, 116*(5), 653-658.

Klein, R., Klein, B.E.K., Linton, K.L.P., and DeMets, D.L. (1991). The Beaver Dam Eye Study: Visual acuity. *Ophthalmology, 98*(8), 1310-1315.

Klein, R., Moss, S.E., Klein, B.E.K., Gutierrez, P.R., and Mangione, C.M. (2001). The NEI-VFQ-25 in people with long-term type 1 diabetes mellitus: The Wisconsin Epidemiologic Study of Diabetic Retinopathy. *Archives of Ophthalmology, 119*(5), 733-740.

Koestler, F.A. (1976). *The unseen minority: A social history of blindness in America.* New York: D. McKay Co.

Kosnik, W., Winslow, L., Kine, D., Rasinski, K., and Sekuler, R. (1988). Visual changes in daily life throughout adulthood. *Journal of Gerontology, 43*(3), P63-P70.

Kremer, I., Nissenkorn, I., Lusky, M., and Yassur, Y. (1995). Late visual field changes following cryotherapy for retinopathy of prematurity stage 3. *British Journal of Ophthalmology, 79*(3), 267-269.

Kuyk, T., and Elliott, J.L. (1999). Visual factors and mobility in persons with age-related macular degeneration. *Journal of Rehabilitation Research and Development, 36*(4), 303-312.

Kuyk, T., Elliott, J.L., and Fuhr, P.S. (1998). Visual correlates of obstacle avoidance in adults with low vision. *Optometry and Vision Science, 75*(3), 174-182.

Kuyk, T., Elliott, J.L., Biehl, J., and Fuhr, P.S. (1996). Environmental variables and mobility performance in adults with low vision. *Journal of the American Optometric Association, 67*(7), 403-409.

Laberge-Nadeau, C., Dionne, G., Maag, U., Desjardins, D., Vanasse, C., and Ekoe, J.M. (1996). Medical conditions and the severity of commercial motor vehicle drivers' road accidents. *Accident Analysis and Prevention, 28*(1), 43-51.

LaForge, R.G., Spector, W.D., and Sternberg, J. (1992). The relationship of vision and hearing impairment to one-year mortality and functional decline. *Journal of Aging and Health, 4*(1), 126-148.

Lakowski, R., and Aspinall, P.A. (1969). Static perimetry in young children. *Vision Research, 9*(2), 305-311.

Lakowski, R., and Oliver, K. (1978). Identification of grades of fuel oil by red-green deficient observers. *Modern Problems in Ophthalmology, 19*, 101-104.

Landy, F.J. (1989). *Psychology of work behavior* (4th ed.). Pacific Grove, CA: Brooks/Cole Publishing Company.

LaPlante, M.P., and Carlson, D. (1996). *Disability statistics report: Disability in the United States: Prevalence and causes, 1992.* (Report No. 7). Washington, DC: U.S. Department of Education, National Institute on Disability and Rehabilitation Research.

Lawton, M.P., and Brody, E.M. (1969). Assessment of older people: Self-maintaining and instrumental activities of daily living. *Gerontologist, 9*(3), 179-186.

Leat, S.J., and Woo, G.C. (1997). The validity of current clinical tests of contrast sensitivity and their ability to predict reading speed in low vision. *Eye, 11*(Pt 6), 893-899.

Leat, S.J., Legge, G.E., and Bullimore, M.A. (1999). What is low vision? A re-evaluation of definitions. *Optometry and Vision Science, 76*(4), 198-211.

Lee, P.P., Spritzer, K., and Hays, R.D. (1997). The impact of blurred vision on functioning and well-being. *Ophthalmology, 104*(3), 390-396.

Legge, G.E. (1984a). Binocular contrast summation - I. Detection and discrimination. *Vision Research, 24* (4), 373-383.

Legge, G.E. (1984b). Binocular contrast summation - II. Quadratic summation. *Vision Research, 24*(4), 385-394.

Legge, G.E., and Rubin, G.S. (1986). Psychophysics of reading. IV. Wavelength effects in normal and low vision. *Journal of the Optical Society of America A. Optics and Image Science, 3*(1), 40-51.

Legge, G.E., Klitz, T.S., and Tjan, B.S. (1997). Mr. Chips: An ideal-observer model of reading. *Psychological Review, 104*(3), 524-553.

Legge, G.E., Madison, C., and Mansfield, J.S. (1999). Measuring Braille reading speed with the MNREAD test. *Visual Impairment Research, 1*, 131-145.

Legge, G.E., Mansfield, J.S., and Chung, S.T.L. (2001). Psychophysics of reading. XX. Linking letter recognition to reading speed in central and peripheral vision. *Vision Research, 41* (6), 725-743.

Legge, G.E., Pelli, D.G., Rubin, G.S., and Schleske, M.M. (1985). Psychophysics of reading. I. Normal vision. *Vision Research, 25*(2), 239-252.

Legge, G.E., Ross, J.A., Isenberg, L.M., and LaMay, J.M. (1992). Psychophysics of reading. Clinical predictors of low-vision reading speed. *Investigative Ophthalmology and Visual Science, 33*(3), 677-687.

Legge, G.E., Ross, J.A., Luebker, A., and LaMay, J.M. (1989). Psychophysics of reading. VIII. The Minnesota Low-Vision Reading Test. *Optometry and Vision Science, 66*(12), 843-853.

Legge, G.E., Ross, J.A., Maxwell, K.T., and Luebker, A. (1989). Psychophysics of reading. VII. Comprehension in normal and low vision. *Clinical Vision Sciences, 4*, 51-60.

Legge, G.E., Rubin, G.S., and Luebker, A. (1987). Psychophysics of reading. V. The role of contrast in normal vision. *Vision Research, 27*(7), 1165-1177.

Legge, G.E., Rubin, G.S., and Schleske, M.M. (1987). Contrast-polarity effects in low-vision reading. In G.C. Woo (ed.), *Low vision: Principles and applications; Proceedings of the International Symposium on Low Vision, University of Waterloo, June 25-27, 1986* (pp. 288-307). New York: Springer-Verlag.

Legge, G.E., Rubin, G.S., Pelli, D.G., and Schleske, M.M. (1985). Psychophysics of reading. II. Low vision. *Vision Research, 25*(2), 253-265.

Lewis, T.L., and Maurer, D. (1992). The development of the temporal and nasal visual fields during infancy. *Vision Research, 32*(5), 903-911.

Liao, F. (1973). Perimetry in young children. *Japanese Journal of Ophthalmology, 17*, 277-289.

Lie, I. (1977). Relation of visual acuity to illumination, contrast, and distance in the partially sighted. *American Journal of Optometry and Physiological Optics, 54*(8), 528-536.

Long, R.G., and Hill, E.W. (1997). Establishing and maintaining orientation for mobility. In B.B. Blasch, W.R. Wiener, and R.L. Welsh (eds.), *Foundations of orientation and mobility* (2nd ed.,). New York, NY: AFB Press.

Long, R.G., Rieser, J.J., and Hill, E.W. (1990). Mobility in individuals with moderate visual impairments. *Journal of Visual Impairment and Blindness, 84*(3), 111-118.

Loomis, J.M., Klatzky, R.L., Golledge, R.G., and Philbeck, J.W. (1999). Human navigation by path integration. In R.G. Golledge (ed.), *Wayfinding behavior: Cognitive mapping and other spatial processes* (pp. 125-151). Baltimore, MD: Johns Hopkins University Press.

Lovie-Kitchin, J.E., and Bowman, K.J. (1985). *Senile macular degeneration: Management and rehabilitation.* Boston, MA: Butterworth Publishers.

Lovie-Kitchin, J.E., and Brown, B. (2000). Repeatability and intercorrelations of standard vision tests as a function of age. *Optometry and Vision Science, 77*(8), 412-420.

Lovie-Kitchin, J.E., and Bailey, I.L. (1981). Task complexity and visual acuity in senile macular degeneration. *Australian Journal of Optometry, 64*, 235-242.

Lovie-Kitchin, J.E., Bowers, A.R., and Woods, R.L. (2000). Oral and silent reading performance with macular degeneration. *Ophthalmic and Physiological Optics, 20*(5), 360-370.

Lovie-Kitchin, J.E., Mainstone, J.C., Robinson, J.C., and Brown, B. (1990). What areas of the visual field are important for mobility in low vision patients. *Clinical Vision Sciences, 5*, 249-263.

Lovie-Kitchin, J.E., Woods, R.L., Hassan, S., and Soong, G. (2001). Visual field size and reduced mobility performance. *Investigative Ophthalmology and Visual Science Supplement, 42*, S857.

Luna, B., Dobson, V., Scher, M.S., and Guthrie, R.D. (1995). Grating acuity and visual field development in infants following perinatal asphyxia. *Developmental Medicine and Child Neurology, 37*(4), 330-344.

Lynn, J.R., Swanson, W.H., and Fellman, R.L. (1991). Evaluation of automated kinetic perimetry (AKP) with the Humphrey Field Analyzer. In R.P. Mills, and A. Heijl (eds.), *Perimetry update 1990/1991* (pp. 433-452). New York, NY: Kugler and Ghedini.

Maag, U., Vanasse, C., Dionne, G., and Laberge-Nadeau, C. (1997). Taxi-drivers' accidents: How binocular vision problems are related to their rate and severity in terms of the number of victims. *Accident Analysis and Prevention, 29*(2), 217-224.

Mackie, R.T., Saunders, K.J., Day, R.E., Dutton, G.N., and McCulloch, D.L. (1996). Visual acuity assessment of children with neurological impairment using grating and vanishing optotype acuity cards. *Acta Ophthalmologica Scandinavica, 74*(5), 483-487.

Mangione, C.M., Berry, S., Spritzer, K., Janz, N.K., Klein, R., Owsley, C., and Lee, P.P. (1998). Identifying the content area for the 51-item National Eye Institute Visual Function Questionnaire: Results from focus groups with visually impaired persons. *Archives of Ophthalmology, 116*(2), 227-233.

Mangione, C.M., Gutierrez, P.R., Lowe, G., Orav, E.J., and Seddon, J.M. (1999). Influence of age-related maculopathy on visual functioning and health-related quality of life. *American Journal of Ophthalmology, 128*(1), 45-53.

Mangione, C.M., Lee, P.P., Pitts, J., Gutierrez, P.R., Berry, S., and Hays, R.D. (1998). Psychometric properties of the National Eye Institute Visual Function Questionnaire (NEI-VFQ). *Archives of Ophthalmology, 116*(11), 1496-1504.

Mangione, C.M., Orav, E.J., Lawrence, M.G., Phillips, R.S., Seddon, J.M., and Goldman, L. (1995). Prediction of visual function after cataract surgery. A prospectively validated model. *Archives of Ophthalmology, 113*(10), 1305-1311.

Mangione, C.M., Phillips, R.S., Lawrence, M.G., Seddon, J.M., Orav, E.J., and Goldman, L. (1994). Improved visual function and attenuation of declines in health-related quality of life after cataract extraction. *Archives of Ophthalmology, 112*(11), 1419-1425.

Mangione, C.M., Phillips, R.S., Seddon, J.M., Lawrence, M.G., Cook, E.F., Dailey, R., and Goldman, L. (1992). Development of the "Activities of Daily Vision Scale": A measure of visual functional status. *Medical Care, 30*(12), 1111-1126.

Mansfield, J.S., Legge, G.E., and Bane, M.C. (1996). Psychophysics of reading. XV. Font effects in normal and low vision. *Investigative Ophthalmology and Visual Science, 37*(8), 1492-1501.

Marottoli, R.A., Cooney, M., Wagner, D.R., Doucette, J., and Tinetti, M.E. (1994). Predictors of automobile crashes and moving violations among elderly drivers. *Annals of Internal Medicine, 121*(11), 842-846.

Marottoli, R.A., Richardson, E.D., Stowe, M.H., Miller, E.G., Brass, L.M., Cooney, L.M., and Tinetti, M.E. (1998). Development of a test battery to identify older drivers at risk for self-reported adverse driving events. *Journal of the American Geriatrics Society, 46*(5), 562-568.

Marron, J.A., and Bailey, I.L. (1982). Visual factors and orientation-mobility performance. *American Journal of Optometry and Physiological Optics, 59*(5), 413-426.

Martin, L. (1999). Computerized method to measure glare and contrast sensitivity in cataract patients. *Journal of Cataract and Refractive Surgery, 25*(3), 411-415.

Marx, M.S., Werner, P., Cohen-Mansfield, J., and Hartmann, E.E. (1990). Visual acuity estimates in noncommunicative elderly persons. *Investigative Ophthalmology and Visual Science, 31*(3), 593-596.

Mash, C., and Dobson, V. (1998). Long-term reliability and predictive validity of the Teller Acuity Card procedure. *Vision Research, 38*(4), 619-626.

Massey, J.T., Moore, T.F., Parsons, V.L., and Tadros, W. (1989). *Design and estimation for the National Health Interview Survey, 1985-1994.* (Report No. PHS 89-1384). Hyattsville, MD: U.S. Department of Health and Human Services.

Massie, D.L., Campbell, K.L., and Williams, A.F. (1995). Traffic accident involvement rates by driver age and gender. *Accident Analysis and Prevention, 27*(1), 73-87.

Matsuo, H., Endo, N., Yokoi, T., and Tomonaga, M. (1998). Visual fields of the children. *L'Annee Therapeutique Et Clinique En Ophtalmologie, 25,* 186-193.

Maurer, D., and Lewis, T.L. (1991). The development of peripheral vision and its physiological underpinnings. In M.J. Weiss, and P.R. Zelazo (eds.), *Newborn attention: Biological constraints and the influence of experience* (pp. 218-255). Norwood, NJ: Ablex Publishing Corporation.

Mayer, D.L., and Dobson, V. (1982). Visual acuity development in infants and young children, as assessed by operant preferential looking. *Vision Research, 22*(9), 1141-1151.

Mayer, D.L., Beiser, A.S., Warner, A.F., Pratt, E.M., Raye, K.N., and Lang, J.M. (1995). Monocular acuity norms for the Teller Acuity Cards between ages one month and four years. *Investigative Ophthalmology and Visual Science, 36*(3), 671-685.

Mayer, D.L., Brar, M., Goldberg, M., and Palafox, G. (1991). Kinetic perimetry for pediatric populations: Humphrey and Goldmann perimetry. In *Technical digest on noninvasive assessment of the visual system* (Vol. 1, pp. 24-27). Washington, DC: Optical Society of America.

McAlpine, L.M., and Moore, C.L. (1995). The development of social understanding in children with visual impairments. *Journal of Visual Impairment and Blindness, 89*(4), 349-358.

McCloskey, L.W., Koepsell, T.D., Wolf, M.E., and Buchner, D.M. (1994). Motor vehicle collision injuries and sensory impairments of older drivers. *Age and Ageing, 23*(4), 267-273.

McCormick, E.J., and Jeanneret, P.R. (1988). Position Analysis Questionnaire. In S. Gael (ed.), *The job analysis handbook for business, industry and government* (pp. 825-842). New York: John Wiley and Sons.

McCormick, E.J., and PAQ Services, Inc. (1977). *Job analysis manual for the position analysis questionnaire (PAQ)*. Logan, UT: PAQ Services, Inc.

McCormick, E.J., Jeanneret, P.R., and Mecham, R.C. (1972). A study of job characteristics and job dimensions as based on the Position Analysis Questionnaire (PAQ). *Journal of Applied Psychology, 56*(4), 347-368.

McCormick, E.J., Mecham, R.C., and Jeanneret, P.R. (1977). *Technical manual for the position analysis questionnaire (PAQ)*. Logan, UT: PAQ Services, Inc.

McCormick, E.J., Mecham, R.C., and Jeanneret, P.R. (1998a). *Technical manual for the position analysis questionnaire (PAQ)* (2nd ed.). Logan, UT: PAQ Services, Inc.

McCormick, E.J., Mecham, R.C., and Jeanneret, P.R. (1998b). *User's manual for the position analysis questionnaire (PAQ)* (revised ed.). Logan, UT: PAQ Services, Inc.

McCulloch, D.L., Orbach, H., and Skarf, B. (1999). Maturation of the pattern-reversal VEP in human infants: a theoretical framework. *Vision Research, 39*(22), 3673-3680.

McDonald, M.A. (1986). Assessment of visual acuity in toddlers. *Survey of Ophthalmology, 31*(3), 189-210.

McDonald, M.A., Ankrum, C., Preston, K., Sebris, S.L., and Dobson, V. (1986). Monocular and binocular acuity estimation in 18- to 36-month-olds: Acuity card results. *American Journal of Optometry and Physiological Optics, 63*(3), 181-186.

McGraw, P.V., and Winn, B. (1993). Glasgow Acuity Cards: A new test for the measurement of letter acuity in children. *Ophthalmic and Physiological Optics, 13*(4), 400-404.

McKnight, A.J., Shinar, D., and Hilburn, B. (1991). The visual and driving performance of monocular and binocular heavy-duty truck drivers. *Accident Analysis and Prevention, 23*(4), 225-237.

McMurdo, M.E., and Gaskell, A. (1991). Dark adaptation and falls in the elderly. *Gerontology, 37*(4), 221-224.

Mihal, W.L., and Barrett, G.V. (1976). Individual differences in preceptual information processing and their relation to automobile accident involvement. *Journal of Applied Psychology, 61*(2), 229-233.

Miller, K.N., Shields, M.B., and Ollie, A.R. (1989). Automated kinetic perimetry with two peripheral isopters in glaucoma. *Archives of Ophthalmology, 107*(9), 1316-1320.

Mohan, K.M., and Dobson, V. (2000). When does measured visual field extent become adult-like? It depends. In V. Lakshminarayanan (ed.), *OSA trends optics and photonics vol. 35: Vision science and its applications* (pp. 2-17). Washington, DC: Optical Society of America.

Mohn, G., and van Hof-van Duin, J. (1986). Development of the binocular and monocular visual fields of human infants during the first year of life. *Clinical Vision Sciences, 1*, 51-64.

Morales, J., and Brown, S.M. (2001). The feasibility of short automated static perimetry in children. *Ophthalmology, 108*(1), 157-162.

Morales, J., Weitzman, M.L., and Gonzales de la Rosa, M. (2000). Comparison between Tendency Oriented Perimetry (TOP) and Octopus Threshold Perimetry. *Ophthalmology, 107*, 134-142.

Mortimer, R.G., and Fell, J.C. (1989). Older drivers: Their night fatal crash involvement and risk. *Accident Analysis and Prevention, 21*(3), 273-282.

Msall, M.E., Phelps, D.L., DiGaudio, K.M., Dobson, V., Tung, B., McClead, R.E., Quinn, G.E., Reynolds, J.D., Hardy, R.J., Palmer, E.A., and Cryotherapy for Retinopathy of Prematurity Cooperative Group. (2000). Severity of neonatal retinopathy of prematurity is predictive of neurodevelopmental functional outcome at age 5.5 years. *Pediatrics, 106*(5), 998-1005.

Munoz, B., West, S.K., Rodriguez, J., Sanchez, R., Broman, A.T., Snyder, R., and Klein, R. (2002). Blindness, visual impairment and the problem of uncorrected refractive error in a Mexican American population: Proyecto VER. *Investigative Ophthalmology and Visual Science, 43*(3), 608-614.

Musch, D.C., Farjo, A.A., Meyer, R.F., Waldo, M.N., and Janz, N.K. (1997). Assessment of health-related quality of life after corneal transplantation. *American Journal of Ophthalmology, 124*(1), 1-8.

Myers, V.S., Gidlewski, N., Quinn, G.E., Miller, D.L., and Dobson, V. (1999). Distance and near visual acuity, contrast sensitivity, and visual fields of 10-year-old children. *Archives of Ophthalmology, 117*(1), 94-99.

Nagi, S.Z. (1965). Some conceptual issues in disability and rehabilitation. In M.B. Sussman (ed.), *Sociology and rehabilitation*. Washington, DC: American Sociological Association.

Nagi, S.Z. (1976). An epidemiology of disability among adults in the United States. *The Milbank Memorial Fund Quarterly. Health and Society, 54*(4), 439-467.

National Materials Advisory Board, and National Research Council. (1995). *Currency features for visually impaired people*. Washington, DC: National Academy Press.

National Research Council. (1980). Recommended standard procedures for the clinical measurement and specification of visual acuity. *Advances in Ophthalmology, 41*, 103-148.

National Research Council. (1994). *Measurement of visual field and visual acuity for disability determination*. Washington, DC: National Academy Press.

Neumann, A.C., McCarty, G.R., Locke, J., and Cobb, B. (1988). Glare disability devices for cataractous eyes: A consumer's guide. *Journal of Cataract and Refractive Surgery, 14*(2), 212-216.

Norcia, A.M. (1994). Vision testing by visual evoked potential techniques. In S.J. Isenberg (ed.), *The eye in infancy* (2nd ed., pp. 157-173). St. Louis, MO: Mosby.

Norcia, A.M., and Tyler, C.W. (1985). Spatial frequency sweep VEP: Visual acuity during the first year of life. *Vision Research, 25*(10), 1399-1408.

Norcia, A.M., Tyler, C.W., and Hamer, R.D. (1990). Development of contrast sensitivity in the human infant. *Vision Research, 30*(10), 1475-1486.

North, R.V. (1985). The relationship between the extent of visual field and driving performance: A review. *Ophthalmic and Physiological Optics, 5*(2), 205-210.

North, R.V. (1993). *Work and the eye*. Oxford, England: Oxford University Press.

O'Dell, C.D., Harshaw, K., and Boothe, R.G. (1993). Vision screening of individuals with severe or profound mental retardation. *Mental Retardation, 31*(3), 154-160.

Odenheimer, G.L., Beaudet, M., Jette, A.M., Albert, M.S., Grande, L., and Minaker, K.L. (1994). Performance-based driving evaluation of the elderly driver: Safety, reliability, and driving. *Journal of Gerontology, 49*(4), M153-M159.

Odom, J.V., Charlton, J., Leys, M., Ellis, B., and Fenstermacher, P. (1998). *A comparison of manual and automated kinetic perimetry.* (Report No. SSA-RFP-98-3537).

Orel-Bixler, D., Haegerstrom-Portnoy, G., and Hall A. (1989). Visual assessment of the multiply handicapped patient. *Optometry and Vision Science, 66*(8), 530-536.

Owsley, C. (1994). Vision and driving in the elderly. *Optometry and Vision Science, 71*(12), 727-735.

Owsley, C., and McGwin, G. (1999). Vision impairment and driving. *Survey of Ophthalmology, 43*(6), 535-550.

Owsley, C., and Sloane, M.E. (1987). Contrast sensitivity, acuity and the perception of "real-world" targets. *British Journal of Ophthalmology, 71*(10), 791-796.

Owsley, C., Ball, K.K., McGwin, G., Sloane, M.E., Roenker, D.L., White, M.F., and Overley, E.T. (1998). Visual processing impairment and risk of motor vehicle crash among older adults. *The Journal of the American Medical Association, 279*(14), 1083-1088.

Owsley, C., Ball, K.K., Sloane, M.E., Roenker, D.L., and Bruni, J.R. (1991). Visual/cognitive correlates of vehicle accidents in older drivers. *Psychology and Aging, 6*(3), 403-415.

Owsley, C., Jackson, G.R., White, M.F., Feist, R., and Edwards, D. (2001). Delays in rod-mediated dark adaptation in early age-related maculopathy. *Ophthalmology, 108*(7), 1196-1202.

Owsley, C., McGwin, G., and Ball, K.K. (1998). Vision impairment, eye disease, and injurious motor vehicle crashes in the elderly. *Ophthalmic Epidemiology, 5*(2), 101-113.

Owsley, C., McGwin, G., Sloane, M.E., Stalvey, B.T., and Wells, J. (2001). Timed instrumental activities of daily living (TIADL) tasks: Relationship to visual function in older adults. *Optometry and Vision Science, 78*(5), 350-359.

Owsley, C., Sekuler, R., and Boldt, C. (1981). Aging and low-contrast vision: Face perception. *Investigative Ophthalmology and Visual Science, 21*(2), 362-365.

Owsley, C., Sloane, M.E., McGwin, G., and Ball, K.K. (2001). Timed instrumental activities of daily living (TIADL) tasks: Relationship to cognitive function and everyday performance assessments. *Journals of Gerontology. Series B, Psychological Sciences and Social Sciences.*

Owsley, C., Stalvey, B.T., Wells, J., Sloane, M.E., and McGwin, G. (2001). Visual risk factors for crash involvement in older drivers with cataract. *Archives of Ophthalmology, 119*(6), 881-887.

Padmos, P., and Milders, M.V. (1992). Quality criteria for simulator images: A literature review. *Human Factors, 34*(6), 727-748.

Papp, A., Kis, K., and Nemeth, J. (2001). Conversion formulas between automated-perimetry indexes as measured by two different types of instrument. *Ophthalmologica, 215*(2), 87-90.

Pardhan, S. (1993). Binocular performance in patients with unilateral cataract using the Regan test: Binocular summation and inhibition with low-contrast charts. *Eye, 7*(Pt 1), 59-62.

Parrish, R.K., Gedde, S.J., Scott, I.U., Feuer, W.J., Schiffman, J.C., Mangione, C.M., and Montenegro-Piniella, A. (1997). Visual function and quality of life among patients with glaucoma. *Archives of Ophthalmology, 115*(11), 1447-1455.

Peli, E., Goldstein, R.B., Young, G.M., Trempe, C.L., and Buzney, S.M. (1991). Image enhancement for the visually impaired: Simulations and experimental results. *Investigative Ophthalmology and Visual Science, 32*(8), 2337-2350.

Peli, E., Lee, E., Trempe, C.L., and Buzney, S.M. (1994). Image enhancement for the visually impaired: The effects of enhancement on face recognition. *Journal of the Optical Society of America A. Optics and Image Science, 11*(7), 1929-1939.

Pelli, D.G. (1987). The visual requirements of mobility. In *Low vision: Principles and application: Proceedings of the International Symposium on Low Vision* (pp. 134-145). New York: Springer-Verlag.

Pelli, D.G., Robson, J.G., and Wilkins, A.J. (1988). The design of a new letter chart for measuring contrast sensitivity. *Clinical Vision Sciences, 2*(3), 187-199.

Petre, K.L., Hazel, C.A., Fine, E.M., and Rubin, G.S. (2000). Reading with eccentric fixation is faster in inferior visual field than in left visual field. *Optometry and Vision Science, 77*(1), 34-39.

Pitts, D.G. (1993). Sunglasses for ocular protection. In D.G. Pitts, and R.N. Kleinstein (eds.), *Environmental vision: Interactions of the eye, vision, and the environment.* Boston, MA: Butterworth-Heinemann.

Pokorny, J., Smith, V.C., Verriest, G., and Pinkers, A. (1979). *Congenital and acquired color vision defects.* New York, NY: Grune and Stratton.

Powls, A., Botting, N., Cooke, R.W., Stephenson, G., and Marlow, N. (1997). Visual impairment in very low birthweight children. *Archives of Disease in Childhood: Fetal and Neonatal Edition, 76*(2), F82-F87.

Quinn, G.E., Dobson, V., Hardy, R.J., Tung, B., Phelps, D.L., Palmer, E.A., and CRYO-Retinopathy of Prematurity Cooperative Group. (1996). Visual fields measured with double-arc perimetry in eyes with threshold retinopathy of prematurity from the cryotherapy for retinopathy of prematurity trial. *Ophthalmology, 103*(9), 1432-1437.

Quinn, G.E., Fea, A.M., and Minguini, N. (1991). Visual fields in 4- to 10-year-old children using Goldmann and double-arc perimeters. *Journal of Pediatric Ophthalmology and Strabismus, 28*(6), 314-319.

Quinn, G.E., Miller, D.L., Evans, J.A., Tasman, W.E., McNamara, J.A., and Schaffer, D.B. (1996). Measurement of Goldmann visual fields in older children who received cryotherapy as infants for threshold retinopathy of prematurity. *Archives of Ophthalmology, 114*(4), 425-428.

Rahmani, B., Tielsch, J.M., Katz, J., Gottsch, J.D., Quigley, H.A., Javitt, J.C., and Sommer, A. (1996). The cause-specific prevalence of visual impairment in an urban population: The Baltimore eye survey. *Ophthalmology, 103*(11), 1721-1726.

Rayner, K., and Bertera, J.H. (1979). Reading without a fovea. *Science, 206*(4417), 468-469.

Regan, D. (1991a). Spatial vision. In J.R. Cronly-Dillon *Vision and visual dysfunction.* Boca Raton: CRC Press.

Regan, D. (1991b). Spatiotemporal abnormalities of vision in patients with multiple sclerosis. In D. Regan (ed.), *Vision and visual dysfunction, Volume 10: Spatial vision* (pp. 239-247). London: MacMillan Press.

Reinach, S.J., Rizzo, M., and McGehee, D.V. (1997). Driving with Alzheimer disease: The anatomy of a crash. *Alzheimer Disease and Associated Disorders, 11*(Suppl 1), 21-27.

Richards, W. (1970). Stereopsis and stereoblindness. *Experimental Brain Research, 10*(4), 380-388.

Rieser, J.J., Hill, E.W., Talor, C.R., Bradfield, A., and Rosen, S. (1992). Visual experience, visual field size, and the development of nonvisual sensitivity to the spatial structure of outdoor neighborhoods explored by walking. *Journal of Experimental Psychology: General, 121*(2), 210-221.

Rizzo, M., Reinach, S.J., McGehee, D.V., and Dawson, J. (1997). Simulated car crashes and crash predictors in drivers with Alzheimer disease. *Archives of Neurology, 54*(5), 545-551.

Rodriguez, J., Sanchez, R., Munoz, B., West, S.K., Broman, A.T., Snyder, R., Klein, R., and Quigley, H. (2002). Causes of blindness and visual impairment in a population based sample of US Hispanics. *Ophthalmology, 109,* 737-743.

Rogers, G.L., Bremer, D.L., and Leguire, L.E. (1987). Contrast sensitivity functions in normal children with the Vistech method. *Journal of Pediatric Ophthalmology and Strabismus, 24*(5), 216-219.

Rogers, P.N., Ratz, M., and Janke, M.K. (1987). *Accident and conviction rates of visually impaired heavy-vehicle operators.* Sacramento, CA: State of California, Department of Motor Vehicles, Research and Development Office.

Rohaly, A.M., and Owsley, C. (1993). Modeling the contrast-sensitivity functions of older adults. *Journal of the Optical Society of America A. Optics and Image Science, 10*(7), 1591-1599.

Rosow, I., and Breslau, N. (1966). A Guttman health scale for the aged. *Journal of Gerontology, 21*(4), 556-559.

Rubin, G.S. (1988). Reliability and sensitivity of clinical contrast sensitivity tests. *Clinical Vision Sciences, 2*(3), 169-177.

Rubin, G.S., and Legge, G.E. (1989). Psychophysics of reading. VI. The role of contrast in low vision. *Vision Research, 29*(1), 79-91.

Rubin, G.S., and Schuchard, R.A. (1989). Does contrast sensitivity predict face recognition performance in low vision observers? In *Noninvasive assessment of the visual system* (pp. 130-133). Washington, DC: Optical Society of America.

Rubin, G.S., and Turano, K.A. (1992). Reading without saccadic eye movements. *Vision Research, 32*(5), 895-902.

Rubin, G.S., and Turano, K.A. (1994). Low vision reading with sequential word presentation. *Vision Research, 34*(13), 1723-1733.

Rubin, G.S., Adamsons, I.A., and Stark, W.J. (1993). Comparison of acuity, contrast sensitivity, and disability glare before and after cataract surgery. *Archives of Ophthalmology, 111*(1), 56-61.

Rubin, G.S., Bandeen-Roche, K., Huang, G.H., Munoz, B., Schein, O.D., Fried, L.P., and West, S.K. (2001). The association of multiple visual impairments with self-reported visual disability: SEE project. *Investigative Ophthalmology and Visual Science, 42*(1), 64-72.

Rubin, G.S., Bandeen-Roche, K., Prasada-Rao, P., and Fried, L.P. (1994). Visual impairment and disability in older adults. *Optometry and Vision Science, 71*(12), 750-760.

Rubin, G.S., Keyl, P.M., Munoz, B., Bandeen-Roche, K., Huang, G.H., West, S.K., and SEE Project Team. (1999). The association of vision, cognition, and attention with crashes in an older American population: SEE Study. *Investigative Ophthalmology and Visual Science Supplement, 40*, S387.

Rubin, G.S., Munoz, B., Bandeen-Roche, K., and West, S.K. (2000). Monocular versus binocular visual acuity as measures of vision impairment and predictors of visual disability. *Investigative Ophthalmology and Visual Science, 41*(11), 3327-3334.

Rubin, G.S., West, S.K., Munoz, B., Bandeen-Roche, K., Zeger, S., Schein, O.D., and Fried, L.P. (1997). A comprehensive assessment of visual impairment in a population of older Americans: The SEE Study: Salisbury Eye Evaluation Project. *Investigative Ophthalmology and Visual Science, 38*(3), 557-568.

Rudberg, M.A., Furner, S.E., Dunn, J.E., and Cassel, C.K. (1993). The relationship of visual and hearing impairments to disability: An analysis using the longitudinal study of aging. *Journal of Gerontology, 48*(6), M261-M265.

Rudel, R.G., and Teuber, H.L. (1963). Discrimination of direction of line in children. *Journal of Comparative and Physiological Psychology, 56*, 892-898.

Rumney, N.J., and Leat, S.J. (1994). Why do low vision patients still read slowly with a low vision aid? In A.C. Kooijman (ed.), *Low vision: Research and new developments in rehabilitation* (pp. 269-274). Amsterdam: IOS Press.

Russell-Eggitt, I.M., Mackey, D.A., Taylor, D.S., Timms, C., and Walker, J.W. (2000). Vigabatrin-associated visual field defects in children. *Eye, 14*(Pt 3a), 334-339.

Rydberg, A., and Han, Y. (1999). Assessment of contrast sensitivity in children aged 3 years 9 months - 6 years with normal vision, visual impairment due to ocular disease and strabismic amblyopia. *Strabismus, 7*(2), 79-95.

Safran, A.B., Laffi, G.L., Bullinger, A., Viviani, P., de Weisse, C., Desangles, D., Tschopp, C., and Mermoud, C. (1996). Feasibility of automated visual field examination in children between 5 and 8 years of age. *British Journal of Ophthalmology, 80*(6), 515-518.

Salive, M.E., Guralnik, J., Glynn, R.J., Christen, W., Wallace, R.B., and Ostfeld, A.M. (1994). Association of visual impairment with mobility and physical function. *Journal of the American Geriatrics Society, 42*(3), 287-292.

Salomão, S.R., and Ventura, D.F. (1995). Large sample population age norms for visual acuities obtained with Vistech-Teller Acuity Cards. *Investigative Ophthalmology and Visual Science, 36*(3), 657-670.

Scharre, J.E., and Creedon, M.P. (1992). Assessment of visual function in autistic children. *Optometry and Vision Science, 69*(6), 433-439.

Scharre, J.E., Cotter, S.A., Block, S.S., and Kelly, S.A. (1990). Normative contrast sensitivity data for young children. *Optometry and Vision Science, 67*(11), 826-832.

Scher, M.S., Dobson, V., Carpenter, N.A., and Guthrie, R.D. (1989). Visual and neurological outcome of infants with periventricular leukomalacia. *Developmental Medicine and Child Neurology, 31*(3), 353-365.

Schiefer, U., Strasburger, H., Becker, S.T., Vonthein, R., Schiller, J., Dietrich, T.J., and Hart, W. (2001). Reaction time in automated kinetic perimetry: Effects of stimulus luminance, eccentricity, and movement direction. *Vision Research, 41*(16), 2157-2164.

Schneck, M.E., Haegerstrom-Portnoy, G., Katz, B., and Brabyn, J.A. (1993). Optic neuritis: Small reductions in luminance cause large losses in vision function. In *Technical digest on noninvasive assessment of the visual system* (Vol. 11pp. 352-355). Washington, DC: Optical Society of America.

Schoelkopf, B., and Mallot, H.A. (1995). View-based cognitive mapping and path planning. *Adaptive Behavior, 3*(3), 311-348.

Scott, I.U., Schein, O.D., West, S.K., Bandeen-Roche, K., Enger, C., and Folstein, M.F. (1994). Functional status and quality of life measurement among ophthalmic patients. *Archives of Ophthalmology, 112*(3), 329-335.

Scott, I.U., Smiddy, W.E., Schiffman, J.C., Feuer, W.J., and Pappas, C.J. (1999). Quality of life of low-vision patients and the impact of low-vision services. *American Journal of Ophthalmology, 128*(1), 54-62.

Sheedy, J.E., Bailey, I.L., and Raasch, T.W. (1984). Visual acuity and chart luminance. *American Journal of Optometry and Physiological Optics, 61*(9), 595-600.

Sheedy, J.E., Bailey, I.L., Buri, M., and Bass, E.B. (1986). Binocular vs. monocular task performance. *American Journal of Optometry and Physiological Optics, 63*(10), 839-846.

Shinar, D. (1977). *Driver visual limitations, diagnosis and treatment.* (Report No. DOT-HS-5-01275). Washington, DC: National Highway Traffic Safety Administration.

Shinar, D., and Schieber, F. (1991). Visual requirements for safety and mobility of older drivers. *Human Factors, 33*(5), 507-519.

Shinar, D., Mayer, R.M., and Treat, J.R. (1975). Reliability and validity assessments of a newly developed battery of driving-related vision tests. Presented at *19th Annual Meeting of the American Association for Automotive Medicine.*

Sloan, L.L. (1959). New test charts for the measurement of visual acuity at far and near distances. *American Journal of Ophthalmology, 48*, 807-813.

Sloan, L.L. (1969). Variation of acuity with luminance in ocular diseases and anomalies. *Documenta Ophthalmologica, 26*, 384-393.

Sloan, L.L., and Brown, D.J. (1963). Reading cards for selection of optical aids for the partially sighted. *American Journal of Ophthalmology, 55*, 1187-1199.

Sloan, L.L., Habel, A., and Feiock, K. (1973). High illumination as an auxiliary reading aid in diseases of the macula. *American Journal of Ophthalmology, 76*(5), 745-747.

Sloane, M.E., Ball, K.K., Owsley, C., Bruni, J.R., and Roenker, D.L. (1992). The Visual Activities Questionnaire: Developing an instrument for assessing problems in everyday visual tasks. In *Noninvasive assessment of the visual system technical digest* (Vol. 1, pp. 26-29). Washington, DC: Optical Society of America.

Sloane, M.E., Owsley, C., and Alvarez, S.L. (1988). Aging, senile miosis and spatial contrast sensitivity at low luminance. *Vision Research, 28*(11), 1235-1246.

Snell, A.C. (1925). Visual efficiency of various degrees of subnormal visual acuity: Its effect on earning ability. *The Journal of the American Medical Association, 85*(18), 1367-1373.

Snell, A.C., and Sterling, S. (1925). The percentage evaluation of macular vision. *Archives of Ophthalmology, 54*, 443-461.

Social Security Administration. (1999). *Social Security and Supplemental Security Income Disability Programs: Managing for today, planning for tomorrow*. Washington, DC: Social Security Administration.

Social Security Administration. (2001). *Disability evaluation under social security.* (Report No. SSA Publication No. 64-039, ICN 468600). Washington. DC: Social Security Administration, Office of Disability.

Social Security Advisory Board. (2001a). *Charting the future of social security's disability programs: The need for fundamental change.* Washington, DC: Social Security Advisory Board.

Social Security Advisory Board. (2001b). *Disability decision making: Data and materials.* Washington, DC: Social Security Advisory Board.

Steinberg, E.P., Tielsch, J.M., Schein, O.D., Javitt, J.C., Sharkey, P., Cassard, S.D., Legro, M.W., Diener-West, M., Bass, E.B., Damiano, A.M., et al. (1994). The VF-14. An index of functional impairment in patients with cataract. *Archives of Ophthalmology, 112*(5), 630-638.

Steinmetz, R.L., Haimovici, R., Jubb, C., Fitzke, F.W., and Bird, A.C. (1993). Symptomatic abnormalities of dark adaptation in patients with age-related Bruch's membrane change. *British Journal of Ophthalmology, 77*(9), 549-554.

Strelow, E.R. (1985). What is needed for a theory of mobility: Direct perception and cognitive maps: Lessons from the blind. *Psychological Review, 92*(2), 226-248.

Sumi, I., Matsumoto, S., Okajima, O., and Shirato, S. (2000). The relationship between visual disability and visual scores in patients with retinitis pigmentosa. *Japanese Journal of Ophthalmology, 44*(1), 82-87.

Szlyk, J.P., and Brigell, M. (1992). Evaluating the driving skills of patients with homonymous hemianopsia using an interactive simulator. *Investigative Ophthalmology and Visual Science Supplement, 33*, 1226.

Szlyk, J.P., Arditi, A., Coffey Bucci, P., and Laderman, D. (1990). Self-report in functional assessment of low vision. *Journal of Visual Impairment and Blindness, 84*(2), 61-66.

Szlyk, J.P., Seiple, W., Fishman, G.A., Alexander, K.R., Grover, S., and Mahler, C.L. (2001). Perceived and actual performance of daily tasks: Relationship to visual function tests in individuals with retinitis pigmentosa. *Ophthalmology, 108*(1), 65-75.

Takayama, S., Tachibana, H., and Yamamoto, M. (1991). Changes in the visual field after photocoagulation or cryotherapy in children with retinopathy of prematurity. *Journal of Pediatric Ophthalmology and Strabismus, 28*(2), 96-100.

Taylor, R.H., Misson, G.P., and Moseley, M.J. (1991). Visual acuity and contrast sensitivity in cataract: Summation and inhibition of visual performance. *Eye, 5*(Pt 6), 704-707.

Teller, D.Y. (1997). First glances: The vision of infants. The Friedenwald lecture. *Investigative Ophthalmology and Visual Science, 38*(11), 2183-2203.

Teller, D.Y., McDonald, M.A., Preston, K., Sebris, S.L., and Dobson, V. (1986). Assessment of visual acuity in infants and children: The acuity card procedure. *Developmental Medicine and Child Neurology, 28*(6), 779-789.

Thinus-Blanc, C., and Gaunet, F. (1997). Representation of space in blind persons: Vision as a spatial sense? *Psychological Bulletin, 121*(1), 20-42.

Thompson, J.R., Woodruff, G., Hiscox, F.A., Strong, N., and Minshull, C. (1991). The incidence and prevalence of amblyopia detected in childhood. *Public Health, 105*(6), 455-462.

Tielsch, J.M., Sommer, A., Witt, K.A., Katz, J., and Royall, R.M. (1990). Blindness and visual impairment in an American urban population: The Baltimore eye survey. *Archives of Ophthalmology, 108*(2), 286-290.

Tinker, M.A. (1963). *Legibility of print.* Ames, IA: Iowa State University Press.

Tolman, E.C. (1948). Cognitive maps in rats and men. *Psychological Review, 55*, 189-208.

Trauzettel-Klosinski, S., and Brendler, K. (1998). Eye movements in reading with hemianopic field defects: The significance of clinical parameters. *Graefes Archive for Clinical and Experimental Ophthalmology, 236*(2), 91-102.

Trauzettel-Klosinski, S., Teschner, C., and Zrenner, E. (1994). Reading strategies in normal subjects and in patients with macular scotoma assessed by two new methods of registration. *Neuro-Ophthalmology, 14*(1), 15-30.

Trupin, L., Sebesta, D.S., Yelin, E., and LaPlante, M.P. (1997). *Disability statistics report: Trends in labor force participation among persons with disabilities, 1983-1994.* (Report No. 10). San Francisco, CA: Disability Statistics Rehabilitation Research and Training Center, Institute for Health and Aging, University of California.

Tschopp, C., Safran, A.B., Viviani, P., Bullinger, A., Reicherts, M., and Mermoud, C. (1998a). Automated visual field examination in children aged 5-8 years. Part I: Experimental validation of a testing procedure. *Vision Research, 38*(14), 2203-2210.

Tschopp, C., Safran, A.B., Viviani, P., Reicherts, M., Bullinger, A., and Mermoud, C. (1998b). Automated visual field examination in children aged 5-8 years. Part II: Normative values. *Vision Research, 38*(14), 2211-2218.

Tschopp, C., Viviani, P., Reicherts, M., Bullinger, A., Rudaz, N., Mermoud, C., and Safran, A.B. (1999). Does visual sensitivity improve between 5 and 8 years? A study of automated visual field examination. *Vision Research, 39*(6), 1107-1119.

Turano, K.A., Dagnelie, G.M., and Herdman, S.J. (1996). Visual stabilization of posture in persons with central visual field loss. *Investigative Ophthalmology and Visual Science, 37*(8), 1483-1491.

Turano, K.A., Geruschat, D.R., and Stahl, J.W. (1998). Mental effort required for walking: Effects of retinitis pigmentosa. *Optometry and Vision Science, 75*(12), 879-886.

Turano, K.A., Herdman, S.J., and Dagnelie, G.M. (1993). Visual stabilization of posture in retinitis pigmentosa and in artificially restricted visual fields. *Investigative Ophthalmology and Visual Science, 34*(10), 3004-3010.

Turano, K.A., Rubin, G.S., and Quigley, H.A. (1999). Mobility performance in glaucoma. *Investigative Ophthalmology and Visual Science, 40*(12), 2803-2809.

U.S. Department of Education, Office of Special Education Programs. (2000). *To assure the free appropriate public education of all children with disabilities: Twenty-second annual report to Congress on the implementation of the Individuals with Disabilities Education Act.* Washington, DC: U.S. Department of Education.

U.S. Employment Service. (1991). *Dictionary of occupational titles* (4th ed.). Washington, DC: U.S. Department of Labor, Employment and Training Administration, U.S. Employment Service.

van Hof-van Duin, J., and Mohn, G. (1984). Visual defects in children after cerebral hypoxia. *Behavioural Brain Research, 14*(2), 147-155.

van Hof-van Duin, J., Cioni, G., Bertuccelli, B., Fazzi, B., Romano, C., and Boldrini, A. (1998). Visual outcome at 5 years of newborn infants at risk of cerebral visual impairment. *Developmental Medicine and Child Neurology, 40*(5), 302-309.

van Hof-van Duin, J., Heersema, D.J., Groenendaal, F., Baerts, W., and Fetter, W.P. (1992). Visual field and grating acuity development in low-risk preterm infants during the first 2 1/2 years after term. *Behavioural Brain Research, 49*(1), 115-122.

Vanhatalo, S., Pääkkönen, L., and Nousiainen, I. (1999). Visual field constriction in children treated with vigabatrin. *Neurology, 52*(8), 1713-1714.

Verghese, P., and Nakayama, K. (1994). Stimulus discriminability in visual search. *Vision Research, 34*(18), 2453-2467.

Viisola, M. (2000). *Statistics on children with visual impairments*. New York, NY: Lighthouse International.

Vingrys, A.J., and Cole, B.L. (1988). Are colour vision standards justified for the transport industry? *Ophthalmic and Physiological Optics, 8*(3), 257-274.

West, S.K., Munoz, B., Rubin, G.S., Schein, O.D., Bandeen-Roche, K., Zeger, S., German, S., and Fried, L.P. (1997). Function and visual impairment in a population-based study of older adults. The SEE project. Salisbury Eye Evaluation. *Investigative Ophthalmology and Visual Science, 38*(1), 72-82.

West, S.K., Rubin, G.S., Broman, A.T., Munoz, B., Bandeen Roche, K., and Turano, K.A. (in press). How does visual impairment affect performance on tasks of everyday life? The SEE project. *Archives of Ophthalmology*.

West, S.K., Rubin, G.S., Munoz, B., Abraham, D., and Fried, L.P. (1997). Assessing functional status: Correlation between performance on tasks conducted in a clinic setting and performance on the same task conducted at home. The Salisbury Eye Evaluation Project Team. *Journals of Gerontology. Series A, Biological Sciences and Medical Sciences, 52*(4), M209-M217.

Westall, C.A., Ainsworth, J.R., and Buncic, J.R. (2000). Which ocular and neurologic conditions cause disparate results in visual acuity scores recorded with visually evoked potential and teller acuity cards? *Journal of the American Association for Pediatric Ophthalmology and Strabismus, 4*(5), 395-301.

Whittaker, S.G., and Lovie-Kitchin, J.E. (1993). Visual requirements for reading. *Optometry and Vision Science, 70*(1), 54-65.

Wiener, W.R., and Lawson, G. (1997). Audition for the traveler who is visually impaired. In B.B. Blasch, W.R. Wiener, and R.L. Welsh (eds.), *Foundations of orientation and mobility* (2nd ed.). New York, NY: AFB Press.

Wild, J.M., Pacey, I.E., O'Neill, E.C., and Cunliffe, I.A. (1999). The SITA perimetric threshold algorithms in glaucoma. *Investigative Ophthalmology and Visual Science, 40*(9), 1998-2009.

Wilson, M.R., Coleman, A.L., Yu, F., Bing, E.G., Sasaki, I.F., Berlin, K., Winters, J., and Lai, A. (1998). Functional status and well-being in patients with glaucoma as measured by the Medical Outcomes Study Short Form-36 questionnaire. *Ophthalmology, 105*(11), 2112-2116.

Wilson, M.R., Quinn, G.E., Dobson, V., and Breton, M. (1991). Normative values for visual fields in 4- to 12-year-old children using kinetic perimetry. *Journal of Pediatric Ophthalmology and Strabismus, 28*(3), 151-153.

Wohlrab, G., Boltshauser, E., Schmitt, B., Schriever, S., and Landau, K. (1999). Visual field constriction is not limited to children treated with vigabatrin. *Neuropediatrics, 30*(3), 130-132.

Wohlwill, W.F. (1960). Developmental studies of perception. *Psychological Bulletin, 57*, 249-288.

Wolbarsht, M.L. (1977). Tests for glare sensitivity and periperal vision in driver applicants. *Journal of Safety Research, 9*(3), 128-139.

Wolfe, K.A., and Sadun, A.A. (1991). Threshold Amsler grid testing in diabetic retinopathy. *Graefes Archive for Clinical and Experimental Ophthalmology, 229*(3), 219-223.

Wood, J.M. (1999). How do visual status and age impact on driving performance as measured on a closed circuit driving track? *Ophthalmic and Physiological Optics, 19*(1), 34-40.

Wood, J.M., and Troutbeck, R. (1992). Effect of restriction of the binocular visual field on driving performance. *Ophthalmic and Physiological Optics, 12*(3), 291-298.

Wood, J.M., and Troutbeck, R. (1995). Elderly drivers and simulated visual impairment. *Optometry and Vision Science, 72*(2), 115-124.

Wood, J.M., Dique, T., and Troutbeck, R. (1993). The effect of artificial visual impairment on functional visual fields and driving performance. *Clinical Vision Sciences, 8*, 563-575.

World Health Organization. (1980). *International classification of impairments, disabilities and handicaps: A manual of classification relating to the consequences of disease.* Geneva: World Health Organization.

World Health Organization. (2001). *International classification of functioning, disability and health.* Geneva: World Health Organization.

Yeargin-Allsopp, M., Murphy, C.C., Oakley, G.P., and Sikes, R.K. (1992). A multiple-source method for studying the prevalence of developmental disabilities in children: The Metropolitan Atlanta Developmental Disabilities Study. *Pediatrics, 89*(4 Pt 1), 624-630.

Zadnik, K., Barr, J.T., Edrington, T.B., Nichols, J.J., Wilson, B.S., Siegmund, K., and Gordon, M.O. (2000). Corneal scarring and vision in keratoconus: A baseline report from the Collaborative Longitudinal Evaluation of Keratoconus (CLEK) Study. *Cornea, 19*(6), 804-812.

Zingirian, M., Gandolfo, E., Capris, P., and Mattioli, R. (1991). Perikon PCL 90: A new automatic perimeter. In R.P. Mills, and A. Heijl (eds.), *Perimetry update 1990/1991* (pp. 403-407). New York, NY: Kugler and Ghedini.

Appendix A

EMPLOYMENT AND ECONOMIC CONSEQUENCES OF VISUAL IMPAIRMENT

Andrew J. Houtenville

School of Industrial and Labor Relations, Cornell University

Working-age people with disabilities work less and have less household income than working-age people without disabilities.[1] There are also dramatic differences in the kinds and levels of disabilities within the working age population with disabilities.[2] Those with severe vision impairments are particularly disadvantaged, for they face many barriers in accessing employment. This paper explores the economic experience and program participation of working-age people with chronic vision-related conditions over the past two decades and compares their experience with those of other working-age people with chronic conditions.

---

[1]See Trupin et al. (1997) and Burkhauser, Daly, and Houtenville (2000).

[2]See Trupin et al. (1997) for a comparison of the labor force participation of people with various disabilities.

DATA AND IMPORTANT SAMPLING ISSUES

The National Health Interview Survey (NHIS) contains the economic and chronic condition information needed to conduct this study. The NHIS is a complex multistage probability sample of the civilian noninstitutionalized population of the United States.[3] The NHIS is collected by the National Center for Health Statistics (NCHS) in the Department of Health and Human Services. The federal government uses data from the NHIS to monitor trends in illness and disability. Researchers use data from the NHIS to analyze access to health care and health insurance and to evaluate federal health programs.

The NHIS collected information on an average of about 60,000 working-age individuals (100,000 individuals in total) annually from 1983 through 1996.[4] This paper separates survey participants into subgroups by chronic condition and gender. Some of these subgroups contain very small numbers of individuals, i.e., very small sample sizes. Smaller sample sizes lead to less precise sample estimates. This paper pools multiple years together to boost the sample sizes in these subgroups.

Specific health conditions and impairments are captured in two distinct methods. The differences between these two methods are very important in the interpretation of statistics generated using the NHIS. Very early the survey participants are randomly asked one of six condition checklists. These checklists directly inquire about

---

[3]The NHIS excludes those on active duty with the armed forces and U.S. nationals living in foreign countries. The dependents of those on active duty with the armed forces are included. The NHIS also excludes those in long-term care facilities, which may disproportionately represent people with disabilities.

[4]The NHIS interviews are performed in person in households. Adult (17 years of age and over) members of the household present at the time of the interview are asked to respond for themselves. A responsible adult (19 years of age and over) answers for children and adults not present at the time of the interview. Between 65 and 70 percent of adults answer for themselves (Massey, Moore, Parsons, & Tadros, 1989).

specific conditions. Table A-1 contains the checklist relevant to vision and the other conditions addressed in this report. In addition to the checklists, in later parts *all* survey participants are asked screening questions to reveal general health, doctor's visits, hospital utilization, sick days, and functioning difficulties. If participants answer yes to these screening questions, they are then asked what conditions caused these issues. The top panel of Table A-2 contains the set of screening questions, while the bottom panel contains an example of the probing questions that follow a screening question.

Thus only one-sixth of NHIS participants are directly asked about blindness and visual impairment and can also reveal blindness or visual impairment if they reveal having general health/functioning difficulties. The remaining five-sixths of NHIS participants reveal blindness or visual impairment *only* if they reveal having general health/functioning difficulties. As a result, the subsample of NHIS participants reporting blindness in the one-sixth sample is a *random* subsample of those reporting blindness. The subsample of NHIS participants reporting blindness in the five-sixths sample is a *choice-based* subsample of those reporting blindness because being in this subsample depends on responses (choices) to the screening questions.[5]

From this point forward, the term "random sample" refers to the one-sixth of the NHIS sample who were directly asked about their condition, and the term "choice-based" sample is used to refer to those who where asked about their condition after having revealed general health/functioning difficulties.

Prevalence, employment, income, and program participation statistics are calculated separately for random and choice-based samples. There are likely to be important differences between the two samples. The prevalence of blindness should be higher in the random sample than in the choice-based sample, because there are likely to be people reporting blindness who do not have general health/functioning difficulties, i.e., who answer "no" to the question in the bottom panel

[5]The same is true for the subsample reporting visual impairment and the other conditions addressed in this paper.

TABLE A-1 Condition Checklist Received by the Random Sample

H1.2a. Does anyone in the family {*read names*} NOW HAVE –
If "Yes," ask 2b and c.
b. Who is that?
c. Does anyone else now have –

A. Deafness in one or both ears?
B. Any trouble hearing with one or both ears?
C. Tinnitus or ringing in the ears?
D. Blind in one or both eyes?
E. Cataracts?
F. Glaucoma?
G. Color blindness?
H. A detached retina or any other condition of the retina?
I. Any other trouble seeing with one or both eyes EVEN when wearing glasses?
J. A cleft palate or harelip?
K. Stammering or stuttering?
L. Any other speech defect?
M. Loss of taste or smell which has lasted 3 months or more?
N. A missing finger, hand or arm, toe, foot, or leg?
O. A missing joint?
P. A missing breast, kidney, or lung?
Q. Palsy or cerebral palsy?
R. Paralysis of any kind?
S. Curvature of the spine?
T. REPEATED trouble with neck, back, or spine?
U. Any TROUBLE with fallen arches or flatfeet?
V. A clubfoot?
W. A trick knee?
X. PERMANENT stiffness or any deformity of the foot, leg, or back?
Y. PERMANENT stiffness or any deformity of the fingers, arm, or hand?
Z. Mental retardation
AA. Any condition caused by an accident or injury which happened more than 3 months ago? *If "Yes," ask: What is the condition?*

Note: In the NHIS, conditions are determined in two ways. First, participants receive one of six condition lists that ask them if they have a specific condition (this table contains list #2). Second, participants are asked broad questions to reveal general health and functioning (see the top panel of Table A-2). If participants reveal they have health or functioning difficulties, they are then asked what conditions cause these difficulties (see the second

continues

TABLE A-1 continued

panel of Table A-2). This method misses those with conditions who have no such difficulties, while the first method captures those with conditions who have no health or functioning difficulties. So only one-sixth of the sample is directly asked about blindness. This one-sixth of the sample is a random sample, because being asked about blindness is not dependent on one's response to another question. The remaining five-sixths of the sample is choice-based, because revealing blindness is dependent on one's response (choice) to another question.

Source: National Health Interview Survey Core Questionnaire, 1985-94, National Center for Health Statistics, Series 10, No. 199.

of Table A-2. Similarly, employment rates and mean incomes are likely to be higher and program participation rates are likely to be lower among random sample members reporting blindness than among choice-based sample members reporting blindness. Choice-based members reporting blindness have already revealed health and functioning difficulties and are thus less likely to work or earn income and more likely to participate in government programs.[6]

[6]In the random sample there could be people who say "no" to the direct question about blindness, but say "yes" to the screening question and reveal blindness as the reason they said "yes." This should not occur if respondents answer correctly when asked directly about blindness. There is no way of measuring how often this occurs. The public release data files include the condition but not whether the condition comes from the direct questions or the screening questions. Responding in this way could lead to an understatement of employment rate because the survey does not capture healthy people with blindness whom for some reason did not say "yes" to the direct question and answered "no" to the screening question. However, even if we did know whether the report of blindness came from the direct answer or screening questions, we would be left with the unanswerable question of which answer is correct.

TABLE A-2 Broad Health Questions Used to Screen for Condition Information

Screening Questions
1. Does any impairment or health problem NOW keep [you] from working at a job or business?
2. Does any impairment or health problem NOW keep [you] from doing any housework at all?
3. Is [you] limited in ANY WAY in any activities because of an impairment or health problem?
4. During those 2 weeks, did [you] miss any time from a job or business because of illness or injury?
5. During those 2 weeks, did [you] miss any time from school because of illness or injury?
6. During those 2 weeks, did [you] stay in bed because of illness or injury?
7. Was there any {OTHER} time during those 2 weeks that [you] cut down on the things [you] usually does because of illness or injury?
8. During those 2 weeks, how many times did [you] see or talk to a medical doctor? {include all types of doctors, such as dermatologists, psychiatrists, and ophthalmologists, as well as general practitioners and osteopaths.}
9. {Besides the time(s) mentioned in [previously]} During those 2 weeks, did anyone in the family receive health care at home or go to a doctor's office, clinic, hospital or some other place? 2b. Who received this care?
10. {Besides the time(s) you already told me about} During those 2 weeks, did anyone in the family get any medical advice, prescriptions or test results over the phone from a doctor, nurse, or anyone working with or for a medical doctor?

An Example of Probing Questions (These are the probing questions for the first screening question above.)
A. What (other) condition causes this? *Ask if injury or operation*: When did [the (injury) occur? / [you] have the operation?] *Ask if operation over 3 months ago*: For what condition did [you] have the operation?
B. Besides (condition) is there any other condition that causes this limitation?
C. Is this limitation caused by any (other) specific condition?
D. Which of these conditions would you say is the MAIN cause of this limitation?

continues

TABLE A-2 continued

Source: Design and Estimation of the 1985-94 National Health Interview Survey, Series 2, No. 110, National Center for Health Statistics, Hyattsville, MD, 1989.

Note: In the NHIS, conditions are determined in two ways. First, participants receive one of six condition lists that ask them if they have a specific condition (see Table A-1). Second, participants are asked broad questions to reveal general health and functioning (the questions in the top panel of this table). If participants reveal they have health or functioning difficulties, they are then asked what conditions cause these difficulties (for example, the questions in the second panel of this table). This method misses those with conditions who have no such difficulties, while the first method captures those with conditions who have no health or functioning difficulties. So only one-sixth of the sample is directly asked about blindness. This one-sixth of the sample is a random sample, because being asked about blindness is not dependent on one's response to another question. The remaining five-sixths of the sample is choice-based, because revealing blindness is dependent on one's response (choice) to another question.

CONCEPTUAL FRAMEWORK AND DEFINITIONS

Nagi (1965) developed a framework for defining disability, in which diseases/disorders result in the impairment of required functions that then interact with the socioeconomic and physical environment and lead to disability. Using the Nagi framework, this paper distinguishes those with chronic vision-related diseases/disorders, such as cataracts, from those with chronic visual impairments, such as being blind in one eye. Those with cataracts are not necessarily visually impaired.[7] This distinction is important in the context of economic experience because impaired function, rather than a specific disease/disorder, is expected to have a greater influence on employment and program participation.

[7]It is also possible for an individual to be visually impaired and not report having a vision-related disease/disorder.

The central focus of this paper is the economic experience of those who are blind in both eyes, for they are the group among people with vision-related conditions at the greatest risk of economic difficulties. They are also most likely to be eligible for Social Security Disability Insurance (SSDI) payments, Supplemental Security Income (SSI) benefits, and other government programs based on their medical conditions. The economic experience of those who are blind in both eyes is compared with that of those with other visual impairments. Economic statistics are also provided for those with vision-related diseases/disorders, which include glaucoma, cataracts, color blindness, and an "other" category, which consolidates conjunctivitis, disorders of the lacrimal system, disorders of binocular eye movements, and diseases of the retina.[8]

For comparison purposes the economic experiences of those with some other functional impairments are provided in this report. These functional impairment groups are also seriously at risk of low rates of employment and diminished economic well-being. These categories are deafness in both ears, other hearing impairment, mental retardation, paraplegia, hemiplegia, quadriplegia, and cerebral palsy.

Defining Chronic Conditions

The NHIS provides extensive information on chronic conditions. The term "condition" refers to diseases/disorders and impairments. Chronic conditions are conditions that exist for three or more months, although some conditions are considered chronic regardless of duration.

As mentioned above, the NHIS captures condition information in two ways: (1) checklists of specific conditions and (2) screening questions followed by open-ended probing questions. The next step is to consolidate and classify survey responses from all points in the survey into a set of condition categories based on the International Classification of Diseases. NCHS hires special medical coders to perform this complex task.

---

[8]This consolidation is required because of the small sample sizes.

According to the NHIS Medical Coding Manual, participants are classified as being blind in both eyes if they describe their condition as blind, no vision, or can't see. If there is no clear indication that only one eye is involved, it is assumed that both eyes are involved.

The NHIS also provides a category entitled "other visual impairments." Participants who are blind in one eye are in this category. This category also includes those who describe their eyesight, seeing, sight, or vision as being bad, blurred, defective, limited, poor, double, problem with, trouble with, or who use phrases like partially blind, blind spots, half-blind. Double-vision, color blindness, night blindness, and day blindness are combined into a single "other visual impairments" group. In addition, any active vision-related diseases/ disorders reported by participants are also classified, regardless of whether they cause visual impairment. The NHIS provides the following categories of diseases/disorders: glaucoma, cataracts, color blindness, conjunctivitis, disorders of the lacrimal system, disorders of binocular eye movements, diseases of the retina, and others vision-related of eye and adnexa.

The NHIS defines other chronic impairments in a similar manner to visual impairments. Participants who are reported as being deaf in both ears, having no useful hearing in both ears, or can't hear in both ears are classified as deaf in both ears. Those reported being partially deaf in both ears or a little deaf in both ears are coded as other hearing impairment. If only one ear is involved, a code of "other hearing impairment" is given. If the medical coder is unable to determine whether one or both ears are involved, the individual is coded as other hearing impairment. Hearing problems relating to allergies or earwax are not classified.

Mental retardation includes mental deficiency or retardation, and those describing themselves as can't learn, slow learner. Mental retardation is considered chronic regardless of onset.

The NHIS codes paralysis as partial or complete and for various parts or portions of the body. Paraplegia is complete paralysis of the lower body, both legs, or from the waist down. Hemiplegia is complete paralysis of one side of the body, including limbs. Quadriplegia is complete paralysis of the entire body or four limbs. Paralysis must exist for three or more months to be considered chronic. Cerebral palsy (and its synonyms) is chronic regardless of date of onset and includes those who describe themselves as congenitally "spastic."

Definitions of Economic Variables

Economic experience is captured via employment rates, mean household size-adjusted income, and receipt of SSDI and SSI payments. The employment rate is based on the following NHIS questions. "During [the past two calendar weeks], did [you] work at any time at a job or business not counting work around the house? (Include unpaid work in family [farm/business].)" Persons not working were asked, "[e]ven though [you] did not work during those 2 weeks, did [you] have a job or business?" Persons who answer "yes" to the first question or "yes" to the second question are considered employed.

Household income is the sum of all income in the household. Households can contain more than one family. The NHIS uses the following questions to determine family income: "Was the total FAMILY income during the past 12 months—that is, yours, [and other family members] more or less than $20,000? Include money from jobs, social security, retirement income, unemployment payments, public assistance, and so forth. Also include income from interest, dividends, net income from businesses, farm, or rent and any other money income received." And then, "[of the income brackets provided] which [bracket] best represents the total combined FAMILY income during the past 12 months—that is, yours, [and other family members]? Include wages, salaries, and other items we just talked about." The respondents can choose from 26 income brackets. To obtain a dollar value for family income, family income is assigned the midpoint of the chosen income bracket. Respondents choosing the top bracket ($50,000 and above) are assigned the mean annual family income among those families above $50,000 as estimated from the Current Population Survey.

Household income is adjusted for household size to get a better measure of an individual's access to household resources. This paper follows the common practice of dividing household income by the square root of household size. This accounts for the fact that $500 per week provides a higher standard of living for a single-person household than it does for individuals belonging to larger households.[9] Because we are comparing income across years, we adjust income using the consumer price index-urban (CPI-U); all income values are in 1998 dollars.

Receipt of SSDI and SSI payments is determined with relatively straightforward questions and refers to receipt of payments in the month prior to the survey. SSDI and SSI recipiency information is available only for 1990-1992, 1994, and 1995.

This paper focuses on working-age men and women (ages 25 to 61). Using this age range avoids confusing reductions in work or economic well-being associated with disability with reductions or declines associated with retirement at older ages or initial transitions in and out of the labor force related to job shopping at younger ages. Men and women are evaluated separately.

RESULTS

To get an idea of the size of populations with the various chronic conditions used in this study, Annex Table A-1 shows the prevalence rates of these chronic conditions in the working-age population in the United States, by gender and the random and choice samples. Annex Tables A-2a through A-2d show the sample sizes used to generate the economic statistics reported below.

Tables A-3 through A-7 compare differences across subgroups. These tables contain employment rates (Table A-3), mean household size-adjusted incomes (Table A-4), the percentages receiving SSDI payments

[9]Using the square root of household size reduces the impact of an each additional household member. An alternative is household income per household member, which places equal weight on adding a second person to a household and adding a sixth person to a household.

(Table A-5), SSI benefits (Table A-6), and either SSDI or SSI payments or both (Table A-7). In these tables, the estimates of those who are blind in both eyes are compared with the estimates of the other groups. Asterisks indicate when the difference between those who are blind in both eyes and another group is statistically significant. The remaining tables illustrate changes over time in employment rates (Table A-8) and mean household size-adjusted income (Table A-9) for the choice-based sample. Sample sizes in the random sample are insufficient to accurately measure changes over time. In these tables, asterisks indicate when the difference between 1983-1987 and 1992-1996 is statistically significant.

Table A-10 compares the employment rates for those who are blind in both eyes and visually impaired with the findings of Trupin et al. (1997) and Kirchner et al. (1999).

Prevalence

As expected, the prevalence rates reported in Annex Table A-1 are higher in the random sample than in the choice-based sample for *all* of the chronic conditions used in this study. This suggests that there are some individuals with chronic conditions who do not have any of the health issues listed in the top panel of Table A-2. This may also suggest that when asked directly about a specific condition, survey participants are more likely to report these conditions.

The relative prevalence rates (Annex Table A-1, columns 3 and 6) reveal that the difference between the random and choice-based samples is least among those with paraplegia/hemiplegia/quadriplegia, mental retardation, cerebral palsy, and those who are blind in both eyes. This suggests individuals with these chronic conditions are more affected by the health issues listed in the top panel of Table A-2. The difference between the random and choice-based samples is dramatically higher among those who report hearing impairments and other visual impairments, diseases, and disorders.

Employment

The discussion of employment, income, and program participation focuses mainly on the random sample. *Unless specified otherwise, all results discussed below refer to the random samples.*

The first column of Table A-3 shows that 88.8 percent of all working-age men without any visual impairment were employed in the period 1983-1996. Over the same period, the employment rate among men who are blind in both eyes was 49.4 percent. The second column of Table A-3 shows that the relative employment rate of men without visual impairments was 1.80, which means that men without visual impairments were 1.80 times as likely to be employed as men who are blind in both eyes.[10] Men with other visual impairments were employed at a rate of 82.3 percent—1.64 times as likely to be employed as men who are blind in both eyes. Similarly, the employment rate of men with vision-related diseases or disorders was 85.0 percent.

Among the other chronic impairments, only men with paraplegia, hemiplegia, or quadriplegia and men with mental retardation were employed at a lower rate than men who are blind in both eyes. Men with paraplegia, hemiplegia, or quadriplegia were about half (0.45) as likely to be employed as men who are blind in both eyes. Similarly, men with mental retardation were about 0.70 times as likely to be employed than men who are blind in both eyes. The employment rate of men with cerebral palsy (58.3 percent) is similar to that of men who are blind in both eyes, and the difference is statistically insignificant. This suggests that there may be no difference or that the sample sizes are insufficient to identify a difference. Men who are deaf in both ears were about one and a half (1.53) times as likely to be employed as men who are blind in both eyes.

In general, the employment rates of working-age women are lower than those of working-age men. However, when comparing across chronic conditions, the employment patterns of women are similar.

---

[10]The relative employment rate is the employment rate of a given group divided by the employment rate of those who are blind in both eyes.

TABLE A-3 Employment Rates of Noninstitutionalized Working-Age Civilians (Ages 25 to 61) with Various Chronic Impairments, Diseases, and Disorders, Pooled Over 1983 Through 1996, by Sample and Gender

	Random Sample[a]	
	Men	
Group	Employment Rate	Relative Rate[b]
No visual impairments	88.8	1.80***
Visual impairments	81.2	1.64***
-Blind in both eyes	49.4	1.00
-Other visual impairments	82.3	1.67***
Vision-related diseases/disorders	85.0	1.72***
-Glaucoma	67.6	1.37***
-Cataracts	67.4	1.36***
-Color blindness	91.4	1.85***
-Other vision-related diseases/disorders[c]	85.1	1.72***
Other impairments		
-Hearing impairments	81.6	1.65***
—Deaf in both ears	75.4	1.53***
—Other hearing impairments	81.9	1.66***
-Mental retardation	34.6	0.70**
-Paraplegia, hemiplegia, or quadriplegia	22.3	0.45***
-Cerebral palsy	58.3	1.18

Note: Asterisks signify when the difference between blind in both eyes and another group is statistically significant at the 99 percent (***), 95 percent (**), and 90 percent (*) levels. NA refers to groups for which sample size is insufficient.

[a] In the NHIS, conditions are determined in two ways. First, participants receive one of six condition lists that ask them if they have a specific condition (see Table A-1). Second, participants are asked broad questions to reveal general health and functioning (see Table A-2, top panel). If participants reveal they have health or functioning difficulties, they are then asked what conditions cause these difficulties (see Table A-2, bottom panel). This method misses those with conditions who have no such difficulties, while the first method captures those with conditions who have no health or functioning difficulties. So only one-sixth of the sample is directly asked

		Choice-Based Sample[a]			
Women		Men		Women	
Employment Rate	Relative Rate[b]	Employment Rate	Relative Rate[b]	Employment Rate	Relative Rate[b]
69.2	2.30***	88.5	2.73***	68.8	2.97***
52.9	1.76***	52.0	1.60***	36.9	1.60***
30.0	1.00	32.4	1.00	23.1	1.00
54.7	1.82***	56.4	1.74***	40.5	1.75***
51.3	1.71***	63.7	1.96***	46.5	2.01***
45.5	1.51***	53.9	1.66***	40.0	1.73***
46.0	1.53***	56.2	1.73***	35.8	1.55***
64.7	2.15***	86.7	2.67***	NA	NA
56.4	1.88***	69.7	2.15***	55.5	2.40***
58.4	1.94***	77.0	2.37***	53.5	2.31***
50.3	1.68***	64.1	1.98***	44.6	1.93***
58.7	1.96***	78.0	2.40***	54.5	2.36***
29.1	0.97	33.0	1.02	27.9	1.21
17.7	0.59	20.4	0.63***	19.4	0.84
27.8	0.93	43.7	1.35**	32.3	1.39*

about blindness. This one-sixth of the sample is a random sample, because being asked about blindness is not dependent on one's response to another question. The remaining five-sixths of the sample is choice-based, because revealing blindness is dependent on one's response (choice) to another question.

[b] The relative employment rate is the employment rate of a given group divided by the employment rate of those who are blind in both eyes.

[c] The category other includes conjunctivitis, disorders of the lacrimal system, disorders of binocular eye movements, and diseases of the retina.

Source: Author's calculations using the National Health Interview Survey, 1983-1996.

TABLE A-4 Mean Household Size-Adjusted Income (HHSAI) of Noninstitutionalized Working-Age Civilians (Ages 25 to 61) with Various Chronic Impairments, Diseases, and Disorders, Pooled Over 1983 Through 1996, by Sample and Gender

	Random Sample[a]	
	Men	
Group	Mean HHSAI	Relative HHSAI[b]
No visual impairments	31,067	1.22***
Visual impairments	29,361	1.15*
-Blind in both eyes	25,503	1.00
-Other visual impairments	29,504	1.16*
Vision-related diseases/disorders	31,655	1.24***
-Glaucoma	28,978	1.14
-Cataracts	26,859	1.05
-Color blindness	32,991	1.29***
-Other vision-related diseases/disorders[c]	33,155	1.30***
Other impairments		
-Hearing impairments	30,954	1.21**
—Deaf in both ears	28,702	1.13
—Other hearing impairments	31,070	1.22***
-Mental retardation	17,382	0.68***
-Paraplegia, hemiplegia, or quadriplegia	20,067	0.79*
-Cerebral palsy	23,614	0.93

Note: Asterisks signify when the difference between blind in both eyes and another group is statistically significant at the 99 percent (***), 95 percent (**), and 90 percent (*) levels. NA refers to groups for which sample size is insufficient.

[a] In the NHIS, conditions are determined in two ways. First, participants receive one of six condition lists that ask them if they have a specific condition (see Table A-1). Second, participants are asked broad questions to reveal general health and functioning (see Table A-2, top panel). If participants reveal they have health or functioning difficulties, they are then asked what conditions cause these difficulties (see Table A-2, bottom panel). This method misses those with conditions who have no such difficulties, while the first method captures those with conditions who have no health or functioning difficulties. So only one-sixth of the sample is directly asked about blindness.

		Choice-Based Sample[a]			
Women		Men		Women	
Mean HHSAI	Relative HHSAI[b]	Mean HHSAI	Relative HHSAI[b]	Mean HHSAI	Relative HHSAI[b]
28,578	1.37***	31,110	1.70***	28,696	1.47***
22,821	1.10	21,631	1.18***	20,624	1.05
20,837	1.00	18,348	1.00	19,567	1.00
22,975	1.10	22,363	1.22***	20,901	1.07
26,516	1.27***	26,627	1.45***	25,149	1.29***
26,246	1.26**	25,385	1.38***	22,019	1.13
24,072	1.16	23,310	1.27***	22,786	1.16*
27,692	1.33**	33,194	1.81***	NA	NA
29,422	1.41***	28,277	1.54***	28,185	1.44***
25,641	1.23**	29,434	1.60***	24,966	1.28***
23,088	1.11	26,098	1.42***	19,888	1.02
25,758	1.24**	29,690	1.62***	25,534	1.30***
18,049	0.87	16,147	0.88***	16,927	0.87**
23,304	1.12	20,245	1.10	20,362	1.04
17,677	0.85	18,438	1.00	19,147	0.98

This one-sixth of the sample is a random sample, because being asked about blindness is not dependent on one's response to another question. The remaining five-sixths of the sample is choice-based, because revealing blindness is dependent on one's response (choice) to another question.

[b] The relative HHSAI is the mean HHSAI of a given group divided by mean HHSAI of those who are blind in both eyes.

[c] The category other includes conjunctivitis, disorders of the lacrimal system, disorders of binocular eye movements, and diseases of the retina.

Source: Author's calculations using the National Health Interview Survey, 1983-1996.

TABLE A-5 Percentage Receiving Social Security Disability Insurance (SSDI) Payments among Noninstitutionalized Working-Age Civilians (Ages 25 to 61) with Various Chronic Impairments, Diseases, and Disorders, Pooled Over 1983 Through 1996, by Sample and Gender

	Random Sample[a]	
	Men	
Group	Percentage Receiving SSDI	Relative Recipi-ency[b]
No visual impairments	1.87	0.08***
Visual impairments	6.61	0.28**
-Blind in both eyes	23.76	1.00
-Other visual impairments	5.79	0.24**
Vision-related diseases/disorders	4.32	0.18**
-Glaucoma	11.64	0.49
-Cataracts	9.72	0.41*
-Color blindness	1.97	0.08***
-Other vision-related diseases/disorders[c]	8.84	0.37*
Other impairments		
-Hearing impairments	4.29	0.18**
—Deaf in both ears	9.80	0.41
—Other hearing impairments	4.02	0.17**
-Mental retardation	37.25	1.57
-Paraplegia, hemiplegia, or quadriplegia	55.05	2.32**
-Cerebral palsy	27.45	1.16

Note: Asterisks signify when the difference between blind in both eyes and another group is statistically significant at the 99 percent (***), 95 percent (**), and 90 percent (*) levels. NA refers to groups where sample size is insufficient.

[a] In the NHIS, conditions are determined in two ways. First, participants receive one of six condition lists that ask them if they have a specific condition (see Table A-1). Second, participants are asked broad questions to reveal general health and functioning (see Table A-2, top panel). If participants reveal they have health or functioning difficulties, they are then asked what conditions cause these difficulties (see Table A-2, bottom panel). This method misses those with conditions who have no such difficulties, while the first method captures those with conditions that have no health or functioning difficulties. So only one-sixth of the sample is directly asked

		Choice-Based Sample[a]			
Women		Men		Women	
Percentage Receiving SSDI	Relative Recipiency[b]	Percentage Receiving SSDI	Relative Recipiency[b]	Percentage Receiving SSDI	Relative Recipiency[b]
1.24	0.03***	2.37	0.05***	1.35	0.04***
8.43	0.21***	23.39	0.49***	14.75	0.38***
39.31	1.00	47.43	1.00	38.66	1.00
6.24	0.16***	16.86	0.36***	8.55	0.22***
6.12	0.16***	16.68	0.35***	9.79	0.25***
5.59	0.14***	22.81	0.48***	10.77	0.28***
6.08	0.15***	12.43	0.26***	11.24	0.29***
2.47	0.06***	NA	NA	NA	NA
11.90	0.30**	22.16	0.47***	9.37	0.24***
3.98	0.10***	5.87	0.12***	3.68	0.10***
23.50	0.60	15.55	0.33***	5.96	0.15***
3.36	0.09**	5.45	0.11***	3.55	0.09***
29.52	0.75	49.31	1.04	40.82	1.06
28.61	0.73	69.07	1.46***	33.37	0.86
11.37	0.29*	40.52	0.85	48.59	1.26

about blindness. This one-sixth of the sample is a random sample because being asked about blindness is not dependent one's response to another question. The remaining five-sixths of the sample is choice-based because revealing blindness is dependent one's response (choice) to another question.

[b] The relative recipiency is the percentage of a given group divided by the recipiency of those who are blind in both eyes.

[c] The category other includes conjunctivitis, disorders of the lacrimal system, disorders of binocular eye movements, and diseases of the retina.

Source: Author's calculations using the National Health Interview Survey, 1983-1996.

TABLE A-6 Percentage Receiving Supplemental Security Income (SSI) among Noninstitutionalized Working-Age Civilians (Ages 25 to 61) with Various Chronic Impairments, Diseases, and Disorders, Pooled Over 1990-1992, 1994, and 1995, by Sample and Gender

	Random Sample[a]	
	Men	
Group	Percentage Receiving SSI	Relative Recipiency[b]
No visual impairments	0.99	0.04***
Visual impairments	3.97	0.16***
-Blind in both eyes	24.69	1.00
-Other visual impairments	2.97	0.12***
Vision-related diseases/disorders	2.28	0.09***
-Glaucoma	9.40	0.38*
-Cataracts	4.97	0.20***
-Color blindness	0.36	0.01***
-Other vision-related diseases/disorders[c]	5.91	0.24**
Other impairments		
-Hearing impairments	1.86	0.08***
—Deaf in both ears	4.41	0.18***
—Other hearing impairments	1.73	0.07***
-Mental retardation	42.73	1.73*
-Paraplegia, hemiplegia, or quadriplegia	34.64	1.40
-Cerebral palsy	31.07	1.26

Note: Asterisks signify when the difference between blind in both eyes and another group is statistically significant at the 99 percent (***), 95 percent (**), and 90 percent (*) levels. NA refers to groups where sample size is insufficient.

[a] In the NHIS, conditions are determined in two ways. First, participants receive one of six condition lists that ask them if they have a specific condition (see Table A-1). Second, participants are asked broad questions to reveal general health and functioning (see Table A-2, top panel). If participants reveal they have health or functioning difficulties, they are then asked what conditions cause these difficulties (see Table A-2, bottom panel). This method misses those with conditions who have no such difficulties, while the first method captures those with conditions that have no health or functioning difficulties. So only one-sixth of the sample is directly asked

		Choice-Based Sample[a]			
Women		Men		Women	
Percentage Receiving SSI	Relative Recipi-ency[b]	Percentage Receiving SSI	Relative Recipi-ency[b]	Percentage Receiving SSI	Relative Recipi-ency[b]
1.46	0.06***	1.08	0.04***	1.39	0.04***
10.38	0.42	9.97	0.36***	15.76	0.46***
24.74	1.00	27.43	1.00	34.57	1.00
9.36	0.38*	5.23	0.19***	10.88	0.31***
8.44	0.34*	7.45	0.27***	9.46	0.27***
8.89	0.36*	9.22	0.34***	12.76	0.37***
10.59	0.43	10.74	0.39**	10.82	0.31***
1.23	0.05***	NA	NA	NA	NA
12.57	0.51	6.03	0.22***	7.50	0.22***
3.35	0.14**	2.34	0.09***	5.93	0.17***
9.19	0.37	4.12	0.15***	12.84	0.37***
3.16	0.13***	2.26	0.08***	5.55	0.16***
52.36	2.12***	45.18	1.65***	40.71	1.18
24.03	0.97	26.51	0.97	17.28	0.50**
40.26	1.63	34.00	1.24	46.27	1.34

about blindness. This one-sixth of the sample is a random sample because being asked about blindness is not dependent one's response to another question. The remaining five-sixths of the sample is choice-based because revealing blindness is dependent one's response (choice) to another question.

[b] The relative recipiency is the percentage of a given group divided by the recipiency of those who are blind in both eyes.

[c] The category other includes conjunctivitis, disorders of the lacrimal system, disorders of binocular eye movements, and diseases of the retina.

Source: Author's calculations using the National Health Interview Survey, 1983-1996.

TABLE A-7 Percentage Receiving Supplemental Security Income (SSI) and/or Social Security Disability Insurance (SSDI) Payments among Noninstitutionalized Working-Age Civilians (Ages 25 to 61) with Various Chronic Impairments, Diseases, and Disorders, Pooled Over 1990-1992, 1994, and 1995, by Sample and Gender

	Random Sample[a]	
	Men	
Group	Percentage Receiving SSDI, SSI	Relative Recipiency[b]
No visual impairments	2.62	0.07***
Visual impairments	9.08	0.24***
-Blind in both eyes	37.38	1.00
-Other visual impairments	7.72	0.21***
Vision-related diseases/disorders	5.88	0.16***
-Glaucoma	15.56	0.42**
-Cataracts	13.55	0.36***
-Color blindness	2.33	0.06***
-Other vision-related diseases/disorders[c]	14.75	0.39**
Other impairments		
-Hearing impairments	5.97	0.16***
—Deaf in both ears	14.21	0.38**
—Other hearing impairments	5.57	0.15***
-Mental retardation	63.56	1.70**
-Paraplegia, hemiplegia, or quadriplegia	79.19	2.12***
-Cerebral palsy	51.34	1.37

Note: Asterisks signify when the difference between blind in both eyes and another group is statistically significant at the 99 percent (***), 95 percent (**), and 90 percent (*) levels. NA refers to groups where sample size is insufficient.

[a] In the NHIS, conditions are determined in two ways. First, participants receive one of six condition lists that ask them if they have a specific condition (see Table A-1). Second, participants are asked broad questions to reveal general health and functioning (see Table A-2, top panel). If participants reveal they have health or functioning difficulties, they are then asked what conditions cause these difficulties (see Table A-2, bottom panel). This method misses those with conditions who have no such difficulties, while the first method captures those with conditions that have no health or functioning difficulties. So only one-sixth of the sample is directly asked

		Choice-Based Sample[a]			
Women		Men		Women	
Percentage Receiving SSDI, SSI	Relative Recipiency[b]	Percentage Receiving SSDI, SSI	Relative Recipiency[b]	Percentage Receiving SSDI, SSI	Relative Recipiency[b]
2.47	0.05***	3.08	0.05***	2.44	0.04***
15.74	0.33***	28.49	0.48***	27.27	0.45***
47.87	1.00	59.75	1.00	60.87	1.00
13.46	0.28***	20.00	0.33***	18.56	0.30***
12.14	0.25***	20.18	0.34***	16.14	0.27***
13.92	0.29***	28.04	0.47***	19.46	0.32***
13.41	0.28***	18.45	0.31***	17.35	0.29***
3.69	0.08***	NA	NA	NA	NA
19.26	0.40**	22.16	0.37***	13.52	0.22***
6.84	0.14***	7.38	0.12***	8.84	0.15***
26.89	0.56	16.98	0.28***	15.97	0.26***
6.20	0.13***	6.96	0.12***	8.45	0.14***
70.29	1.47*	72.75	1.22**	67.72	1.11
52.64	1.10	84.37	1.41***	41.68	0.68**
51.63	1.08	63.01	1.05	77.28	1.27*

about blindness. This one-sixth of the sample is a random sample because being asked about blindness is not dependent one's response to another question. The remaining five-sixths of the sample is choice-based because revealing blindness is dependent one's response (choice) to another question.

[b] The relative recipiency is the percentage of a given group divided by the recipiency of those who are blind in both eyes.

[c] The category other includes conjunctivitis, disorders of the lacrimal system, disorders of binocular eye movements, and diseases of the retina.

Source: Author's calculations using the National Health Interview Survey, 1983-1996.

TABLE A-8 Employment Rates of Noninstitutionalized Working-Age Civilians (Ages 25 to 61) in the Choice-Based Sample with Various Chronic Impairments, Diseases, and Disorders, Pooled Over 1983-1987 and 1992-1996 and Percentage Changes, by Gender

Group
No visual impairments
Visual impairments
-Blind in both eyes
-Other visual impairments
Vision-related diseases/disorders
-Glaucoma
-Cataracts
-Color blindness
-Other vision-related diseases/disorders[b]
Other impairments
-Hearing impairments
—Deaf in both ears
—Other hearing impairments
-Mental retardation
-Paraplegia, hemiplegia, or quadriplegia
-Cerebral palsy

Note: Asterisks signify when the difference between 1983-1987 and 1992-1996 is statistically significant at the 99 percent (***), 95 percent (**), and 90 percent (*) levels. NA refers to groups where sample size is insufficient.

In the NHIS, conditions are determined in two ways. First, participants receive one of six condition lists that ask them if they have a specific condition (see Table A-1). Second, participants are asked broad questions to reveal general health and functioning (see Table A-2, top panel). If participants reveal they have health or functioning difficulties, they are then asked what conditions cause these difficulties (see Table A-2, bottom panel). This method misses those with conditions who have no such difficulties, while the first method captures those with conditions that have no health or functioning difficulties. So only one-sixth of the sample is directly asked

Men			Women		
1983-87	1992-96	Percentage Change[a]	1983-87	1992-96	Percentage Change[a]
88.6	87.9	-0.79***	65.2	71.1	8.66***
54.5	48.5	-11.65*	34.5	39.9	14.52
34.8	27.3	-24.15	19.5	27.8	35.10
58.7	53.2	-9.83	38.1	43.6	13.46
62.7	63.3	0.95	41.1	48.8	17.13
50.6	52.0	2.73	33.3	40.5	19.51
53.3	59.4	10.83	33.3	34.2	2.67
92.0	77.2	-17.49	NA	NA	NA
71.5	69.6	-2.69	50.1	59.8	17.65
65.9	65.2	-1.07	43.6	48.2	10.02
61.1	58.8	-3.84	37.6	44.4	16.59
66.8	66.1	-1.05	45.0	49.1	8.71
32.9	34.3	4.17	23.6	31.5	28.68**
19.1	22.7	17.22	7.2	29.5	121.53***
44.2	33.8	-26.67	35.6	27.7	-24.96

about blindness. This one-sixth of the sample is a random sample because being asked about blindness is not dependent one's response to another question. The remaining five-sixths of the sample is choice-based because revealing blindness is dependent one's response (choice) to another question.

[a] The percentage change is the difference between the two periods divided by the average of the two periods multiplied by 100.

[b] The category other includes conjunctivitis, disorders of the lacrimal system, disorders of binocular eye movements, and diseases of the retina.

Source: Author's calculations using the National Health Interview Survey, 1983-1996.

TABLE A-9 Mean Household Size-Adjusted Income of Noninstitutionalized Working-Age Civilians (Ages 25 to 61) in the Choice-Based Sample with Various Chronic Impairments, Diseases, and Disorders, Pooled Over 1983-1987 and 1992-1996 and Percentage Changes, by Gender

Group
No visual impairments
Visual impairments
-Blind in both eyes
-Other visual impairments
Vision-related diseases/disorders
-Glaucoma
-Cataracts
-Color blindness
-Other vision-related diseases/disorders[b]
Other impairments
-Hearing impairments
—Deaf in both ears
—Other hearing impairments
-Mental retardation
-Paraplegia, hemiplegia, or quadriplegia
-Cerebral palsy

Note: Asterisks signify when the difference between 1983-87 and 1992-96 is statistically significant at the 99 percent (***), 95 percent (**), and 90 percent (*) levels. NA refers to groups where sample size is insufficient.

All dollar values are adjusted for inflation to 1998 dollar values. In the NHIS, conditions are determined in two ways. First, participants receive one of six condition lists that ask them if they have a specific condition (see Table A-1). Second, participants are asked broad questions to reveal general health and functioning (see Table A-2, top panel). If participants reveal they have health or functioning difficulties, they are then asked what conditions cause these difficulties (see Table A-2, bottom panel). This method misses those with conditions who have no such difficulties, while the first method captures those with conditions that have no health or functioning difficulties. So only one-sixth of the sample is directly asked about blindness. This one-

Men			Women		
1983-87	1992-96	Percentage Change[a]	1983-87	1992-96	Percentage Change[a]
29,574	31,885	7.52***	27,082	29,608	8.91***
21,110	21,349	1.13	19,339	21,152	8.96
16,969	17,741	4.45	20,925	18,613	–11.70
21,989	22,149	0.72	18,952	21,947	14.65**
24,270	28,104	14.64**	24,321	24,432	0.46
21,423	27,657	25.40**	21,143	20,775	–1.76
23,668	24,375	2.94	20,663	24,464	16.85
34,189	32,155	-6.13	NA	NA	NA
24,484	29,204	17.58*	28,234	27,058	–4.25
24,027	26,532	9.91*	22,321	22,580	1.15
26,077	22,847	–13.20	19,832	18,181	-8.69
23,682	27,102	13.47**	22,911	23,597	2.95
15,593	15,234	-2.33	15,451	17,102	10.14
17,702	22,264	22.83**	17,844	21,849	20.18
19,116	17,698	-7.70	20,477	16,655	-20.59

sixth of the sample is a random sample because being asked about blindness is not dependent one's response to another question. The remaining five-sixths of the sample is choice-based because revealing blindness is dependent one's response (choice) to another question.

[a] The percentage change is the difference between the two periods divided by the average of the two periods multiplied by 100.

[b] The category other includes conjunctivitis, disorders of the lacrimal system, disorders of binocular eye movements, and diseases of the retina.

Source: Author's calculations using the National Health Interview Survey, 1983-1996.

TABLE A-10 Comparison with Results from Other Study of Vision-Related Conditions and Labor Market Attachment

Descriptions	Study of Vision-Related Conditions and Labor Market Attachment — This Study			
Dataset	National Health Interview Survey			
Time period	Pooled over 1983-96			
Age group	Aged 25 to 61			
Measure of labor market attachment[b]	Have a job in the previous two weeks			
Secondary restrictions	Random sample[c]		Choice-based sample[c]	
Measures of vision-related conditions	Blind in both eyes	Other visual impairments	Blind in both eyes	Other visual impairments
Percentage attached to the labor market	39.5	73.1	28.2	49.8

[a] Trupin et al. (1997) report annual estimates from 1983-1994. The pooled results below are my calculations using their annual estimates.

[b] All three studies are based on the same set of questions. Trupin et al. (1997) include those who are looking for work but mention similar estimates are obtained when excluding those who are looking for work.

[c] In the NHIS, conditions are determined in two ways. First, participants receive one of six condition lists that ask them if they have a specific condition (see Table A-1). Second, participants are asked broad questions to reveal general health and functioning (see Table A-2, top panel). If participants reveal they have health or functioning difficulties, they are then asked what conditions cause these difficulties (see Table A-2, bottom panel). This method misses those with conditions who have no such difficulties, while the first method captures those with conditions that have no health or functioning difficulties. So only one-sixth of the sample is directly asked

Trupin et al. (1997)		Kirchner et al. (1999)
National Health Interview Survey on Disability, Phase I		National Health Interview Survey
Pooled over 1983-94[a]		Pooled over 1994-95
Aged 18 to 64		Aged 18 to 54
Have a job or looking for work in the previous two weeks		Have a job in the previous two weeks
Condition is the main cause of work and/or activity limitations[d]		None
Blind in both eyes	Other visual impairments	Serious visual impairment even when wearing glasses[e]
30.1	61.0	59.0

about blindness. This one-sixth of the sample is a random sample because being asked about blindness is not dependent one's response to another question. The remaining five-sixths of the sample is choice-based because revealing blindness is dependent one's response (choice) to another question.

[d] Trupin et al. (1997) restrict their sample to only those who report blindness as the main source of work and/or activity limitation, which is a subset of the prompting questions referred to in Table A-2. This allows them to disregard the distinction between recipients and nonrecipients of List #2, yet they ignore those with conditions who are not limited.

[e] In Kirchner et al. (1999) individuals are considered to have a "serious visual impairment" if they have "SERIOUS difficulty seeing even when wearing glasses or contact lenses" and then identify themselves as "legally blind" or expect themselves "to have SERIOUS difficulty seeing, for at least the next 12 months."

The third column of Table A-3 shows that 69.2 percent of working-age women without visual impairments were employed in the period 1983-1996. The employment rate among women who are visually impaired is 52.9 percent and the rate for women who are blind in both eyes is 30.0 percent. The fourth column of Table A-3 reveals that women without visual impairments were over twice (2.30) as likely to be employed as women who are blind in both eyes. Women with other visual impairments were employed at a rate of 54.7 percent. The employment rate of women with vision-related diseases or disorders is 51.3 percent.

Among the other chronic conditions, the employment rates of women with cerebral palsy, paraplegia/hemiplegia/quadriplegia, and mental retardation are statistically indistinguishable from the employment rates of women who are blind in both eyes. This suggests that there may be no difference or that the sample sizes are insufficient to identify a difference. All other groups were employed at higher rates than women who are blind in both eyes.

As expected, among all groups, the employment rate of men in the random sample is higher than the employment rate of men in the choice-based sample. This is also true among women, except for women with cerebral palsy and paraplegia/hemiplegia/quadriplegia.[11] Comparing the employment rates of the random sample and the choice-based sample, it appears that four groups always had the lowest employment rate: (1) those who are blind in both eyes and those with (2) cerebral palsy, (3) paraplegia/hemiplegia/quadriplegia, and (4) mental retardation. This is consistent with the finding that these groups are more affected by the health issues listed in Table A-2.

[11]The difference between the employment rates of women with cerebral palsy in the random sample and the employment rates of women with cerebral palsy in the choice-based sample is likely to be within the margin of error, likewise for women with paraplegia/hemiplegia/quadriplegia.

Household Size-Adjusted Income

Unless specified otherwise, all results discussed below refer to the random samples. The mean household size-adjusted income among working-age men without visual impairments was $31,067 (Table A-4, column 1) for the period 1983-1996. This figure is 1.22 times higher than the mean household size-adjusted income among men who are blind in both eyes ($25,503). Men with other visual impairments had a mean household size-adjusted income of $29,504, which is 1.16 times the mean household size-adjusted income of men who are blind in both eyes. The mean household size-adjusted income of men with vision-related diseases or disorders was $31,655.

Among the other chronic conditions, mean household size-adjusted incomes lower than that of men who are blind in both eyes are found among men with mental retardation and paraplegia/hemiplegia/quadriplegia. Men with cerebral palsy and men who are deaf in both ears have similar mean household size-adjusted income; the differences are statistically insignificant.

The cross-condition comparisons are fairly similar for working-age women. The third column of Table A-4 reveals that the mean household size-adjusted income among working-age women without visual impairments was $28,578, compared with $20,837 among working-age women who are blind in both eyes. Mean household size-adjusted income of women with other visual impairments ($22,975) was slightly higher than that of women who are blind in both eyes. Interestingly, the mean household size-adjusted income of women who are deaf in both ears is not statistically different than that of women who are blind in both eyes.

As expected, among all groups, the mean household size-adjusted income of those in the random sample was higher than the mean household size-adjusted income of those in the choice-based sample, except for men with paraplegia/hemiplegia/quadriplegia and women with cerebral palsy.

Program Participation

Unless specified otherwise, all results discussed below refer to the random samples. Table A-5 shows the percentage of men and women receiving SSDI payments and their rates relative to those who are blind in both eyes. (Note that SSDI eligibility must be established by working for a prescribed length of time.) These results are based on data pooled over the years 1990-1992, 1994, and 1995. Few working-age men without visual impairments received SSDI, 1.87 percent (Table A-5, column 1). Among men who are blind in both eyes, only about a quarter (23.76 percent) received SSDI payments. Only 5.79 percent of men with other visual impairments received SSDI payments, which may reflect the severity of these impairments.

Among other groups, only men with paraplegia/hemiplegia/ quadriplegia received SSDI payments at a higher rate (55.05 percent); they were 2.32 times as likely to receive SSDI payments. The difference in SSDI recipiency between men who are blind in both eyes (23.76 percent) and men with mental retardation (37.25) is not statistically significant. Men who are deaf in both ears received SSDI payments at a rate of 9.80 percent and were thus 0.41 times as likely to receive SSDI payments as men who are blind in both eyes, although the difference between the two groups is statistically insignificant.

The third column of Table A-5 shows that 39.31 percent of women who are blind in both eyes received SSDI payments. No other group has a higher recipiency, although the difference is statistically insignificant for women who are deaf in both ears and women with mental retardation or paraplegia/hemiplegia/quadriplegia.

Table A-6 reveals similar patterns for SSI recipiency. Among men who are blind in both eyes, 24.69 percent received SSI. Men with other visual impairments participated at a rate of 3.97 percent, which again may reflect the severity of other visual impairments. Men with mental retardation were 1.73 times as likely to receive SSI benefits as men who are blind in both eyes. Interestingly, men who are deaf in both ears were much less likely (0.18 times) to receive SSI benefits than men who are blind in both eyes. SSI recipiency is generally higher among women than among men (Table A-6, columns 3 and 4).

The patterns across conditions are similar to the patterns shown for men.

Dual eligibility for SSDI and SSI is possible, as long as SSDI payments do not cause an individual to go over the SSI means test. Table A-7 shows that 37.38 percent of men who are blind in both eyes participated in SSDI and/or SSI, which indicates that 11.07 percent participated in both programs.

Consistent with previous findings, the recipiency rates for SSDI and SSI are generally higher for those in the choice-based sample than for those in the random sample. Again, this may reflect the severity of the disability.

Changes Over Time

Due to sample size constraints, the over-time results were generated only for the choice-based sample. Tables A-8 and A-9 illustrate changes in employment rates and mean household size-adjusted income over time for the choice-based sample. Pooled results from 1983-1987 are compared with pooled results from 1992-1996. These years are chosen because they represent similar phases of the business cycle. Both represent recovery periods in the U.S. economy. The NHIS began collecting SSDI and SSI information in 1990; therefore changes in SSDI and SSI participation over time cannot be measured.

Those in the choice-based sample who are blind in both eyes can be thought of as those who are blind in both eyes and report being constrained by their condition. Recall from Table A-5 that when comparing the employment rates of the random sample and the choice-based sample, it appears that four groups always have the lowest employment rate: (1) those who are blind in both eyes and those with (2) cerebral palsy, (3) paraplegia/hemiplegia/quadriplegia, and (4) mental retardation.

The employment rate of working-age men in the choice-based sample without visual impairments was 88.6 percent in the period 1983-1987, and 87.9 percent in the period 1992-1996, which represents a statistically significant decline of 0.79 percent (Table A-8, columns 1, 2, and 3). The employment rate of men in the choice-based sample with visual impairments declined by much more (11.65 percent), from 54.5 percent in the period 1983-1987 to 48.5 percent in the period 1992-1996. The changes in the employment rates for all other groups of men are not statistically significantly different from zero, which suggests that there may be little change or the sample sizes are insufficient to identify a change.[12]

The last three columns of Table A-8 show that the employment rates of working-age women in the choice-based sample without visual impairments rose by 8.66 percent, from 65.2 percent in 1983-1987 to 71.1 percent in 1992-1996. However, the change in the employment rates among women in the choice-based sample who are blind in both eyes is not statistically different from zero. Interestingly, the employment rates of women in the choice-based sample increased for those with mental retardation (23.6 to 31.5 percent) and paraplegia/hemiplegia/quadriplegia (7.2 to 29.5 percent).

The third and sixth columns of Table A-9 show that the mean household size-adjusted income increased between the periods 1983-1987 and 1992-1996 by 7.52 percent among men in the choice-based sample without visual impairments and 8.91 percent among women in the choice-based sample without visual impairments. Changes in the mean household size-adjusted income among men and women in the choice-based sample who are blind in both eyes are not significantly different from zero.

[12]Comparison of six-year periods (1983-1988 and 1991-1996) and seven-year periods (1983-1989 and 1990-1996) without a significant change in patterns across subgroups. And even though more years are pooled, there are no substantial changes in statistical significance.

COMPARISON WITH OTHER STUDIES

Table A-10 compares the employment results in this paper to the results of two other studies. The results are remarkably close. Trupin et al. (1997) used the NHIS over the period 1983-1994; thus they should find lower rates of labor force attachment than the ones reported here—1995 and 1996 were growth years in the overall economy. Trupin et al. (1997) report labor force participation rates, which include people who are actively looking for a job; thus their estimates should be higher than the employment rates presented in this paper. They analyzed the population for whom being blind in both eyes is the main cause of activity limitations; thus their sample is similar to the results from the choice-based sample for which main cause of activity limitations is one way of revealing blindness (see Table A-2). They evaluated those ages 18 to 64 and thus should capture lower rates of labor force attachment than those reported here. They combined women and men. Table A-10 adjusts the results of Table A-5 to pull together the results for men and women.

As is shown in the fifth column of Table A-10, Trupin et al. (1997) found a 1983-1994 labor force participation rate of 30.1 percent among those ages 18 to 64 for whom being blind in both eyes is the main cause of activity limitations. This is remarkably similar to the 1983-1996 employment rate of 28.2 percent for those age 25 to 61 in the choice-based sample who are blind in both eyes.

Kirchner et al. (1999) used the National Health Interview on Disability pooled over 1994-1995; thus they should find higher rates of labor force attachment than the ones reported here—they did not cover the recession of the early 1990s. They use exactly the same definition of employment used here. In their study, individuals were considered to have a "serious visual impairment," if they have "SERIOUS difficulty seeing even when wearing glasses or contact lenses" and then identify themselves as "legally blind" or expect themselves "to have SERIOUS difficulty seeing, for at least the next 12 months." Their results should fall between the random sample results for those who are blind in both eyes and those with other visual impairments. They evaluated those ages 18 to 54 and thus should also find lower rates of labor force attachment than those reported here. They also combined women and men.

Kirchner et al. (1999) found a 1994-1995 employment rate of 59.9 percent among those ages 18 to 54 who are severely visually impaired. This is between the 1983-1996 employment rates of 39.5 and 73.1 percent for those ages 25 to 61 in the random sample who are blind in both eyes and who have other visual impairments, respectively.

A Canadian study by Fawcett (1996) estimated labor force participation (employed or actively looking for work) rates for the population with disabilities in Canada. Among working-age persons with "seeing disabilities," 45.6 percent participated in the labor force in 1991. Similar rates were found among those with disabilities related to mobility (43.3), agility (46.0), speaking (41.8), and mental function/learning (47.5). The labor force participation of those with hearing disabilities in Canada (62.7 percent) was higher than that of those with seeing disabilities in Canada. These cross-disability patterns are similar to employment patterns shown in Table A-3 for the United States.

CONCLUSION

This paper provides a statistical description of the economic experience of working-age individuals with chronic vision-related conditions over the period 1983-1996 using the NHIS. The economic experience of individuals who are blind in both eyes is compared with the economic experience of those with other chronic conditions. The economic experience of those who are blind in both eyes is worse than those with less severe visual impairments but similar to those with other serious chronic conditions (e.g., paraplegia/hemiplegia/quadriplegia, mental retardation, and cerebral palsy).

ACKNOWLEDGMENT

The author thanks Richard V. Burkhauser and Corrine Kirchner for their helpful comments.

REFERENCES

Burkhauser, R. V., Daly, M. C., & Houtenville, A. J. (2000). How working age people with disabilities fared over the 1990s business cycle. In P. P. Budetti, R. V. Burkhauser, J. M. Gregory, & H. A. Hunt (eds.), *Ensuring health and income security for an aging workforce* . Kalamazoo, MI: W.E. UpJohn Institute for Employment Research.

Fawcett, G. M. (1996). *Living with disability in Canada: An economic portrait.* Hull, Quebec: Human Resources Development Canada, Office for Disability Issues.

Kirchner, C., Schmeidler, E., & Todorov, A. (1999). *Looking at employment through a lifespan telescope: Age, health, and employment status of people with serious visual impairment.* New York, NY: American Foundation for the Blind (subcontractor to Rehabilitation Research and Training Center on Bindness and Low Vision, Mississippi State University).

Massey, J. T., Moore, T. F., Parsons, V. L., & Tadros, W. (1989). *Design and estimation for the National Health Interview Survey, 1985-1994.* (Report No. PHS 89-1384). Hyattsville, MD: U.S. Department of Health and Human Services.

Nagi, S. Z. (1965). Some conceptual issues in disability and rehabilitation. In M. B. Sussman (ed.), *Sociology and rehabilitation.* Washington, DC: American Sociological Association.

Trupin, L., Sebesta, D. S., Yelin, E., & LaPlante, M. P. (1997). *Disability statistics report: Trends in labor force participation among persons with disabilities, 1983-1994.* (Report No. 10). San Francisco, CA: Disability Statistics Rehabilitation Research and Training Center, Institute for Health and Aging, University of California.

Annex Table A-1 Prevalence Rates of Various Chronic Impairments, Diseases, and Disorders Among Noninstitutionalized Working-Age Civilians (Ages 25 to 61) Pooled Over 1983 Through 1996, by Sample and Gender

Group
Visual impairments
-Blind in both eyes
-Other visual impairments
Vision-related diseases/disorders
-Glaucoma
-Cataracts
-Color blindness
-Other vision-related diseases/disorders[c]
Other impairments
-Hearing impairments
—Deaf in both ears
—Other hearing impairments
-Mental retardation
-Paraplegia, hemiplegia, or quadriplegia
-Cerebral palsy

Note: Asterisks signify when the difference between the random sample and choice-based sample is statistically significant at the 99 percent (***), 95 percent (**), and 90 percent (*) levels. NA refers to groups where sample size is insufficient.

[a] In the NHIS, conditions are determined in two ways. First, participants receive one of six condition lists that ask them if they have a specific condition (see Table A-1). Second, participants are asked broad questions to reveal general health and functioning (see Table A-2, top panel). If participants reveal they have health or functioning difficulties, they are then asked what conditions cause these difficulties (see Table A-2, bottom panel). This method misses those with conditions who have no such difficulties, while the first method captures those with conditions that have no health or functioning difficulties. So only one-sixth of the sample is directly asked

Men			Women		
Random Sample[a]	Choice-Based Sample[a]	Relative Prevalence[b]	Random Sample[a]	Choice-Based Sample[a]	Relative Prevalence[b]
4.89	0.57	0.12***	2.38	0.39	0.17***
0.17	0.10	0.60***	0.17	0.08	0.48***
4.71	0.47	0.10***	2.21	0.31	0.14***
4.16	0.31	0.08***	1.97	0.36	0.18***
0.50	0.09	0.17***	0.47	0.11	0.24***
0.62	0.10	0.16***	0.82	0.10	0.12***
2.68	0.02	0.01***	0.27	0.00	0.00***
0.48	0.12	0.25***	0.51	0.16	0.32***
10.75	1.14	0.11***	5.94	0.62	0.10***
0.53	0.08	0.15***	0.26	0.06	0.24***
10.22	1.06	0.10***	5.68	0.55	0.10***
0.46	0.35	0.76***	0.35	0.25	0.71***
0.20	0.16	0.81*	0.09	0.06	0.66**
0.11	0.07	0.64**	0.09	0.06	0.63**

about blindness. This one-sixth of the sample is a random sample because being asked about blindness is not dependent one's response to another question. The remaining five-sixths of the sample is choice-based because revealing blindness is dependent one's response (choice) to another question.

[b] The relative prevalence is the prevalence in the random sample divided by the prevalence in the choice-based sample.

[c] The category other includes conjunctivitis, disorders of the lacrimal system, disorders of binocular eye movements, and diseases of the retina.

Source: Author's calculations using the National Health Interview Survey, 1983-1996.

Annex Table A-2a Sample Size of Noninstitutionalized Working-Age Civilian Men (Ages 25 to 61) in the Random Sample with Various Chronic Impairments, Diseases, and Disorders, 1983-1996

	Year					
Group	1983	1984	1985	1986	1987	1988
No visual impairments	3,652	3,599	3,130	2,128	4,344	4,281
Visual impairments	204	187	180	113	219	233
Blind in both eyes	2	5	4	3	8	11
Other visual impairments	202	182	176	110	211	222
Vision-related diseases/ disorders	184	148	150	93	219	193
Glaucoma	14	20	22	8	23	24
Cataracts	29	27	32	11	28	27
Color blindness	126	90	83	67	144	126
Other vision-related diseases/disorders[a]	19	16	17	8	28	26
Other impairments						
Hearing impairments	454	412	389	237	494	483
Deaf in both ears	29	29	21	12	21	23
Other hearing impairments	425	383	368	225	473	460
Mental retardation	15	12	14	16	14	21
Paraplegia, hemiplegia, or quadriplegia	6	5	8	7	10	3
Cerebral palsy	3	6	1	5	3	6

Note: In the NHIS, conditions are determined in two ways. First, participants receive one of six condition lists that ask them if they have a specific condition (see Table A-1). Second, participants are asked broad questions to reveal general health and functioning (see Table A-2, top panel). If participants reveal they have health or functioning difficulties, they are then asked what conditions cause these difficulties (see Table A-2, bottom panel). This method misses those with conditions who have no such difficulties, while the first method captures those with conditions that have no health or functioning difficulties. So only one-sixth of the sample is directly asked about blindness. This one-sixth of the sample is a random sample because

1989	1990	1991	1992	1993	1994	1995	1996	Sum
4,146	4,270	4,225	4,569	3,945	4,255	3,709	2,341	52,594
194	205	218	257	220	217	188	108	2,743
1	10	9	11	5	12	8	6	95
193	195	209	246	215	205	180	102	2,648
149	165	171	218	184	193	176	95	2,338
17	20	26	26	22	31	15	16	284
29	23	27	39	24	25	33	16	370
90	109	103	147	123	118	109	56	1,491
18	19	20	22	21	25	25	9	273
421	491	442	558	465	485	409	235	5,975
17	19	14	36	16	31	23	10	301
404	472	428	522	449	454	386	225	5,674
16	29	21	20	18	19	24	12	251
3	7	5	9	13	12	8	10	106
2	6	3	5	4	4	5	4	57

being asked about blindness is not dependent on one's response to another question. The remaining five-sixths of the sample is choice-based because revealing blindness is dependent on one's response (choice) to another question.

[a] The category other includes conjunctivitis, disorders of the lacrimal system, disorders of binocular eye movements, and diseases of the retina.

Source: Author's calculations using the National Health Interview Survey, 1983-1996.

Annex Table A-2b Sample Size of Noninstitutionalized Working-Age Civilian Men (Ages 25 to 61) in the Choice-Based Sample with Various Chronic Impairments, Diseases, and Disorders, 1983-1996

	Year					
Group	1983	1984	1985	1986	1987	1988
No visual impairments	19,018	19,154	16,561	11,286	22,453	22,731
Visual impairments	120	122	104	66	127	135
Blind in both eyes	27	16	20	11	18	22
Other visual impairments	93	106	84	55	109	113
Vision-related diseases/ disorders	87	58	61	30	51	71
Glaucoma	25	12	17	6	14	22
Cataracts	32	15	23	13	22	21
Color blindness	7	6	1	3	3	2
Other vision-related diseases/disorders[a]	27	25	24	11	12	29
Other impairments						
Hearing impairments	100	87	74	50	116	107
Deaf in both ears	21	12	17	5	7	9
Other hearing impairments	79	75	57	45	109	98
Mental retardation	65	41	45	42	64	90
Paraplegia, hemiplegia, or quadriplegia	40	38	29	16	36	30
Cerebral palsy	12	14	10	6	10	10

Note: In the NHIS, conditions are determined in two ways. First, participants receive one of six condition lists that ask them if they have a specific condition (see Table A-1). Second, participants are asked broad questions to reveal general health and functioning (see Table A-2, top panel). If participants reveal they have health or functioning difficulties, they are then asked what conditions cause these difficulties (see Table A-2, bottom panel). This method misses those with conditions who have no such difficulties, while the first method captures those with conditions that have no health or functioning difficulties. So only one-sixth of the sample is directly asked about blindness. This one-sixth of the sample is a random sample because

1989	1990	1991	1992	1993	1994	1995	1996	Sum
21,553	22,469	22,502	23,771	20,743	21,864	19,118	12,175	275,398
109	126	130	171	135	123	111	63	1,642
19	25	28	33	22	25	18	10	294
90	101	102	138	113	98	93	53	1,348
69	69	76	122	63	62	68	32	919
22	19	26	34	23	17	21	5	263
23	22	17	52	15	17	14	9	295
1	3	6	12	2	3	7	2	58
25	30	29	32	26	27	29	17	343
93	2,278	103	118	90	104	76	55	3,451
12	81	11	13	15	11	12	7	233
81	2,197	92	105	75	93	64	48	3,218
67	82	75	109	96	78	77	54	985
33	29	30	35	40	36	34	21	447
17	19	23	19	18	18	16	5	197

being asked about blindness is not dependent on one's response to another question. The remaining five-sixths of the sample is choice-based because revealing blindness is dependent on one's response (choice) to another question.

[a] The category other includes conjunctivitis, disorders of the lacrimal system, disorders of binocular eye movements, and diseases of the retina.

Source: Author's calculations using the National Health Interview Survey, 1983-96.

Annex Table A-2c Sample Size of Noninstitutionalized Working-Age Civilian Women (Ages 25 to 61) in the Random Sample with Various Chronic Impairments, Diseases, and Disorders, 1983-1996[a]

	Year					
Group	1983	1984	1985	1986	1987	1988
No visual impairments	4,219	4,211	3,657	2,491	5,020	4,929
Visual impairments	118	89	81	65	146	121
Blind in both eyes	5	6	1	4	15	6
Other visual impairments	113	83	80	61	131	115
Vision-related diseases/ disorders	89	75	66	52	101	93
Glaucoma	15	14	21	9	29	25
Cataracts	30	32	30	23	33	44
Color blindness	12	9	4	9	13	11
Other vision-related diseases/disorders[a]	36	23	14	12	31	22
Other impairments						
Hearing impairments	275	263	246	149	304	294
Deaf in both ears	23	11	10	10	18	10
Other hearing impairments	252	252	236	139	286	284
Mental retardation	9	13	6	9	15	15
Paraplegia, hemiplegia, or quadriplegia	1	10	2	3	2	7
Cerebral palsy	2	4	1	2	6	3

Note: In the NHIS, conditions are determined in two ways. First, participants receive one of six condition lists that ask them if they have a specific condition (see Table A-1). Second, participants are asked broad questions to reveal general health and functioning (see Table A-2, top panel). If participants reveal they have health or functioning difficulties, they are then asked what conditions cause these difficulties (see Table A-2, bottom panel). This method misses those with conditions who have no such difficulties, while the first method captures those with conditions that have no health or functioning difficulties. So only one-sixth of the sample is directly asked about blindness. This one-sixth of the sample is a random sample because

1989	1990	1991	1992	1993	1994	1995	1996	Sum
4,750	4,916	4,890	5,256	4,586	4,811	4,267	2,704	60,707
106	110	123	137	118	113	106	71	1,504
6	9	4	12	8	5	16	7	104
100	101	119	125	110	108	90	64	1,400
96	105	102	130	95	103	101	53	1,261
31	25	26	32	22	29	35	13	326
37	42	50	58	41	37	33	27	517
10	13	18	20	9	21	14	5	168
25	31	17	25	28	22	24	12	322
265	283	312	330	300	296	238	156	3,711
13	6	10	13	9	10	6	10	159
252	277	302	317	291	286	232	146	3,552
12	23	26	22	10	17	22	16	215
0	6	3	4	6	2	5	4	55
3	4	3	2	4	5	5	7	51

being asked about blindness is not dependent on one's response to another question. The remaining five-sixths of the sample is choice-based because revealing blindness is dependent on one's response (choice) to another question.

[a]The category other includes conjunctivitis, disorders of the lacrimal system, disorders of binocular eye movements, and diseases of the retina.

Source: Author's calculations using the National Health Interview Survey, 1983-1996.

Annex Table A-2d Sample Size of Noninstitutionalized Working-Age Civilian Women (Ages 25 to 61) in the Choice-Based Sample with Various Chronic Impairments, Diseases, and Disorders, 1983-1996

	Year					
Group	1983	1984	1985	1986	1987	1988
No visual impairments	20,934	21,214	18,429	12,658	25,058	25,278
Visual impairments	91	100	85	47	99	84
Blind in both eyes	16	16	14	12	23	11
Other visual impairments	75	84	71	35	76	73
Vision-related diseases/ disorders	98	66	83	45	103	82
Glaucoma	31	17	23	15	39	22
Cataracts	36	22	28	16	28	27
Color blindness	0	0	0	0	0	0
Other vision-related Diseases/disorders[a]	34	29	37	20	47	39
Other impairments						
Hearing impairments	63	58	63	33	77	60
Deaf in both ears	15	6	11	7	18	4
Other hearing impairments	48	52	52	26	59	56
Mental retardation	44	51	37	40	57	66
Paraplegia, hemiplegia, or quadriplegia	12	19	16	5	16	20
Cerebral palsy	8	12	9	5	14	13

Note: In the NHIS, conditions are determined in two ways. First, participants receive one of six condition lists that ask them if they have a specific condition (see Table A-1). Second, participants are asked broad questions to reveal general health and functioning (see Table A-2, top panel). If participants reveal they have health or functioning difficulties, they are then asked what conditions cause these difficulties (see Table A-2, bottom panel). This method misses those with conditions who have no such difficulties, while the first method captures those with conditions that have no health or functioning difficulties. So only one-sixth of the sample is directly asked about blindness. This one-sixth of the sample is a random sample because

1989	1990	1991	1992	1993	1994	1995	1996	Sum
24,070	25,056	25,039	26,326	22,980	24,308	21,317	13,300	305,967
94	88	97	133	100	114	88	56	1,276
16	20	17	30	24	25	22	15	261
78	68	80	103	76	89	66	41	1,015
82	93	76	121	82	70	66	50	1,117
27	35	30	40	23	25	31	17	375
27	23	18	47	20	11	10	6	319
0	0	0	2	0	0	0	0	2
36	38	31	39	41	36	27	29	483
84	1,150	62	95	87	82	76	38	2,028
11	36	12	22	14	14	13	10	193
73	1,114	50	73	73	68	63	28	1,835
75	66	52	76	66	64	55	38	787
14	15	20	24	7	13	13	8	202
11	17	14	15	17	20	14	7	176

being asked about blindness is not dependent on one's response to another question. The remaining five-sixths of the sample is choice-based because revealing blindness is dependent on one's response (choice) to another question.

[a]The category other includes conjunctivitis, disorders of the lacrimal system, disorders of binocular eye movements, and diseases of the retina.

Source: Author's calculations using the National Health Interview Survey, 1983-1996.

Appendix B

PUBLIC FORUM ON VISUAL DISABLILITY DETERMINATION METHODS AND ISSUES

The Committee on Disability Determination for Individuals with Visual Impairments held a public forum on November 15, 2000, at the National Academy of Sciences in Washington, DC. This appendix includes:

- A list of all organizations invited to nominate speakers, indicating which ones provided nominations;
- The questions the committee sent to nominating organizations and to speakers;
- A list of speakers, their affiliations, and major topics each addressed;
- Information on where the full text of the speakers' presentations is filed.

ORGANIZATIONS INVITED TO NOMINATE FORUM SPEAKERS

The following organizations were invited to nominate speakers for the forum. Those that responded with nominations are in **boldface.**

American Academy of Disability Evaluating Physicians

American Academy of Ophthalmology

American Board of Independent Medical Examiners

American Council of the Blind

American Diabetes Association

American Foundation for the Blind

American Macular Degeneration Foundation

American Medical Association

American Occupational Therapy Association

American Optometric Association

Association for Education and Rehabilitation of the Blind and Visually Impaired

Blinded Veterans Association

Center for the Partially Sighted

Columbia Lighthouse for the Blind

Council of Citizens with Low Vision International

Foundation Fighting Blindness

Glaucoma Foundation

Glaucoma Research Foundation

Jewish Guild for the Blind

Job Accommodation Network

Lighthouse International

Macular Degeneration Foundation

Macular Degeneration Partnership

National Association for Parents of the Visually Impaired

National Association of the Visually Handicapped

National Association of Disability Evaluating Professionals

National Association of Disability Examiners

National Council of State Agencies for the Blind

National Federation of the Blind

National Institute on Disability and Rehabilitation Research

Prevent Blindness America

Rehabilitation Research and Training Center on Blindness and Low Vision

Research to Prevent Blindness

Sensory Access Foundation

Social Security Administration

QUESTIONS TO BE ADDRESSED BY FORUM PARTICIPANTS

We are interested in your responses to the following questions. Please respond both for adults, under DI and SSI,[1] and for children under SSI.

1. Do the current vision tests and criteria[2] adequately assess a claimant's ability to engage in gainful employment (adults) or age-appropriate activities (children)?

   a. If not: Are there weaknesses in the particulars of the visual functions being measured, in the particular tests used, or in the criteria for presumptive disability? (For adults? For children?)

   b. If other visual functions could and should be tested to provide an adequate assessment, what functions are they? (For adults? For children?)

   c. If particular tests are inadequate, what tests would provide a better assessment? (For adults? For children?)

   d. If the criteria are inappropriate, what criteria would permit a better determination? (For adults? For children?)

2. What everyday tasks that require vision (e.g., reading, driving) best represent the range of visual demands of employment (adults) or age-appropriate activities (children)?

---

[1]DI: Disability Insurance, under Title II of the Social Security Act; SSI: Supplemental Security income, under Title XVI of the Social Security Act. See the *Social Security Handbook* or *Disability Evaluation Under Social Security* for details.

[2]The current tests are Snellen or comparable acuity and Goldmann or comparable perimetry. Tests are performed monocularly. The current criteria for presumptive disability are acuity ≤ 20/200 or visual field ≤ 20° diameter or 10° minimum radius from fixation, in better eye. See 20CFR §404 Appendix 1, medical listings, or *Disability Evaluation Under Social Security*, for details.

3. Overall, what specific recommendations would you make for improvements to the SSA's tests and/or criteria for determining visual disability? (For adults? For children?)

4. If the tests or criteria were to be changed, what are the most important factors to consider in selecting and evaluating new tests or criteria? (For adults? For children?)

SPEAKERS

Roy Cole, OD
Director, Vision Program Development
Jewish Guild for the Blind
New York, NY
Inadequacy of current tests; need to test broader range of functions; need to test contrast sensitivity. (Addressed committee questions directly.)

August Colenbrander, MD
Director, Low Vision Service
California Pacific Medical Center
San Francisco, CA
Presented justification for Functional Vision Score methodology

Anne Corn, EdD
Professor of Special Education
Peabody College of Vanderbilt University
Nashville, TN
Difficulty of predicting functional capacity from current tests; desirability of testing function.

Charles R. Fox, OD, PhD, FAAO
Fox & Associates
Baltimore, MD
Difficulty of predicting functional capacity from current tests; need for standardization; possibly mobile test facilities; analyze visual requirements of work.

Gregory W Good, OD, PhD
Chief of Vision Rehabilitation Services
Professor of Clinical Optometry
College of Optometry, Ohio State University
Columbus, OH
Need to standardize acuity testing for uniform, fair determination; possibly test contrast sensitivity; issues of combining measures; need to test binocularly.

Corinne Kirchner, PhD
American Foundation for the Blind
New York, NY
Social factors in vision testing; variables not currently considered; societal conditions affecting disability criteria.

Robert Massof, PhD
Director, Lions Vision Research and Rehabilitation Center, Wilmer Ophthalmological Institute
Professor of Ophthalmology
Johns Hopkins University School of Medicine
Baltimore, MD
Need to relate vision measures and impairments to real-life functions and methods for doing so; survey on vision requirements for jobs and daily tasks, indicating that 20/200 criterion is too strict.

Lylas Mogk, MD
Henry Ford Health Care System
Grosse Pointe, MI
Needs for: additional and different measures of visual function and task performance; temporary and partial disability benefits; coordination of benefits with rehabilitation services.

Bruce P. Rosenthal, OD, FAAO
Chief of Low Vision Programs
Lighthouse International
New York, NY
Change criteria for definition of visual impairment; use ETDRS chart for acuity; revise visual field testing and criteria; test contrast sensitivity.

Sidney Schreiber, MD
Scientific Advisor
American Macular Degeneration Foundation
Northampton, MA
Additional tests needed; tests should reflect real-world conditions; consider individual's functional requirements for vision.

Ron Schuchard, PhD
Associate Director, VA Geriatric Rehabilitation Center
Associate Professor, Emory University School of Medicine
Decatur, GA
Insensitivity of current tests to central scotomas; need to measure real-life task performance to determine disability; need for binocular testing. Suggested specific tests. Allow partial/temporary disability and coordinate benefits with rehab.

Mary Warren, MS, OTR/L
Director, Visual Independence Program
The Eye Foundation of Kansas City
Kansas City, MO
Weaknesses of current tests and criteria. Need to measure functional vision, including reading acuity; measure binocularly; consider individual factors in determination.

Karen Wolffe, PhD
Career Counseling and Consultation
Austin, TX
Variables beyond those currently tested that affect employment and employability; need to consider these in disability determination. Need for research to determine whether objective tests can be developed for these.

Further information, including the papers submitted by forum participants, is on file at:

Public Access Records Office
The National Academies
2101 Constitution Avenue NW
Room NAS 204
Washington, DC 20418
Tel: (202) 334-3543
FAX: (202) 334-1580
Email: publicac@nas.edu

Appendix C

GLOSSARY OF SOCIAL SECURITY TERMS RELATED TO DISABILITY

Administrative law judge (ALJ)—Administrative law judges in the Office of Hearings and Appeals of the Social Security Administration conduct hearings and make decisions on cases that are appealed by individuals whose claims have been denied by state agencies.

Administrative review process—The procedures followed in determining eligibility for, and entitlement to, benefits. The administrative review process consists of several steps, which usually must be requested within certain periods and in the specified order.

Allowance rate—The percentage of claims allowed in a given time period. At the hearing level, allowance rates are computed either as a percentage of dispositions (including dismissals) or as a percentage of decisions (excluding dismissals).

Appeals Council—The organization within the Office of Hearings and Appeals of the Social Security Administration that makes the final decision in the administrative review process. When an individual disagrees with the decision or dismissal of the ALJ, he or she may, within 60 days of receiving the hearing decision, request that the Appeals Council review the decision. The Appeals Council may deny or dismiss the request for review, or it may grant the request and either issue a decision or remand (return) the case to an ALJ. The Appeals Council may also review any ALJ action on its own motion within 60 days after the ALJ's action.

Award—An action adding an individual to the Social Security benefit rolls.

Beneficiary—An individual on the Social Security benefit rolls.

Claimant—An individual who has applied for benefits and whose claim is still pending.

Concurrent claim—A claim for both Title II (Old Age Surveys and Disability Insurance) and Title XVI (Supplemental Secuity Income) benefits.

Continuing disability review—An evaluation of a disabled beneficiary's impairments to determine if the person is still disabled within the meaning of the law.

Conversion—The simultaneous cessation of payment of a specific type of benefit and entitlement of the beneficiary to another type of benefit. Title II disabled worker beneficiaries are converted to retirement benefits when they attain normal retirement age.

DI—Disability Insurance under Title II of the Social Security Act.

Disability—For purposes of Title II (Old Age Surveys and Disability Insurance) benefits and Title XVI (Supplemental Security Income) benefits for adults, disability is the inability to engage in any substantial gainful activity by reason of any medically determinable impairment that can be expected to result in death or can be expected to last for a continuous period of not less than 12 months. A person must not only be unable to do his or her previous work but cannot, considering age, education, and work experience, engage in any other kind of substantial gainful work that exists in the national economy. It is immaterial whether such work exists in the immediate area, or whether a specific job vacancy exists, or whether the worker would be hired if he or she applied for work. For SSI disabled child benefits, a child under age 18 is considered disabled if he or she has any medically determinable physical or mental impairment(s) that result(s) in marked and severe functional limitations and that can be expected to last for a continuous period of not less than 12 months.

Disability Determination Services (DDS)—The state agency that makes the initial and reconsideration determination of whether a claimant is disabled or a beneficiary continues to be disabled within the meaning of the law.

Disability examiner—An employee of a state's Disability Determination Services who collects medical evidence and, usually in conjunction with a physician, makes a determination on a claimant's disability.

Duration—A factor in the determination of disability. To be eligible for benefits, a claimant must have a disability that has lasted, or is expected to last, 12 months or to end in death. See Sequential evaluation process.

Equals listing—A step in the sequential evaluation process. Regulations issued by the Social Security Administration include a Listing of Impairments, which describes, for each major body system, impairments that are considered severe enough to prevent a person from doing any substantial gainful activity. A determination that an impairment is equal in severity to the criteria in the listings is sufficient to establish that an individual who is not working is disabled within the meaning of the law. See Sequential evaluation process.

Hearing—The level following reconsideration in the administrative review process. The hearing is a de novo procedure at which the claimant and/or the claimant's representative may appear in person, submit new evidence, examine the evidence used in making the determination under review, give testimony, and present and question witnesses. The hearing is on the record but is informal and nonadversarial.

Hearing office—One of the 138 locations of the Office of Hearings and Appeals of the Social Security Administration at which hearings are held.

Medical expert (ME)—A physician or mental health professional who provides impartial expert opinion at the hearing level of the disability claims process. MEs either testify at hearings or provide written responses to interrogatories.

Medical listings—A common term for the Listing of Impairments issued by the Social Security Administration as part of the regulations on determining disability. The listings describe, for each major body system, impairments that are considered severe enough to prevent a person from doing any substantial gainful activity. An impairment that meets or equals the criteria in the listings is sufficient to establish that an individual who is not working is disabled within the meaning of the law.

Meets listing—A step in the sequential evaluation process. Regulations issued by the Social Security Administration include a Listing of Impairments, which describes, for each major body system, impairments that are considered severe enough to prevent a person from doing any substantial gainful activity. An impairment that meets the criteria in the listings is sufficient to establish that an individual who is not working is disabled within the meaning of the law. See Sequential evaluation process.

Nonsevere impairment—An impairment that does not significantly limit a person's physical or mental ability to perform basic work activities. See Sequential evaluation process.

Other work—Work that exists in the national economy, other than the work a person has done previously. See Sequential evaluation process.

Reconsideration—An independent reexamination by state agencies of all evidence on record related to a case. It is based on the evidence submitted for the initial determination plus any further evidence and information that the claimant or the claimant's representative may submit in connection with the reconsideration. A reconsideration determination is made by a different disability examiner and physician/psychologist from the ones who made the original determination.

Sequential evaluation process—The five-step process used in determining whether an individual meets the definition of disability in the law. A determination at any step that an individual is disabled or not disabled ends the process.

Supplemental Security Income (SSI)—Supplemental Security Income, Title XVI of the Social Security Act, a program that provides benefits to low-income aged, blind, and disabled individuals who meet income and resource requirements.

Substantial gainful activity (SGA)—Remunerative work that is substantial, as determined from consideration of the amount of money earned, the number of hours worked, and the nature of the work. The dollar amount is established by regulations.

Termination—The ending of entitlement to a type of benefit. Disabled workers' benefits are most commonly terminated because of death, conversion to a retirement benefit at age 65, or recovery from their disabling condition.

Usual work—A claimant's past relevant work. See Sequential evaluation process.

Vocational considerations—Age, education, and work experience, considered at the final step of the sequential evaluation process.

Vocational expert (VE)—Professional who provides factual information and expert opinion relevant to particular vocational questions, which may be raised at the hearing level of the disability claims process.

Source: List of SSA terms related to Disability Insurance taken from glossaries in Social Security Advisory Board (2001a, 2001b).

Appendix D

BIOGRAPHICAL SKETCHES

Peter Lennie is professor at the Center for Neural Science and dean for science at New York University. He is a member of the Association for Research in Vision and Ophthalmology and has obtained multiple research grants from the National Institutes of Health for his studies on vision and other related topics. Other memberships include the Experimental Psychology Society, the Optical Society of America (Fellow), the Physiological Society, and the Society for Neuroscience. He has been appointed to various international committees, such as the Organizing Committee of European Conference on Visual Perception and the UK Image Interpretation Initiative External Review Board. He received the Merit Award from the National Eye Institute in 1992 and 1997. He was chair of the National Research Council's Committee on Vision from 1991 to 1995 and more recently served as a member of the Board on Behavioral, Cognitive, and Sensory Sciences. He has a PhD from the University of Cambridge, England.

Ian L. Bailey is professor of optometry and vision science and director of the Low Vision Clinic for the School of Optometry, University of California, Berkeley. He has been one of the pioneers in the development of many of today's more scientifically based approaches to visual acuity measurement and the prescribing of low vision aids, publishing numerous articles or chapters in the scientific and professional literature. Bailey was chair of the low vision section and the low vision diplomat program of the American Academy of Optometry. He served for 10 years on the National Research Council's Committee on Vision as the joint representative of the American Optometric Association and the American Academy of Optometry. Bailey served for eight years on the editorial board of *Optometry and Vision Science.* He has a higher diploma of the British Optical Association from the City University in London, an MS from Indiana University, and a diploma in low vision from the American Academy of Optometry.

John A. Brabyn is a senior scientist at the Smith Kettlewell Eye Research Institute and the director of its Rehabilitation Engineering Research Center on blindness and low vision. His interests are in rehabilitation engineering research for blind, visually impaired, deaf, and multihandicapped people; low vision research; transfer of technology to industry; and human factors engineering. He is a member of the Institute of Electrical and Electronic Engineers, the Rehabilitation Engineering and Assistive Technology Society of North America, and the American Association for the Advancement of Science. He was a member of the National Research Council's Committee on Currency Features Usable by the Visually Impaired. He has a PhD in electrical engineering from the University of Canterbury, New Zealand.

Richard V. Burkhauser is chair of the Department of Policy Analysis and Management and the Sarah Gibson Blanding professor of policy analysis in the College of Human Ecology at Cornell University. His current research interests focus on the importance of social environment on the work outcomes of people with disabilities; how disability influences economic well-being; how Social Security reforms affect the work and economic well-being of older persons; and cross-national comparisons of the economic well-being and work of older persons. He is the head of the Panel Study on Income Dynamics Board of Overseers and on the editorial boards of *The Journal of Disability Policy Studies, The Review of Income and Wealth, Labor Economics, Research on Aging,* and *The Journal of Applied Social Science Studies.* He was a member of the Technical Panel of the 1994-1996

Advisory Council on Social Security and the 1994-1996 National Academy of Social Insurance Panel on Disability Policy Reform. He is currently a member of the Ticket to Work/Work Incentives Improvement Act Advisory Board. He has a PhD in economics from the University of Chicago.

Velma Dobson is a professor in the Departments of Ophthalmology and Psychology at the University of Arizona. An experimental psychologist who specializes in the assessment of vision in infants and young children, she is currently conducting research on visual acuity and visual fields in infants and young children. She was involved in the development of the Teller acuity cards and has conducted studies of visual development in infants treated in a neonatal intensive care unit. She holds research grants from the National Eye Institute for the study of visual acuity and visual fields in infants and young children. She also collaborates on two studies funded by the National Eye Institute to examine the diagnosis and treatment of astigmatism and refractive amblyopia in Native American preschool- and school-age children. She has a PhD in experimental psychology (1975) from Brown University. She directs visual acuity testing in two multicenter studies of retinopathy of prematurity and serves as adviser for a multicenter National Eye Institute study to determine effective and cost-efficient methods for screening vision in 3- to 5-year-old children.

Richard D. Gonzalez is a professor in the Department of Psychology at the University of Michigan. He is associate director of the department's decision laboratory and has a joint appointment in the Department of Statistics. His research interests are in judgment and decision making, while his current focus is on generalizations of expected utility theory and developing algorithms for testing generalized theories. Drawing from traditional work in psychophysics, his research centers on how people distort probabilities in decision making. Other research interests include basic psychological measurement (psychometrics) and the development and use of statistical models in testing psychological theory. He is on the editorial boards of four journals including *Psychological Review* and *Journal of Experimental Psychology: Learning, Memory and Cognition.* He has a PhD in psychology from Stanford University.

Karen Jacobs is a clinical associate professor of occupational therapy at Boston University. In addition to being a registered occupational therapist, she is a board-certified professional ergonomist and the founding editor of the international and interdisciplinary journal *WORK: A Journal of Prevention, Assessment and Rehabilitation*. One of her research interests is "healthy computing," as more Americans, children and adults, spend increasing time working at computer keyboards, putting themselves at risk for repetitive strain injuries and other conditions that can result from overuse. Other research and scholarly projects include occupational safety and health for the dental professional using web-based continuing education. A fellow of the American Occupational Therapy Association, she served as president 1998-2001. She has an EdD from the University of Massachusetts.

Chris A. Johnson is director of diagnostic research and senior scientist at Devers Eye Institute in Portland, Oregon, as well as the Oregon Lions' Anderson-Chenoweth-Ross vision research chair. He has conducted research on the visual requirements for a wide variety of occupations and currently is involved in research on diagnostic tests, especially visual field testing and analysis of peripheral visual function. He is a member of the American Academy of Ophthalmology, the American Academy of Optometry, the Association for Research in Vision and Ophthalmology, the American Glaucoma Society, the Optical Society of America, and the International Perimetric Society. He is also a member of the Glaucoma Advisory Committee, the editorial board of the *Journal of Glaucoma* and *Optometry and Vision Science*, the scientific advisory board for the Glaucoma Foundation, and co-founder/co-chair of the North American Perimetry Society. He served on the National Research Council's Committee on Vision 1985-1988 and on its working group on night vision. He has a PhD in psychology from the Pennsylvania State University.

Frank J. Landy is professor emeritus at the Pennsylvania State University and chief executive officer of the litigation support division of SHL/Landy Jacobs, a consulting firm. He has been an active consultant for 29 years for both public- and private-sector clients. His consulting has addressed issues of human performance in applied settings, often including issues related to vision. He has served as an expert witness in various state and federal courts and has been retained as an expert by the Department of Justice—disability rights section—to testify on issues related to vision and the Americans with Disabilities Act. The Equal Employment Opportunity Commission and the Department of Labor commissioned him to chair a group of scientists to investigate the effect of aging on the performance of public safety officers. He has published widely in the area of human performance and validation as well as other areas of psychology. He is a member of the Human Factors Society and the American College of Sports Medicine. He founded the journal *Human Performance,* served on the council of representatives of the American Psychological Association, and was president of its Division 14. He was a member of the National Research Council's Committee on Performance of Military Personnel and has served as a consultant for the Institute of Medicine. He has a PhD in industrial and organizational psychology from Bowling Green State University.

Paul P. Lee is professor of ophthalmology at Duke Medical Center, senior fellow in the Duke Center on Aging and Human Development, and consultant in the Health Services Program at RAND in Santa Monica, California. He also serves as chairman of Duke Eye Care, LLC. His research activities center on collaborative efforts to examine health services issues in care delivery and to develop methods to improve the care that patients receive in the community setting. He was a contributor to the development of the National Eye Institute visual function questionnaire. He serves on the board of trustees of the American Academy of Ophthalmology, the writing committee for the board recertification examination, and as an associate examiner for the American Board of Ophthalmology. He is the socioeconomics and health services section editor for the *Archives of Ophthalmology* and is on the editorial board of *Evidence-Based Eye Care.* He has an MD from the University of Michigan and a JD from Columbia University.

Gordon E. Legge is the distinguished McKnight university professor of psychology and director of the Center for Cognitive Sciences at the University of Minnesota. His primary research interests are in the problems encountered by people with low vision in performing important visual tasks, such as reading, object recognition, and spatial navigation. He has published an extensive series of articles on the psychophysics of reading, many concerned with low vision, and has developed a reading-acuity eye chart. He is currently a member of the National Advisory Eye Council at the National Institutes of Health and the *Vision Research* editorial board. He was a member of the National Research Council's Committee on Currency Features Usable by the Visually Impaired and was a member of the Committee on Vision 1990-1995. He has a PhD in psychology from Harvard University.

Dennis M. Levi is dean of the School of Optometry at the University of California, Berkeley. Prior to this, he was the associate dean for research and graduate studies and a professor of optometry and physiological optics at the University of Houston College of Optometry. His work emphasizes the use of psychophysical techniques to study the mechanisms that limit spatial vision in both the normal and amblyopic visual systems, and he has an active research program in spatial vision and amblyopia. He was a member of the National Eye Institute Visual Science B study section and served as chair for the last two years of his tenure. He has served on the editorial boards of *Vision Research* and *Investigative Ophthalmology & Visual Science*. He has OD, MS, and PhD degrees from the University of Houston College of Optometry.

Cynthia Owsley is professor and director of the clinical research unit in the Department of Ophthalmology, School of Medicine at the University of Alabama at Birmingham and also serves as co-director of the Center for Research on Applied Gerontology there. She has been the principal investigator on several projects funded by the National Institute on Aging and the National Eye Institute on aging-related vision impairment, eye disease, and their impact on everyday life. She was chair of the planning panel on vision impairment and rehabilitation for the National Eye Institute's National Plan for 1999-2003. She is currently a member of the editorial board of *Vision Research*. She was a member of the Committee on Vision that produced the 1994 report *Measurement of Visual Field and Visual Acuity for Disability Determination* and worked with the Committee for Safe Mobility of Older Persons of the National Research Council's Transportation Research Board. She has a PhD in experimental psychology from Cornell University.

Susan Van Hemel is a senior program officer in the behavioral, cognitive, and sensory sciences and education unit of the Division of Behavioral and Social Sciences and Education at the National Research Council. She has 22 years of experience in studies and analytic work related to human performance, human resource management, and training. Recent work includes studies of vision requirements for commercial drivers and of commercial driver fatigue, including experimental simulator-based studies of factors affecting fatigue and a survey of driver knowledge and beliefs about fatigue. Previously she managed and performed studies related to human performance in work and everyday tasks; job performance test development; training analysis, design, and evaluation; and organizational factors in nuclear power plant safety. She is a member of the Human Factors and Ergonomics Society and its technical groups on visual perception and aging. She has a PhD in experimental psychology from the Johns Hopkins University.

Sheila K. West is El-Maghraby professor of preventive ophthalmology in the Department of Ophthalmology at the Johns Hopkins School of Medicine. In addition, she holds an appointment in the Department of Epidemiology at the Johns Hopkins School of Public Health. Her research has been in the field of public health ophthalmology. She has been the principal investigator on several grants researching the role of visual impairment in disability among older Americans, prevention of blindness from trachoma, and the epidemiology of cataract and macular degeneration. She has published widely in epidemiology, ophthalmology, and vision impairments and is principal investigator on the Salisbury Eye Evaluation (SEE) project. She has a PhD in epidemiology from the Johns Hopkins University School of Hygiene and Public Health.

M. Roy Wilson is dean of the School of Medicine and vice president for health sciences at Creighton University. His major scientific contributions have been in bridging the fields of epidemiology and ophthalmology. A nationally recognized ophthalmologist, he has delivered numerous invited lectures and has published many articles, book chapters, and abstracts. He is a reviewer for all of the major ophthalmic journals, is on the editorial board of the *Archives of Ophthalmology*, and is section editor for the *Journal of Glaucoma*. He currently serves as a member of the basic and clinical science curriculum committee of the American Academy of Ophthalmology, the scientific advisory committee for the American Health Assistance Foundation, and the scientific advisory boards of both the Glaucoma Foundation and the Glaucoma Research Foundation. He has an MS in epidemiology from the University of California, Los Angeles, and an MD from the Harvard Medical School.

INDEX